AT HOME IN EXILE

A Memoir

AT HOME IN EXILE

A Memoir

Helga M. Griffin

Because they ask me questions about my life and family, and because some of them may also one day face an uncertain future, I dedicate this book to my grandchildren:

Julian, Laura, Patrick, Priscilla, Alexis, Sam and Giovanna

Published by ANU Press
The Australian National University
Acton ACT 2601, Australia
Email: anupress@anu.edu.au

Available to download for free at press.anu.edu.au

ISBN (print): 9781760464264
ISBN (online): 9781760464271

WorldCat (print): 1232435948
WorldCat (online): 1232438554

DOI: 10.22459/AHE.2021

This title is published under a Creative Commons Attribution-NonCommercial-NoDerivatives 4.0 International (CC BY-NC-ND 4.0).

The full licence terms are available at creativecommons.org/licenses/by-nc-nd/4.0/legalcode

Cover design and layout by ANU Press.

Cover photograph: The recently released Girschik family with Konrad Pick (ex-internee engineer from Iran) outside Melbourne's Botanical Gardens on 5 January 1947.

First edition © 2006 Pandanus Books
This edition © 2021 ANU Press

Contents

Author's Note to the 2021 Edition ix
Foreword to the 2021 Edition xi
Foreword and Acknowledgements xv
1. A Fountain in the Square 1
2. The Lost Homeland 5
3. Steinkirche 13
4. A Jewel in the Austrian Crown 19
5. Meeting the Relatives 37
6. For the Love of Iran 41
7. To the Bottom of the World 53
8. *Das Lager* 65
9. His Majesty's Guests 79
10. The Imaginary Homeland 91
11. Shadows and Flames 119
12. After the War 123
13. Stranded in Exile 127
14. Swimming for the Eucharist 139
15. *Ad Maiorem Dei Gloriam* 155
16. Mirror Without Identity 173
17. *The Wreck of the Deutschland* 191
18. Intelligence Testing 209
19. A Banquet of Life 223
20. Marriage in Rome 249
21. Integration 257

Author's Note to the 2021 Edition

This book is a minimally amended, reprinted version of *Sing me that lovely song again* (Pandanus Press, 2006). The title was chosen by Ian Templeman, the publisher, because he was more interested in its literary merits than in academic history. For that reason, many of my dates were removed from the original manuscript during editing.

My original intention was to get my parents and the elder of my two brothers to write their own memories of how they experienced their internment in Persia and five years behind barbed wire in Australia during World War II, focusing on individual memory by gender and age. It seemed a remarkable opportunity to make this anecdotal and analytical contribution to social science: they had each lived in the same space with the same people for the same period. It was to be an experiment made in heaven, that is, within an impeccable laboratory. But my parents had been too distressed by their loss of freedom and the congested and pressured atmosphere of life in camp to collaborate.

Because I wanted to keep the focus on my own memories, and the tone of voice my own, I wrote my own book with only minimal research in various archives in Australia and abroad. I did some research as a check on some important facts.

Asked to speak about my book at an academic conference at the University of Queensland in 2006, I did some further research to validate my contribution. My speech was then published in *National Socialism in Oceania* (edited by Emily Turner-Graham and Christine Winter, Peter Lang, 2010) with the title I had originally suggested to Pandanus Press, 'At Home in Exile: Ambiguities of wartime patriotism'. When in 2015 I was asked by Japanese scholars to speak at Cowra, NSW, at a conference on internment, I suggested that my younger brother, Peter, also be invited to speak, using half my allocated 20 minutes because he had a different memory of our internment. As a young boy he had a wonderful time in camp, getting up to mischief, playing games, feeling adventurous. Girls are more vulnerable. Puberty can be a greater problem for them.

Another interesting matter associated with this book is that the Iranian-born anthropologist Dr Pedram Khosronejad contacted me in 2019 after reading my book in the house of a friend. Pandanus Press having ceased to exist, Pedram took considerable trouble to locate and invite me to join a small group for a project he was devising. Their parents had also been interned from Persia during the period covered by my book. The group is now aged between 64 and 85 years of age – the 'children of internees from Persia'. The group works collectively and individually in association with Dr Khosronejad's experiment of a reciprocal anthropology of the aged. Outcomes of their work will include a publication as well as documentary film. This book remains one of several unique contributions within the development of the project.

With the literary title used in its initial hard copy, this book has not been part of bibliographies on civilian or refugee internment in Australia, although it is unusual as an account of a female's personal experiences.

Foreword to the 2021 Edition

After World War I, at the time of the period of the great depression in Europe and also of the national infrastructure development projects by Reza Shah (1878–1944), the King of Persia (1925–1941), between 1930 and 1941 many young and talented civilian Germans considered Persia as their land of opportunity. After moving there, they established a large expatriate community, settled down and became friends with Persian communities in cities, rural areas and also the territories of pastoral nomads. The majority of the civilian German expatriates of Persia came to the country as young, first-rate scholars, engineers, technicians, architects and trader-salesmen.

The British Government, and especially the prime minister, Winston Churchill (1874–1965), were against the residency of this specific group of civilian Germans in Persia, and since their arrival in the country put pressure on Reza Shah to expel them. Churchill strongly believed and propagated the fallacious theory that all civilian Germans were fifth columnists and secret members of the Gestapo who would help Hitler invade Asia and South Asia through Persia in the event of another world war conflict.

Under this excuse, and after the outbreak of World War II, in a joint intervention on 25 August 1941, the Russian and British armies invaded neutral Persia and captured the majority of the civilian Germans in the country. German women and children under the age of sixteen were brutally separated from their husbands and fathers and expelled by force to their countries of origin. The men, after a few weeks of interrogation in temporary military tented camps in Basra (Iraq), were transferred to the war internment camps of Australia where they spent the rest of their captivity until 1946.

There were six family groups including four children among those 494 civilian German internees of Persia who were brought to the Australian war internment camps. After the end of the war, many of the civilian German internees from Persia, including families and their children, were granted leave to stay in Australia, while some of them were deported or repatriated to European countries, and a few of them decided to return to Iran, probably to continue their professional activities.

Until today there has been no academic contribution or public news regarding this specific group of civilian Germans of Persia and their lives before, during and after World War II.

Helga was six years old when she and her family were captured in Persia in 1941 and brought with other German families as prisoners of war to the Tatura war internment camp. Her family was released in 1946 and decided to stay in Australia.

Helga was born in Çankiri Village in Turkey on 27 June 1935 and moved to Persia with her family in early 1936 because her father was assigned to pioneer parts of the Trans-Iranian Railway system. During their sojourn in Iran, Helga's family became friends with many Persians and her parents adored the country and its people. But with the outbreak of World War II, like other civilian Germans of Persia, their beautiful life became a nightmare. They were captured by the British Army in their home in the west of Persia, and after weeks of interrogation sent to the Australian internment camps. This book, which comprises the memoirs of Helga since her childhood in Persia, her life experiences as a child prisoner in the Tatura internment camp in Australia and her life after the war, should be considered the only book written by one of the few survivors of the civilian Germans of Persia.

Beside her personal memories and hard life experiences, to write this book Helga used her superb talents in history and anthropology, two major fields that she admired during her academic education. Therefore, the reader should consider this book as an important contribution to the field of historical anthropology. For this reason, She checked her work for factual accuracy in local and international archives and spoke to a number of persons who had survived the war.

This book is a unique example of academic scholarship depicting one of the unknown human disasters and catastrophes of World War II, the life story of one of the thousands of innocent German civilians who escaped Hitler and moved to Persia to find a peaceful shelter for their family.

Pedram Khosronejad
Associate Professor
Western Sydney University
October 2020

Foreword to the 2021 Edition

با اتمام جنگ جهانی اول و طرح توسعه ایران توسط رضاشاه، مهندسان جوان آلمانی و سایر کشورهای آلمانی زبان همجوار که در دوران افسردگی بزرگ اروپای بعد از جنگ بسر می‌بردند برای یافتن شرایط کاری بهتر در سال‌های ۱۳۱۵ تا ۱۳۱۹ با خانواده خود به ایران مهاجرت کردند. این گروه از آلمانی‌های غیر نظامی مقیم ایران متخصصان متبحری در رشته‌های گوناگون چون مهندسی ساختمان و عمران، مهندسی مکانیک و صنایع، مهندسی آب و خاک و یا متخصصان تجارت و اقتصاد بودند و در مناطق شهری، روستایی و عشایری کشور سکونت داشتند. این افراد به ایران و ایرانیان و نیز فرهنگ این سرزمین علاقه زیادی داشتند به طوری که در دوران اقامتشان در ایران دوستان و نزدیکان بسیاری پیدا کرده بودند.

دولت بریتانیا بخصوص وینستون چرچیل نخست وزیر وقت انگلستان، از حضور این گروه از آلمانی‌ها در ایران خشنود نبود و از هنگام ورود آنها به کشور، تلاش کرد تا فشار مضاعفی را بر رضاشاه وارد کند تا از این طریق آلمانی‌های مقیم را از ایران خارج کند. اعتقاد چرچیل بر این بوده است که این دسته از آلمانی‌ها، مأموران مخفی و ستون پنجم هیتلر و آلمان نازی در ایران هستند و در صورت وقوع جنگی دیگر این افراد به آلمان کمک خواهند کرد تا ایران را اشغال کرده و از طریق مرز پاکستان به هند و سایر کشورهای آسیای جنوبی حمله کند.

پس از شروع جنگ جهانی اول، در سال ۱۳۲۰، دولت روسیه و انگلیس به بهانه حفظ بیطرفی ایران و دفاع از ایران در قبال حمله احتمالی آلمان، دست به اشغال ایران زدند و سریعا آلمانی‌های غیر نظامی ایران را بازداشت کردند. زنان و فرزندان با سن کمتر از ۱۶ سال به آلمان فرستاده شدند و مردان مجرد پس از چندین هفته بازجویی به بازداشتگاه‌های جنگی استرالیا انتقال داده شدند. در بین بازداشت شدگان آلمانی‌های مقیم ایران که به زندان‌های استرالیا انتقال داده شدند، هشت زندان به همراهی همسر و فرزندانشان به این کشور آمدند. همه این زندانیان آلمانی بازداشت شده در ایران در بین سال‌های ۱۳۲۰ و ۱۳۲۵ در زندان‌های جنگی استرالیا عمر خود را سپری کردند و بعد از جنگ بسیاری از آنها تصمیم گرفتند که در استرالیا بمانند و تعداد اندکی نیز به آلمان برگشتند و تعدادی نیز برای ادامه فعالیت خود به ایران بازگشتند.

تا به امروز هیچگونه تحقیق علمی و یا گزارش خبری از زندگی و شرح حال آلمانی‌های مقیم ایران در بین دو جنگ جهانی اول و دوم و سرنوشت این افراد، همسر و فرزندانشان در دوران جنگ و بعد از آن صورت نگرفته است.

هلگا گرشیک گریفن شش ساله، یکی از چهار بچه اسیر شده شش خانواده آلمانی ایران است که به همراه والدین، برادرش پیتر و ۴۹۴ اسیر آلمانی مقیم ایران در ۲۸ آبان ۱۳۲۰ شمسی به بازداشتگاه‌های جنگی استرالیا انتقال داده شد و تا سال ۱۳۲۵ در اسارت باقی ماند.

هلگا در پنجم تیرماه ۱۳۱۴ در ترکیه متولد شد و در سال ۱۳۱۵ برای پروژه جدید کاری پدرش که در رابطه با طرح توسعه راه آهن ایران بود به همراه خانواده‌اش عازم تهران شد. هلگا و خانواده‌اش در طی اقامتشان در ایران زندگی شاد و سرشار از آسایش را تجربه و دوستان و آشنایان زیادی پیدا کرده بودند. ولی با شروع جنگ جهانی دوم و اشغال ایران توسط روسیه و انگلیس زندگی و سرنوشت هلگا و خانواده‌اش نیز تغییری بنیادین کرد. پس از اسارت در خاک ایران توسط ارتش

xiii

At Home in Exile

مهاجم انگلیس، جدایی از پدر و اسارت چند هفته‌ای در یک کمپ صحرایی در بصره کشور عراق، هلگا و خانواده‌اش به همراهی سایر اسرای آلمان ایران به زندان‌های جنگی استرالیا انتقال یافتند و تا پایان جنگ در اسارت باقی ماندند.

کتاب حاضر که شامل خاطرات هلگا از زمان کودکی وی در ایران، تجربیات و مشاهدات او و از دوران اسارت در کمپ‌های جنگی استرالیا، و همچنین سال‌های پس از جنگ است، تنها کتاب معتبر و موجود است که توسط یکی از تنها بازماندگان آلمانی‌های مقیم ایران نگاشته شده است.

هلگا در نوشتن این کتاب در کنار بهره بردن از خاطرات و تجربیات شخصی، از آموخته‌هایی که به صورت آکادمیک در زمینه مطالعات تاریخی و انسان‌شناسی داشته، استفاده کرده و همین امر اثر او را از یک رمان به یک پروژه کاملا علمی تبدیل کرده است. هلگا برای نوشتن این کتاب در طی سالیان متوالی در آرشیوهای استرالیا و سایر کشورهای دنیا به دنبال اسناد و مدارک مربوطه گشته و همچنین ساعت‌های متمادی به مصاحبه با محققین، بازماندگان جنگ جهانی دوم و اسرای کمپ‌های جنگی پرداخته است.

کتاب حاضر یکی از منحصر بفرد ترین کتاب‌های دانشگاهی است که به یکی از ناشناخته‌ترین فجایع انسانی جنگ جهانی دوم می‌پردازد و سرنوشت هزاران نفر از آلمانی‌های بیگناه را که از ترس هیتلر و برای آسایش و امنیت خود و خانواده‌شان به ایران مهاجرت کرده بودند را بازخوان می‌کند و به این مهم می‌پردازد که این افراد چگونه طعمه سیاست بازی‌های غیر انسانی چرچیل قرار گرفتند و سیر زندگی و سرنوشتشان به یکباره تغییر کرد.

پروفسور پدرام خسرونژاد
۱۰ آبان‌ماه ۱۳۹۹ سیدنی، استرالیا

Foreword and Acknowledgements

I first began to write this book in 1996, every day for an hour or two before work, over a period of about four months. At the time I was employed on the research and editorial staff of the *Australian Dictionary of Biography* at The Australian National University in Canberra. I then circulated my manuscript widely to friends and acquaintances with different personal and professional backgrounds.

What came back to me was a surprising set of responses, different and contradictory even when applied to the same chapters. While one person did not want me to change one word of what I had said about the War, others loathed my exposure of Nazi activity in our camp, as if I was making it up. One person thought that writing about a Catholic education was nowadays an overworked exercise, while others liked those chapters particularly, for 'being exactly as [they] remember it', or for the 'ethnography', or for being written by a young 'convert' to Catholicism crossing the exotic Tridentine Catholic bridge in secular Australia. Some readers wanted to edit out the German influences evident in my English language, although this is itself an indicator of the problem of assimilating new language patterns.

In 1996 my English language was also suffering from the professional straitjacket of having worked for eighteen years with a project that published reference books. I decided to put the manuscript aside, allowing it to lie fallow, waiting for the book to germinate subconsciously. I also wanted to internalise some of the good advice I had been given without losing my own way of speaking. Above all, I wanted to combine open truthfulness about my memories of an earlier life and the way I now reflect on it.

I want to acknowledge by name those people who in 1996 generously gave me in writing or verbally their enthusiastic support and constructive criticism: Anne Boyd, Debra Dwyer, Morag Fraser, Amirah and Ken Inglis, Ann McCulloch, Jan and Hank Nelson, Joy Hooton and Marivic Wyndham. While I subsequently did not follow their advice directly, its value to me has nevertheless been great. I have left out the names of readers of the first manuscript who were kind, but who concealed their honest reactions. I understand that politeness precluded them from being frank. Their reservations seemed to include distaste for an allegedly romantic style; that my story was too personally revealing; that there was too much religion in it; that my memory could not have been as vivid as it seems; and that later incidents must have influenced my interpretation of the past. Such reactions were all worthy of consideration.

I revised this memoir in 2004. Although it relies substantially on my own reminiscences, I am grateful to my brothers Peter and Herbert Girschik and cousins Christine Robertson and Peter Erlanger who, at my request and without their having read any of the story, provided details of the family of my mother and her sister. My brother Peter corrected a couple of details about the camp. I expect that their recollections and interpretations do not correspond completely with mine.

What follows, then, are the thoughts of an ageing woman reminiscing about her young life—a life that was in part fractured but not permanently damaged. It expresses my compulsion to speak about circumstances about which my elders kept silent for almost forty years. Displaced as a child to a foreign land far away, with parents who were tarred as 'enemy aliens', I now know that my fate and such stereotyping were the result of a chance combination of politics and culture. It had nothing to do with the sorts of people we were. By sheer accident, I was privileged to have come out of it all relatively unscathed when so many others all over the world suffered terribly through no fault of their own. A philosophy of hope is therefore implicit in this story of my youth.

Denials sometimes persist for a long time. When my mother in the early 1980s wrote a letter to a German newspaper to support the view that Nazi activities did exist in Australian internment camps, her letter was not published. Powerful lobbies got in the way. Readers might ask why I still dwell on painful experiences that were all over and done with so long ago. I think that there is in many of us a drive to expose the secrets of the past and to learn from them. And, indeed, through the 1980s and into the

1990s, Germany has been at the forefront of acknowledging her crimes against humanity during the Nazi time. With my German and Austrian background, I retain some sense of communal responsibility for the past; just as with my Australian naturalisation, I have also inherited Australia's communal responsibility for its past history.

My particular thanks for bringing this project to fruition go to the Pandanus Books team: Ian Templeman, Justine Molony and Emily Brissenden, for their enthusiastic and generous professional encouragement. In the always risky editing process, I am grateful for the meticulous hand of consultant editor, Jan Borrie. Then came work in detail. To collaborate with Diana Giese brought reassurance, nurture, instruction and pleasure. Like a discriminating gardener, she pruned many tangled passages while leaving my blooms, my best sentences, completely unaltered, so that I felt I still owned the text. She also matched pictures and text with both serious and playful purpose.

My generous and perceptive husband, Jim Griffin, has always been my most steadfast and loving support, but also my most incisive critic. More than anyone throughout my married life, he has challenged my originally narrower view of things and stimulated my social conscience and psychological outreach. I am immensely grateful to my immediate family, their partners and my close friends. It is a source of sorrow that some of my offspring and their families now live so far away. My often unspoken gratitude to my family and friends lives always in my heart.

Helga Griffin
2006

1

A Fountain in the Square

I begin my perceived existence in a railway carriage. I do not as yet know precisely who I am or how old. I am still a bundle of feelings who parrots the talk of her parents. I am so little and my mother is so tall beside me in her soft, grey, black-flecked coat. I lean against her reassuring, warm and fragrant body. We travel backwards. The train wheels rumble along the lines below us. On my lap is a light-green Iranian tea set in baked clay. I love it. I love it because my father gave it to me when we said goodbye by the Caspian Sea.

Fragments of my remembered past are so vivid that I enter particular episodes of that life as if I were there now, at this very moment, on an island floating in its own enclosed immutable space and time. But then the larger story unfolds gently in its telling. All my personal islands are linked to other people and large communities over whom I, as a child, had no decisive control.

Now I am standing near a window in my grandmother's apartment in Breslau. It is well above ground and overlooks the square below. Children ride their tricycles around an empty fountain. Some leap in and out of its dry basin. There is a statue, identified for me as King Neptune, in the centre of it. I long to join the play. My young aunt is brushing my hair and promises to take me downstairs. The sky is a bright blue. The snow has not yet come.

Uncle Otto takes me to see the *Konditorei* (sweets and cake shop) nearby. In the shop window a whole gingerbread village is covered in sugar snow. Who buys such large treats? The scene is too perfect to eat.

One day I am surrounded by crowds in a Breslau square. The day is grey. Marching people enter from a side street. Trumpeters perform lively music as they move along. Some marchers carry large decorated flags. Children swarm beside the procession. I also leap along with them to the sound of the music. There is nothing sinister in what I observe. But mother tells me to come quickly, and takes me away.

Early one morning, in grandmother's flat, my bent-over *Omi* (grandmother's mother) brings a cup of warm milk to the cot in which I am standing. She is gentle and kind to me.

Now we are in Vienna with my father's people. We walk across a bridge that spans the Danube. I am frightened of the water below. My grandfather holds my hand lovingly, securely. I look up at the patterns made by the bridge. My heart soars with these strong supports and the patterns they make. One day I will be told by my father that the bridge is called a 'hanging bridge'. So grand is the memory that I look for it many years later. But I cannot find it again.

My father's sisters take mother and me to the *Prater*, the Luna Park of Vienna. At the entrance is a *Watschen Mann* (ear-cuff man), a large rubber doll in the shape of a man. People come and whack him across the face. A needle inside a tube tells how strong the blow has been. I feel sick as I watch a strong man hit the *Watschen Mann* across his face. Then, in a little open train we move through a tunnel and observe amazing scenes in grottoes. Girls hang from hooks by their plaits above burning coals, while devils with pitchforks stand below them. They do not move. I shiver as the train moves on.

Mother then takes me up on the Ferris wheel.

Later in life I was able to date these scenes, these unconnected fragments of memory so solidly fixed in my mind over the years. They happened when my mother took me back home to her folk in Germany for Christmas. Six months later, in 1938, my brother was born in Iran's Tehran just before I turned three. Although these are my only memories between the ages of two-and-a-half and three, they are not without their implications for the future. They may well illustrate that in early childhood a sudden change of residence helps to anchor memories that are governed by feelings and perceptions rather than by thought. While this set of images has become a fixture of my mind, labelled as 'my first memories', I assume that they were once even simpler. Over time they grew in subtlety and size. Fashioned as my own seamless garment, they may have in fact been sewn from the unremembered talk of others. My mother forgot some things I recall, while she remembered different parts of this story for much longer.

2

The Lost Homeland

Since the death of my mother, Elfriede, ten years ago, I have been haunted by the desire to visit the homeland, the *Heimat*, that she never saw again after her fifty years in Australia. In more ways than one, Germany had become her lost homeland, the spiritual place of her ancestors from which she was exiled. I sensed the pain she felt over the tangible loss of connection to her own past. For me to be able to go so far away and pay tribute to her German home in what is now Poland, to savour the environment of her childhood, at first seemed impossible. I nevertheless hoped for the opportunity to do so, although I expected to find all the names of the places changed, and that people spoke a language I did not understand. It would be confronting to go there, I thought.

When in 1997 I visited Vienna, my father's Austrian birth city, and after that my German cousins in Germany, I was not regarded as a stranger. Despite being an almost lifelong Australian, I spoke their language and somehow belonged. I was accepted by people as someone who had come home to reclaim my heritage. I could merge with crowds unobtrusively, like a 'local'. The only subtle tremors of feeling generated by what people are used to were shown up in my too-German ways for the Austrians, and my too-Austrian ways for the Germans. The Austrians reacted more firmly. This suggests that my mother's influence on me was strongest.

I was born in Turkey, north of Ankara, in 1935, and when I also went there on my trip home, I was treated to a special welcome by each Turk who found this out, from my passport or my conversation. My birth in Turkey entitled me to Turkish citizenship. Naturally I was delighted, though somewhat embarrassed as well, by such trust. I knew only too well that the families of guest workers of Turkish origin, even those residing in Germany for several generations, did not qualify for German citizenship.

Now, in 2005, this rule has been changed. At the time of my visit, in so many places in the world, bloodlines counted most. In Turkey, geography seemed more important.

In 1992, as an Australian citizen, I visited parts of the United States with my eldest son, Justin. Australians seemed hardly known there. 'Where is that place Australia?' they would ask. 'You mean Austria?' Since the war in Iraq, with Australia's involvement, some of this has changed. Now many more Americans know about us.

When my eldest daughter Anthea and her partner John invited me to stay with them in London, and offered to accompany me on my quest for mother's lost homeland, I used the city as a springboard from which to visit the place where Elfriede, her brother Otto and much younger sister Else had been born and raised. After World War II, no member of the family of their mother, Emma Bittnar, went back to Steinkirche, once a German village in rural Silesia.

The reason for this is part of the complex modern history of that troubled part of the world. At the end of the War, in 1945, letters from my mother's family from Breslau, where some had settled after 1930, told how my mother's mother and her sister lived through incendiary bombing raids and the artillery battle over Breslau between Nazi German forces and the advancing Soviet Army. Thousands of Breslau's refugees fled to Dresden before the Red Army's advance. Most of them were then incinerated in the firestorm from the bombing of the city.

The consequences of the invasion of Breslau by Soviet troops were personal secrets too dreadful to speak of in our family. Elfriede's younger sister, Else, stayed behind in Breslau to protect her ailing mother. After the shooting had ceased, she and other women were forced to clear rubble from the streets.

They were then dragooned into gangs to break rocks. Her subsequent terrified flight westwards towards Zwickau with her sick mother became one of Else's most traumatic nightmares. The starving refugees were shot at in farmers' fields as they scavenged for food. Her end-of-War experiences led to Else's hospitalisation for almost a whole year.

2. The Lost Homeland

During and after the War's end, those people in German Silesia who had not already fled the Russian advance in early 1945 were subsequently evicted from their farms, homes and city residences to make room for people displaced in eastern Poland by Soviet conquest. It was not what Churchill wanted; this was his ally Stalin's demand.

For many exiled Silesians and their descendants, the pain of loss has lingered. Their attachment to their heritage was steeped in custom, literature and legends. Although one can argue that the resettlement of displaced Poles on once-German territory was justified compensation for the horrific crimes committed against Poland by the criminal Nazis, the issue was not settled by this simple, brutal, diplomatic solution. As a great English writer of Polish history, Norman Davies, has recorded, Silesians were singled out to pay the end-of-War costs for atrocities perpetrated by the whole German nation.

My father's relatives in Vienna suffered less acutely than my mother's during the War. Members of the family of my father's eldest sister, however, were to experience the consequences of her mental instability after she was twice sexually assaulted by Allied soldiers while a patient in hospital. Both my parents, especially Elfriede, were spared this terror. Their misfortunes were to begin in an entirely different place, far away from 'home'.

Knowing how my mother's family had suffered, I intended to visit both metropolitan Wroclaw (Breslau) in Poland and the rural birthplace of my mother's family. But I could not find the obscure village that was once Steinkirche in relation to what was once Breslau. What was its Polish name? How large or small a place was it? Did it still exist in any form? Was any part of Wroclaw still identifiable as the old Breslau I had seen in books?

No German family photographs had survived the War to guide me. I keenly remembered the Neptune fountain in Breslau in the Neumarkt Platz, visible from the upper-floor apartment where my grandmother lived. But my mother had no recollection of such a fountain. My daughter Anthea also doubted the accuracy of so old a memory. Would I be able to find that fountain in the city? Would I be able to find the name for the village where my relatives had lived? Would anyone still speak German in Lower Silesia?

To prepare myself for the journey from my home in Canberra, Australia, I visited the National Library's vast collection of maps. But I could not find Steinkirche, even in old German records of Silesia. The Polish-German Gazeteer, which has a remarkable list of old German place-names in relation to their Polish replacements, and vice versa, gave the names for many places, including Märzdorf where my mother had worked as a young woman, on an estate near the Oder River. But there was nothing for Steinkirche. The people assembling the directory must have thought it simply the description of a stone church, as the name suggests, rather than the actual name for the place where the church stood.

Obviously it was not an important village. No one in our extended family could give me the Polish names for rural Steinkirche or of Neumarkt Platz in the Silesian metropolis. Had Steinkirche been north, east, west or south of Breslau? In my mind's eye I assumed it to be east—towards Posen—mistakenly, so I was to discover. In answer to one of my many questions, I recalled that my mother had once told me that it had taken her about an hour by train to travel to the school she attended briefly in Breslau. It was an important clue.

I then rang my cousin, Peter Erlanger, but neither he nor his older sister could help me. Peter advised me to try to find Steinkirche using my computer's Internet search engine. It was enlightened advice, and was to provide me with a key clue. The website yielded a huge list of entries, mostly concerning stone churches in present-day Germany. But there was also a reference to a 1928 visit by a church official inspecting a number of communities overseen by the Lutheran Church at Strehlen. I had often heard my mother and her sister refer to acquaintances in Strehlen.

The article about Steinkirche described it as having a 1264 Polish Catholic foundation, on a site where pagan sacrifices had taken place. This seemed to have the ring of truth. The description offered a brief history of the church and gave illustrations of it in various stages of alteration. By the seventeenth century, the place had become Lutheran and in the following 200 years the community's religious confidence expressed itself architecturally, through continual improvements. A church tower with baroque spire was raised and the interior refurbished with an upper-storey balcony with pews on three sides.

2. The Lost Homeland

This description told me that Steinkirche was somewhere in the vicinity of Strehlen. Then, according to Elfriede's stories about walking her animals, ducks, geese and a goat to the railway station to meet visitors, a station once existed near the village. I wondered whether it had survived the bombing. I have seen films of the utter devastation along the Oder River in early May 1945, just before the War in Europe ended. Did the railway still pass Steinkirche? My mother's father had been a railway line pointsman, a signal attendant. From a station close to home he would have undertaken the long journeys his work demanded.

I went back to the old German maps in the National Library and located Steinkirche on one of several contiguous contour maps perhaps designed for military purposes. They covered Lower Silesia in 1938 in·remarkable detail, although such detail also helped obscure the printed names of villages, which were lost in the depictions of miniature hills, rivers, quarries, castles, lakes and even houses.

Eventually I did locate the village through this superb map. Steinkirche was off the main road near the second railway station south of Strehlen, probably on a hill, something my mother had never mentioned. If one passed it, one could also locate it as station number two of the seven between Strehlen and Milnsterberg, on the railway running south of Breslau towards the Carpathian Mountains. Then I noted the Polish names for the two townships south of Wroclaw (Breslau). In the German-to-Polish Gazetteer they are given as Strzelin and Ziebice.

My intention was to take a train or a car to the new Polish ex-Steinkirche, visit it discreetly, and search the old cemetery for family connections. I wanted to photograph my two-year-old granddaughter beside my own grandfather Friedrich's grave. I wanted to look for other evidence of family history, and just savour the atmosphere of the place. I also wanted to see what had happened to Neumarkt Platz.

It was difficult to achieve anything in a hurry. In London, my daughter, granddaughter and I visited the office of the Polish Consulate. Tourist brochures were generously given to us, but none of the authoritative road maps of Poland showed the villages between Strzelin and Ziebice. Did our village still exist? And by what name?

After flying to Berlin, we set out in a hire car for Wroclaw on 13 September 2003. Beside the Hitler-era Autobahn, there are still extensive forests, between flat farmlands. It was raining when we entered Poland.

We received the clear impression from grim customs officials and money-changers at the border that we had entered a part of the world still not entirely recovered from post-War economic depression. Roadside stands sold plaster garden statues, especially gnomes, and other wares were also for sale, judging by the surreptitious lifting of skirts to reveal totally bare flesh, from women sheltering under their umbrellas. I wondered where they would take their truck driver customers in a place where there seemed to be only road and forest.

Anthea's navigation skills took us promptly to the clean and pleasant Tumski Hotel on the Sand Island near the oldest part of Wroclaw. I was immensely moved when I found that my room overlooked a canal of the Oder. This was a place of which mother had often spoken. Maria on the Sand (*die Sandkirche*) is still there, one of the large old Gothic red-brick churches that escaped bombing.

That Saturday afternoon, too late for lunch, we sampled Polish beer and vodka. We explored the famous Rynek, the central seventeenth-century market square with its famed Gothic town hall where American soldiers had stolen the gold from the astrological clock. The bombed-out buildings had been restored, but they were too garishly painted to revive a sense of their history. The adjoining salt square now mostly sells flowers.

We wondered at how few smiling faces there were, and were puzzled by how little German or English anyone spoke. Why was there so little tourism? Only a pair of elegant teenagers had fluent German. We turned down their offers of pornographic pictures and sexual experiences.

We covered enough of the area to get a strong impression of a once-lively city devastated by War and hastily repaired. These were convenient reconstructions, done without an eye to matching styles.

I was especially anxious to find out where Neumarkt Platz had been. That evening at the hotel, I kept going to the window and trying to imagine my mother as a young woman taking an evening stroll with a companion along the banks of the Oder. But this was autumn. Thick mists hung above the water. Few people were out walking.

On Sunday we set out seriously to find the location of the old square. We walked through once-stately streets, past the Metropole Hotel from where Hitler had addressed the crowds, to the Ethnographic Museum. This proved disappointing. The contents of two rooms were a mere gesture in honour of local culture. Few of the artefacts were authentically part of this area. It told us nothing of any interest or with any authority. We wondered whose culture we were looking at.

At the central railway station, we tried to question officials, in German and English, about the location of Steinkirche. But only Polish was spoken at the information office and other counters. Nor could we locate the correct train line on the information screens.

On our walk back to the centre of town, past the dilapidated theatre where my mother had attended performances, John spotted another bookshop. Surprisingly it was trading busily on a Polish Catholic Sunday. It sold old maps and books. We found old pictures of Breslau labelled in Polish and English. We found descriptions in both Polish and English of Neumarkt Platz (Novi Targ). Various maps showed clear plans of its location. They also showed the Neptune fountain I had been seeking. For centuries it had a conspicuous place in town maps as a well drawing water from the Oder, whose tributaries flowed together and separated the town into different quarters, spanned by a multitude of bridges.

I was thrilled. Before this find, my family had begun to question whether the fountain had actually existed. 'You and your fountain!' they cried. But I always knew it was there, in my memory and beyond.

When we walked to Novi Targ, we found the old houses by the square had been destroyed totally by the War. So, to my disappointment, had the Neptune fountain . In *Microcosm*, his history of Wroclaw, Norman Davies tells how, after the War, the rubble of Breslau had been removed in trainloads to rebuild Warsaw in its original style. Some fine Breslau buildings left standing by War were even knocked down for their old bricks.

I viewed this horrible information as being akin to the punishment Dante dished out to sinners in his Purgatory. Atonement was to be made only by suffering punishment that fitted the spirit of a crime.

We then looked for the air-raid shelters in which my grandmother and aunt Else had sheltered from the fire-bombs that rained down on the city in early 1945.

Else had told us how phosphorescence burning on human skin could not be put out, and how a seventeen-year-old soldier, weak from starvation, had been fed at a stranger mother's breast in the bunker before he returned to fight Russian soldiers in the final Breslau street battles. She had told us how a fat man had wedged himself into the shelter's entrance, and had been mown down by the hysterical mob. She had told us how she herself had carried her sick mother across a burning rooftop.

Beneath the reconstructed Novi Targ square, John identified shelters in two places, downstairs bolted against public entry. Plain and ugly high-rise public housing of cheap materials now stood around the bare square, where once interesting seventeenth-century merchant houses had stood amid a lively marketplace. People had lived in apartments even before the Communist-style transformations. Before their destruction, the old buildings of Breslau were of stately proportions, made of good material by experienced artisans who valued their talents and who took pride in a town with depth to its history.

Novi Targ now looks much sadder and more neglected than my glossy photos show. Breslau's lively markets that were once a feature of the city, as shown in my photographs of 1905, were relocated by the council in the second half of the twentieth century to a large new market hall. This was allegedly because of the congestion caused in the city's central squares by traders with their cars, animals and stalls.

I was nevertheless deeply moved. This ugly restoration was on ground where my grandmother and her children had walked so many times. Grandmother Emma and my beloved aunt Else had lived there for fifteen years before 1945. My mother had corresponded with them from far away.

Had we stayed longer, we would have enjoyed other moments of pleasure in a city that remains drab, and in which not even the theatre has been restored. The original buildings, and what they stood for, were German. The culture of Silesia before 1945 has not yet been generally acknowledged. It is also part of Polish history. I am sure this will change.

3

Steinkirche

We had still not found the Polish name for my mother's village. Anthea and John were beginning to doubt that it still existed, since nothing appeared on reputable tourist maps of Poland. But another moment of good fortune supported my own confidence. After we had paid the hotel bill that Monday morning, I tried my German one last time on a more senior man behind the counter. I had not seen him before. He said he had never heard of the place, but asked me to show him where I thought it was on the detailed map he had of Lower Silesia.

I showed him somewhere just south of Strzelin. He said immediately: 'That has to be it. Bialy Kosciol. It means White Church!'

Still sceptical, Anthea announced to her young daughter: 'Be happy. We are about to take you on a mystery tour!'

The following day, on a bright autumn morning, John drove us south of Wroclaw on a sealed road that skirted the railway line beside flat farmlands. It was country that still looked part of what used to be known as the great north-eastern German plain. Sweet-corn stubble and potatoes yet to be harvested revealed that there were not many crops growing that autumn.

Wartime bombing had obviously reduced Strehlen to a much smaller city. After Strzelin, the landscape began to undulate. We passed a settlement on the left, then noticed the land turn to hills as we approached where we understood Bialy Kosciol to be. We could make out the steeple of a church on a hill.

We turned left again and followed the road beneath a raised railway track. Then we drove up the gentle slope of a hill, along an avenue of old trees, crossed a bridge over a stream (the Olawa) and entered the village.

A single row of houses flanked the road on either side. Most had red tiled roofs, and appeared to be fairly new. There were about eighteen in all. But the village seemed deserted. I saw no cars and no shops. Nor did the church towards the end of the road where the hill peaked match the latest picture I had printed from the Internet. Had we come to the wrong place?

Then, as we wandered about, Anthea found a poster that showed the church had been rebuilt. Between 1987 and 1994, it had been restored according to its original mediaeval Catholic design.

An elderly Polish woman appeared in the churchyard. But she did not understand our questions. She indicated through gestures that the place had been bombed in the War and the church almost totally destroyed. What remained had been hacked to pieces by 'Russkis', leaving only a shell standing. This had been used in the reconstruction, with what was obviously more recently quarried stone of the region.

John pointed out to me that some of the stones had been numbered for correct repositioning.

While the old woman went to collect her husband, who had learned to speak some German, Anthea discovered a small stack of green paper with a brief illustrated history of the church, in Polish. We took some and both placed donations in the money box.

Inside the church, by the altar, was a painting of a Black Madonna in a golden frame. Like its mediaeval model, the church was once again a Catholic place of worship.

The friendly old woman returned. She had not located her husband. Had he really gone away? Or did he just not want to meet us? She told us, again through gestures, that the wrought iron internal gates of the church were the only fittings that had survived the bombing.

Again, I was moved. Those gates would have been there when our relatives were christened, confirmed and married in this church, and when they were buried from it. Anthea photographed me on the pebbled path down which they had walked to the church for so many years.

3. Steinkirche

But where was the cemetery?

The old woman did not understand through my drawings of graves that I wanted to see the old burial place. But there were a number of large weathered tombstones resting against the wall that enclosed the church. The inscription on one of them was clear. It recorded a death in the 1660s. Were these tablets preserved from the time when the church had first become Protestant? What had happened to the earlier Catholic graves? The place was full of the questions of history.

We stopped in the churchyard to look at a memorial plot adorned with fresh flowers and candles. It was placed under a tree, and seemed to be dedicated to those who had suffered the atrocities of the War. We thanked the kind woman for her concern for us and she and I embraced symbolically across the years, aware of the troubled pasts of both our families.

We felt like foreign intruders in our smart little red German hire car. We had arrived in this very silent and rather poor place to find few people. Only dogs barked their disapproval at our presence. I regret now that I did not enter the shop Anthea pointed out. But she took down the Polish website address of the village, and as we left, we hoped we could use it for future correspondence.

Anthea and I wanted to explore the village a little further, but John informed us that the road ended just beyond where we had driven, behind a house. Our presence would be too intrusive in this deserted place. It was as if everyone had taken flight at our arrival. Were we just another lot of Germans looking for traces of family land that had been confiscated?

The old woman indicated what seemed to be a shrine to the Black Madonna further along the road. After taking photos of the distant forested slopes where my mother's people had collected wild food, and of the river and lakes beyond the village, where she and her siblings had no doubt learned to swim, we drove back to the park-like retreat John had seen.

Sure enough, it was the disused cemetery. It had been badly vandalised. Only four or five tombstones were legible, and even they were badly defaced and corroded. The broken tombstones stood above the encroaching shrubs and tough ivy that covered everything else. I noted the dates 1914 and 1918, but no family names. The period I needed for the deaths of our grandfather and his daughter, 1918, was a time when the cemetery was still in use. Right at the back were some empty graves.

It never occurred to me that there might be unexploded War-time ammunition buried under all that vegetation. What did dawn on me was that the picture my mother always used to draw for her children, whenever she needed to claim our attention, was an abbreviated record of her own village. She drew a church with a steeple on a hill, sheep grazing below, and a cemetery with tombstones down the slope.

John stopped the car at the bottom of the hill so that I could photograph the village from afar. I was surprised how much bigger it looked from this angle. On our route to our next destination in the mountains, planned purely for pleasure, we noted that the railway line—'Fred's line' I called it, after our grandfather's work—ran from Wroclaw to Klodzko, and towards the base of the mountains. We didn't know whether trains still ran on that single track.

After a brief tour of the mountain district, we returned for another look at Bialy Kosciol. Each of us wanted to follow the road below the village to the nearby lakes. The two lakes were larger than we had thought, and there was a barrier between them, a kind of causeway. The map shows an arm of the Olawa River flowing into it beneath a bridge that was part of the main village road.

The southern bank of the lake offered a fine view of the village, and showed it to be much larger than we had initially thought. Now there seemed to be some sixty or seventy houses. Another cluster of buildings was strung along the ridge, as a separate section. Perhaps they were holiday houses. On the shores of the lake a number of A-frame holiday huts were available for rent. Since the warmer months were over, however, the place was closed. Later when we studied the village website, it informed us that nowadays a Polish grand tour for cyclists runs through the village.

John drove us up to the village again to show me the quarry I now felt compelled to find. Probably the stones for the village houses and its roads had been extracted from it. Steinkirche was supported by agriculture and stone masonry.

The quarry was on the one road through the settlement, just beyond the church, fenced off and filled with water, just as it must have been when it lured our grandmother to a swift deliverance from her insupportable grief. I'll tell that story in my next chapter.

3. Steinkirche

My mother Elfriede worked on an estate near the river, from where she could see the steeple of her church on the horizon. It made her homesick.

This was also where she left home for Stamboul (Istanbul). But we were unable to find any signpost with the Polish name (Zelazna, between Olawa and Jelcz) on it. The whole area has been subjected to major roadworks. The highway to Krakow now runs where one assumes the village to have been.

I had often thought Elfriede must have invented her impression of the sight of the church steeple. Surely it was too far away to be seen? But no. Eerily, through the haze, it stayed with us as a ghostly presence along the edge of the ridge beyond the fields. It was visible as far as the place we thought Märzdorf must once have stood.

I regretted that our visit was too short to explore the surrounding countryside on foot. Forests clung to the distant slopes of foothills leading to ranges. Anthea said that it was fortunate I had seen the lost homeland of my forebears at a time before Poland joined the European Union. Rapid change will erase still further the landscape and traditions familiar to them.

4

A Jewel in the Austrian Crown

My mother, Elfriede, was two-and-a-half years older than my father, Rudolf Girschik. She had the more constant influence on her children when we were growing up. He set a fine example of dedication in his responsibility for his family and in how he performed his work. During informal moments of endearment, they were Friedel and Rudi, although my mother preferred her formal name.

While they came from German and Austrian backgrounds where the same basic language was spoken, by temperament, environmental influence and acculturation they were quite different people. It is interesting to think that Hitler wanted to reunite Germans and Austrians as the 'one people' he believed them to be. He was, of course, Austrian himself. He used a false mythic conceptualisation that bypassed historical and cultural realities to justify his invasion of Austria, and to create in 1938 the notorious *Anschluss* (connection).

There was little opposition. People knew of the great Holy Roman Empire that in the distant past had encompassed both areas. The shared language of modern Austria and Germany gave Hitler a mandate for unification. Contemporary pictures suggest that Austrians in Vienna gave the *Anschluss* overwhelming support.

But there were incipient cultural faultlines between the two countries. These were found in microcosm in the relationship between Rudi and Friedel. They increasingly surfaced as conflict during World War II, which deepened the differences. We children often cringed as we watched this Austro-German alliance between two volatile people of forceful character descend into frustration and misunderstanding. A typical exchange would go like this: 'But you are only a German country girl, Elfriede!' 'And you Viennese, Rudolf, have the greatest talent in the world for advertising yourselves and Vienna!'

My father's words used to fall like bricks. My mother's were shot as keen arrows to the heart of her antagonist. 'You're so crude! Your manners belong to the language used by labourers on a building site,' was one riposte.

Beyond the walls of their home they were all charm. As one of my friends was to put it in the 1960s: 'I love your parents. The energy levels always rise a few degrees when they enter the room.' That's how they ended up: too forceful for their children.

In the early years of their marriage, fractures between them were cemented over. Her Protestant upbringing and his Catholicism were lesser obstacles than Rudolf's career. The most damaging influence on them, however, was the vengeful intervention of what may be seen as 'other people's wars'. My parents were essentially private citizens within their respective nationalities. They never participated in political activity or public warfare in any sense of the word. Like so many disengaged people, they were caught up in the larger currents of the twentieth century, like leaves ripped by autumn winds from the trees. This is not special pleading on their behalf. They, like me and so many others, lacked the understanding and the courage to deal with the negative forces unleashed by the War. I cannot leave a truthful memory of them presenting me with a shining example of political courage. I lack the evidence to offer them either praise or blame. During that War, I was a child to whom much adult activity was like the title on the spine of a book. The text, the heart of their thoughts and feelings, was closed to me.

I have nevertheless been able to piece together, from their own spare and occasional words, the circumstances that led them to a life away from 'home'. Mother was the more obliging storyteller.

What drew their paths together? They both had family roots in Czechoslovakia. In Europe, a road can now be followed between their homelands, and it moves through that former nation. As young adults, they worked in the same distant foreign country. Yet nothing could have been more different than their experience in the years when they were growing up.

4. A Jewel in the Austrian Crown

Born on 5 August 1907, Elfriede was raised in the agricultural village of Steinkirche in German Lower Silesia. She was the eldest child of Emma, born Friebe, who married the widower Friedrich Bittnar. Elfriede was born into a close-knit family. Friedrich had brought a daughter into the household, and he appears also to have had an older son.

Ancestors seem to have been settled in that part of the world for a long time. The village was named after its mediaeval church, and became for a period a Bohemian possession. Later, during the seventeenth century, it was staunchly Protestant. By then it was also Prussian. Still later, it became part of a united Germany.

Is it possible that before Elfriede's mother's marriage an association already existed between her mother's father, Gustav Friebe, and her own? Both men worked as railway pointsmen, or signal attendants. Perhaps the stress of caring for a stepchild and a baby led Emma to give Elfriede over to be raised by her parents, who lived in another part of the village.

To be given away like that was one of the grievances Elfriede carried over into later life.

While the Bittnar family had once enjoyed a degree of wealth because of their involvement in the weaving for which Silesia was noted, by Elfriede's time, her family no longer benefited from this cottage industry.

Her father spoke fluent Russian, a useful talent in a place as vulnerable as Lower Silesia. The great Russian bear of Eastern Europe was both feared and admired. Russia itself was too close for comfort.

Friedrich's work often kept him away from home for long periods, as he travelled to the country's borders. His son Otto was born to Emma two years after Elfriede.

Friedrich owned a simple two-storey whitewashed stone house without running water. The family had to lug in water for cooking, bathing, cleaning and washing. From an early age, the children acquired habits of thrift and knew the value of work. In winter, the Bittnar washing was dried in the attic. The family was, however, sufficiently well-off not to have to share the ground floor with their animals.

While Friedrich brought in wages, the family lived in modest comfort, although World War I made things difficult and the post-War Depression caused periods of real hardship. The family owned or had access to a plot of land beyond the village where vegetables were grown. They were thus sometimes better off than their urban-based relatives.

Family bonds appear to have been strong in the Friebe–Bittnar alliance. Emma had at least four brothers. Her children had 'aunts' who visited her home, but I do not know whose sisters or wives they were. Emma's brother Wilhelm had set himself up as a baker in Berlin and married the beautiful fair-haired daughter of two of his customers, an expatriate Ukrainian couple. Ties with relatives in Berlin always remained strong. Connections to urban life and Friedrich's interest in Russia (which his daughter Elfriede absorbed) brought the cultural currents of the day into the family's parochial existence. For instance, Elfriede's grandmother had a habit of sulking and not speaking when she was offended. Her husband used to coax her into a better mood with songs from Johann Strauss' operetta, *Nights in Venice*: '*Komm in die Gondel mein Liebchen, oh steige doch ein!*'

Elfriede inherited her grandmother's propensity for not speaking for long periods when hurt. It is a product, I believe, of a repressive upbringing. But she absorbed enough of her grandfather's sense of humour, which her own father shared, to enable her to rise, resourcefully and imaginatively, above these disapproving sulks. Elfriede's character also made her strong enough to overcome catastrophes in later life.

The Lutheran Church strongly influenced village life. The members of Emma's family not only regularly attended church, but were taught from the Bible to live by Christian precepts. Elfriede spoke of her mother as a good Samaritan to strangers. Later in life, she recalled that Emma never turned away hungry people from her door. She sat them at her table, whether beggar or friend. Thus began a tradition of hospitality from which both her daughters were to draw inspiration that reached women of subsequent generations.

Elfriede's father had been raised a Hussite, a follower of Jan Huss, the most important Czech religious reformer of the fifteenth century, who died in 1415. He also belonged to *die Brüderschaft*, the Moravian Brotherhood. Although Friedrich was said to have been a man of deep humanity and gentleness in his dealings with his wife and children, Elfriede remembered that his religious formation determined that a Sunday at home was observed as seriously as a funeral.

The family's Lutheran members, however, exercised the dominant influence. Pagan superstitions had not been eliminated from rural Silesia despite centuries of Christian teaching. The two systems co-existed. It was considered dangerous to hang out washing for some days after Christmas in case the god Odin's horses caught their hooves in the washing lines as they galloped by. They could bring tragedy to a family. Animals were always to be treated with care. On Christmas Eve, all farm animals were to be indulged with special food in honour of their presence during the birth of Jesus in the Bethlehem stable.

When Elfriede was nine years old, during Christmas 1916, Russian soldiers came to Steinkirche. They picked the little girl up off the street and carried her aloft through the snow-bound village, as the Christ child. This was a Russian custom. The Russians were prisoners-of-war, assigned to work in the fields of local farmers. Friedrich Bittnar had given them permission to carry his daughter as part of their traditional ritual. He could converse with them in their own language.

In 1918 tragedy struck the family. Friedrich and his two children were wrongly diagnosed as having typhus, and were taken back to the hospital where they were then said to have contracted the illness. It was lice-borne, carried by soldiers returning from World War I. They died within a fortnight. Emma was said to have lost so many relatives that the undertaker wept at the graveside. Elfriede still experienced fits of melancholy fifty years afterwards, every time she heard the train driver blow his whistle passing by the village. It was the custom to acknowledge a death and a burial in this manner in these tightly knit village communities.

Emma, who was pregnant at this time, was so shocked by the disaster that her hair turned white 'overnight'. She even tried to drown herself in the local quarry. Twelve-year-old Elfriede ran after her mother in her nightdress, pleading with her to return home. For a long time after that, Elfriede feared going to sleep at night.

Much later in life, a train blowing its whistle near her home in rural Western Australia in the 1960s could transport Elfriede back to Steinkirche and the deaths in her family.

On 14 November 1918, Emma gave birth to a daughter whom she named Else after her dead stepdaughter. Strange as it may seem to us, it was then not unusual to name a newborn child after one who had died earlier. There was a high rate of infant mortality, and certain names recurred in families. Elfriede had admired her stepsister with her Titian auburn hair. She was said to have been a beauty. Elfriede mourned her death and also the loss of her father, to whom she had always been closest. At a time when children were frequently beaten, he had only ever smacked her once when, with her customary quick tongue, she had called him a 'three-coloured tomcat' because of the red streaks in his beard and the two shades of brown in his hair and eyebrows.

When Emma lost her husband and stepdaughter, Elfriede was obliged to leave the high school in Breslau she had started that year, as well as her home with her grandparents. She had to come back to look after her mother. The loss of her schooling and the way she felt she was being pushed around contributed to further feelings of grievance. She also felt displaced by the birth of the baby.

Baby Else seemed to be showered with loving protection. She was a sweet-natured child. As Elfriede was to recall, while she herself was used to wearing the hand-me-down clothes of her older sister, Else was dressed in 'new silk and velvet'. Given Elfriede's talent for dramatisation, one can substitute 'new cotton and wool'.

Elfriede saw herself as put upon. As she remembered it, she was always being reprimanded by visiting aunts for her sharp tongue and the wilful behaviour which could 'bring trouble to her mother'. She increasingly saw herself as an alienated rebel. In later life she experienced recurring fits of melancholia. Perhaps this was rooted in the tragedy of 1918 and its consequences. It was no doubt nourished by a typical diet of Silesian Romantic literature, of which Joseph von Eichendorff was the most noted exponent. These writings were infused with a love of Nature, and romanticised the freedom of the wanderer. Elfriede devoured such work as her spiritual sustenance.

In her early thirties, another blow would further blight her spirit.

But as a teenager, she had little time to wallow in self-pity. She was part of a hard-working household without water. Her mother took to her bed for long periods, both before and after the birth of the baby, suffering fits of depression despite the joy of her splendid new child. When baby

Else was old enough to be left in the care of her older sister, at about the age of two, Emma would set off on occasional long journeys in the company of friends to visit two of her brothers. Her thirteen-year-old daughter would be left in charge of her two siblings as well as the young children of the travel companions.

Elfriede resented this arrangement. She remembered it as scandalously irresponsible. As she saw it, Emma sacrificed her daughter's education to her own needs. Daunted by being called on to be so responsible so young, she remembered being scornful when her mother returned from her long absences. Elfriede had made the little ones happy by re-arranging the furniture and sleeping with everyone together on the floor. Then suddenly her mother would take over again, and reimpose her own arrangements.

The idea for the communal sleeping is a clue to my mother's resourcefulness. It demonstrates her talent for improvisation. As a teenager, she sewed clothes and hats, hoping to become a dress designer. When her twelve-year-old cousin Gertrud arrived alone from distant Berlin with a placard around her neck announcing 'Steinkirche via Breslau', passengers looking out were astonished to see Elfriede, a young teenager, with her family's goat and ducks dressed up in the jackets and hats she had sewn for them.

When the situation at home became more stable, Elfriede was sent to acquire secretarial skills in the nearest city. Emma knew of the hardships faced by a widow after her husband dies. Since 1918, she had scratched together a living by taking in washing, ironing and sewing to make ends meet. She argued that a woman had a better chance for independence with ready access to paid work, rather than from mere education.

Elfriede must already have been quite independent in character. She cut her long hair short in the new manner of city girls, even though this was considered 'in the manner of tarts'. She kept up her interest in fine literature and, once she began to earn wages, collected books. The village school had taught the girls well. Elfriede could recite long narrative poems many years after she had left. The school laid the foundations for her respect for learning and her love of literature.

She was about eighteen, I think, when she took up a position on an estate at Märzdorf. There she did secretarial work and became the companion of an eighty-year-old woman of aristocratic lineage. She travelled with her in her carriage to social functions. The old woman taught her all manner of domestic refinements and thrifty budgeting for a large aristocratic household. All clothing was mended with such artistry that additions became invisible. Even bedsheets were darned.

From parts of the estate, Elfriede could see the steeple of her village church. She was beset with nagging *Heimweh* (homesickness). Her stories suggest she may not have gone home very much. Märzdorf was perhaps six kilometres away as the crow flies, but much further when following the road, which wound in part along the flood-prone banks of the Oder. Her work arrangements seem to have provided little regular time off.

Through Elfriede's talent for vivid description, I later got to know something about the older women of my mother's family. They laughed and sang with open-throated ease, using humour and repartee to lighten the domestic routine, which they approached with almost religious zeal. They created clean, comfortable spaces in their houses, not so much to be admired as to offer *Gemutlichkeit*, comfortable, cosy conviviality. My mother told me: 'We were expected to become *Herdetiere* (herd animals)'—that is, people with a strong sense of community, a strong culture.

After World War II, when Silesia had been handed over to Poland, and Elfriede's sister Else had joined our household in Australia, the sisters indulged their predilection for wine and spirits and nostalgic reminiscences about their days in Silesia. They admired the fine craftsmanship of its artisans and the way in which the seasons were celebrated. They remembered the celebration of a fruitful harvest or the winter solstice which used to hail 'the return of the sun' with huge bonfires and burning cartwheels that were rolled down the hill. My mother spoke of the fragrance of pine branches brought indoors at Christmas when snow lay thick on the ground. They were decorated with the finest strips of silver 'angels' hair' and dotted with real wax candles in little tin stands. Polished fresh apples that had been stored in the barn beneath a layer of hay adorned the tree, together with gingerbread hearts coated in chocolate.

In winter when times were good the cosy *Kacheloven* or tile oven warmed the house day and night. Spring arrived with such exuberant return of growth that 'the oldest donkey kicked his legs in the air'. On 1 May, the young ones danced around the maypole in their regional costumes.

These were seasonal festivals celebrated all over Europe. But everyone valued what was special to their region.

Girls were all brought up in the same way as my mother. Acculturation involved habit-forming activities such as the scrubbing of floors, the starching and ironing of all bed linen, and the baking of honey-based *Bienenstich* and butter-crumbed *Streusel* cakes for Sunday's breakfast after church. *Das Schlesische Himmelreich*, a regional specialty of pork stewed with dried fruits, was less remarkable for its flavours than for the many occasions on which it appeared on the table. Some of my great-grandmother's aphorisms have endured over four generations. I recall my mother's exchange with one of my daughters in the 1970s: 'Do not allow anger to erupt. Do as my grandmother cautioned: "Take a mouth full of cold water and wait until it boils!"'

Young Anthea's retort, some hours later, was: 'Grandmama—the water!'

The women of my family excelled as cooks and sewed and gardened with enthusiasm. Conversely, they also shared a pervasive melancholy, a talent for withdrawing into protracted silences, of making others guilty by their refusal to be open about what had gone wrong. My brothers and I have acquired some of their reclusive melancholy.

But there was always an over-arching pleasure in the companionship of that rural environment, of groups of people picking mushrooms and berries in the forests and going on excursions into the mountains singing in harmony to lutes as they walked.

It was into this robust, but often temperamentally ambiguous environment, that my mother was born. She absorbed its essence as she grew up.

I now ask myself why, if Elfriede found this environment so oppressive, in later life I only ever heard her speak the dialect of her people with her sister Else.

I know she looked back on those days in the village with mixed feelings. Both sadness and love suffused her memories. She found an oppressive 'parish pump' atmosphere of gossip, of people 'minding other people's business' and of dictating how others should behave. Central to this was what people assumed to be the 'pillow talk' between the pastor and his wife. They seemed to know what everybody had told her husband in confidence before it became common knowledge. The pressures of a married clergyman and his wife, together with other constraints, made village life stifling for Elfriede. She often recalled how poor the family became after her father's death, and the limitations this imposed on their lives.

Emma always wanted to join the young ones, whether welcome or not. She accompanied them to local dances, taking part in the fun as well as acting like a chaperone. Grandmother, too old to come along, would gaze enviously from the attic window.

Around 1930 the members of Emma's household moved into an apartment in Neumarkt Platz, the market square of Breslau. Possibly Elfriede and Otto, the wage-earners, contributed to the rent. Breslau was a vibrant, cultured city with a theatre, opera house, book and craft shops, botanic gardens, zoo and public baths. The Austrian empress Maria Theresa had once exclaimed that Silesia was the jewel in Austria's crown. Breslau was prosperous because it lay between trade routes. It benefited from abundant natural resources, especially coal from Upper Silesia. So many traders and their animals moved into parts of the city from the country each week that the council had to control them.

During the 1930s, Hitler's crazy regime harnessed the groundswell of Germanic feeling and mythology in the re-education and re-tribalisation of the German nation. Set on the eastern frontier of Germany, Silesia was vulnerable to foreign invasion and ethnic cleansing. Traditions contributed to a sense of identity. The children of Steinkirche had been raised with a strong love of their locality and a sense of being Silesian German.

It is interesting to note how long traces of Silesian culture have endured in South Australia's Barossa Valley. Back 'home' even local landforms had mythological significance, like the western mountain range known as *das Riesengebirge* (the mountains of the giants) in which the gentle giant *Rübezahl* strode with seven-league boots. You had to be careful not to get trampled. *Das Eulengebirge* (the mountains of the owls) were also a talking point. There was mystery and there was magic beyond natural life.

I do not know what year it was when Elfriede went to work in Stamboul (Istanbul). It could not have been later than 1933. She got a position there on the recommendation of her employers at Märzdorf. Their illustrious relative, Baron von Tucher, whose family had been painted by Holbein and Goya, was the German envoy to Turkey. With their base in Hamburg, the Tucher family had won its standing through the Hanseatic League's cloth trade, just as merchants elsewhere had achieved aristocratic standing through fortuitous trading and as pioneer bankers.

Before her departure for Turkey, Elfriede spent time with her cousins in Berlin and with a close friend from Steinkirche, Johannes Müller, who was studying law (probably in Breslau) and who introduced her to other law students. With them she tasted the heady cabaret life of Berlin's fashionable city centre, on *Unter den Linden* (under the linden trees).

Elfriede later said that to be part of that scene between the Wars was like 'dancing on top of a volcano'. One of her close friends was her cousin Vera, a successful dress designer who was to migrate to the United States. Elfriede's closest female friend also migrated there and was to end up in prison for participating in civil rights activities.

Elfriede herself was much taken by the powerful anti-Fascist art of Käthe Kollwitz, the wife of a doctor who treated the poor of Berlin. At the same time, the girl from Steinkirche began to dress fashionably, in the urban style. While an element of sophisticated snobbery appeared in Elfriede's demeanour, she never lost her attachment to the land.

Her talent for quick-witted repartee and her fondness for reciting from memory passages from literature prepared her for the company she was to keep among expatriates in Turkey. She was employed in Stamboul to supervise the domestic staff of the German legation and to deal with the envoy's personal correspondence. Despite her domestic role, she mixed freely with visiting diplomats from other nations with whom she was sometimes invited to sit at table. She also cooked for them when the legation's cook took maternity leave. With her Turkish boyfriend, she visited the local restaurants, getting him to purchase recipes for her to cook at the legation.

Elfriede mixed with German academics from the university. She often spoke of the classy boating parties she went to on the Bosporus and the Sea of Marmara. She never mentioned party politics. (After she had left, the next envoy was a political appointee of Hitler's.)

This is the time my parents met. When Rudolf, the young civil engineer from Vienna, called at the legation, she compared his unaffected charm with the seedy sophistication of diplomats and academics. That was how she was to explain it to me some forty years later. 'He was like a fresh mountain spring, unaffected and spontaneous.' Her rural childhood had left deep roots.

Rudolf and Elfriede became lovers. I was born four months into their marriage.

Rudolf was born on 3 March 1910 in Vienna into a pious Catholic family. He had been raised with the indulgence often accorded a youngest child. While his older brother Karl was destined to take over the family workshop, where small leather goods were manufactured to be sold at their retail outlet in central Vienna, Rudolf was lucky. He attended a Technical High School and then the Museum of Technology, to qualify for a diploma in civil engineering.

His mother left her mark on the family's domestic life, but her husband ruled the household with strict Catholic authority. Before her marriage to Karl, Maria (born Bresnitzer) had performed in repertory in the city of Graz, as an actress and singer.

Since her family lived off their leathercraft business in the spa resort of Bad-Ischl in the larger neighbourhood of Salzburg, Maria's family may well have had business connections with the Girschiks of Vienna. On the *Ahnen Pass* (genealogical passport), which Hitler made obligatory after Germany's *Anschluss*, Karl's family is traced back to the eighteenth century, always with Austrian residence.

The name Girschik obviously has an older Slavonic origin. Its Czech equivalent means butcher, although there were no butchers in my father's family, who almost all made a living from working with leather. I am not aware of any Jewish connections, although Girsch sometimes appears as a Jewish name elsewhere.

In 1956, when I visited relatives in Vienna, that family was the only one in the Vienna phone book. I sometimes wonder whether tinkering with evidence was possible, since I see no evidence in this document that—according to my father—one male elder of the direct branch of his family came from Prague, with antecedents in Moravia. Perhaps this was his mother's father.

At least two, or maybe all three of Rudolf's sisters were given sound instruction in music. Their eldest daughter, Maria Anna ('Marianne'), was taught the piano by a pupil of Franz Liszt. She was already an accomplished pianist before her marriage to Oswald Dittrich, whose father, Franz Rudolf Dittrich (1861–1919), had studied under Anton Bruckner, whom he succeeded as court organist in Vienna. Franz Dittrich's first musical appointment was to Kyoto where, as musician and impresario at the court of the Emperor, he was the first person to introduce Western classical music to Japan. No one in my family knows why his marriage or cohabitation with a Japanese woman, Kiku Mori, ended, or what happened to his two children, Otto Mori (born 1892) and Yashiko Miyoko (born 1894). We know that his son became a violinist, probably Japan's first. Franz Dittrich remarried in 1900, to the twenty-year-old Katherine Kriegl who, in 1901, produced Oswald Dittrich, his only offspring in Vienna.

While the family life of my father Rudolf was closely and rigidly supervised, under his father's Catholic piety and rigid paternalism, the cosmopolitan influence of Viennese urban life left sufficient mark on Rudolf for him to be able to happily leave home. He was not dependent on either his family or what Vienna stood for. He nevertheless retained a singular fondness for both when he lived abroad.

Rudolf Girschik's sister Anna ('Annie'), the second oldest, was to become—until she turned fifty—the leading soprano in concert-style orchestral Masses by Schubert and Bruckner, Mozart and Haydn. She performed in the city's neo-Gothic Votifkirche. She could not become 'professional' since she was obliged to work in the family's shop during the week.

Karoline ('Li'), Rudolf's third sister, was to marry a teacher and cellist, Franz Berg. Rudolf himself learnt to play the violin. He admired the music of his city's great composers, but made nothing special of it. The religion and music of my father's family were just another part of ordinary living: something people took for granted, not something to boast about, or to acknowledge with passion in times of cultural drought. The distinction between 'classical' high-brow, and popular 'folk' music was not significant. Familiar with classical music, Rudolf was just as likely to be enlivened by a proficient brass band as by a visit to the Volksoper up the hill from where he lived.

He was equally relaxed about his Catholic religion, proving himself over time a convert to pragmatic rationalism. He was a collector of 'correct information', never a dogmatic idealist.

As a teenager after World War I, young Rudolf had been boarded out every summer at the rural retreat of a Protestant Danish doctor's family, which had claimed him on behalf of a Scandinavian aid project. This supported children from central Europe left destitute at the end of the War. He learned to speak simple conversational Danish. Rudolf remained in grateful contact with these people all his life. Like most western European high school children, he studied languages: French, English, Italian, in that order. He thought it necessary that everyone learn more than one language and also kept in touch with Professor Pucci, his French and Italian teacher, all his life.

Rudolf loved observing and experiencing foreign ways. After he graduated in civil engineering, he found work on buildings around Vienna uninspiring, with secure work hard to come by.

When he heard about the expansion of railways in the Middle East, in 1933 he rode his bicycle from Vienna to Baghdad in search of opportunity. No stories survive from that marathon. One cannot even be certain that he rode all rhe way, as he later inferred. On the one hand I came to know him years later as an honest man of few, blunt words interlaced with moments of sentimentality; on the other, I discovered his penchant for joking, and for telling the occasional tall story to test our faith in him.

The prospect of working in a Muslim country did not deter him. Arriving in Baghdad, he was told to try his luck in neighbouring Turkey. He came to Stamboul with a camera, a sketchbook diary and the notebooks in which he composed 'verses'. Perhaps they were written to a distant beloved, for his only daughter was named in part, so he said, after one of his Danish girlfriends.

His first assignment was to supervise the construction of the Swedish embassy in Ankara, the new Turkish capital. Either before or during this project, he must have met Elfriede Bittnar at the German legation in Stamboul.

4. A Jewel in the Austrian Crown

After the embassy was completed, he was awarded membership of the Knights of Vasa from the King of Sweden, in person. This no doubt guaranteed him further work. When a contract was signed for his supervision of a railway project, about 100 kilometres north of Ankara, he was able to offer Elfriede financial security.

But there was no smooth passage to their long-term relationship. As Elfriede was to comment ruefully in later life, suggesting the historical basis of conflict between Austria and Germany: 'The war between the Empress Maria Theresa and the Prussian King Frederick II continued into our marriage.'

Rudolf's patriotic Austrian family opposed his marriage to his German lover vehemently, by letter. This was in spite of the fact (or perhaps because) she was expecting his child. They argued against her Protestant upbringing, and that she was unconventionally older than he and a sophisticated woman of the world who had 'led the innocent Rudolf astray'.

My mother reluctantly agreed to convert to Catholicism to placate them, though this offended her sense of fairness.

Rudolf remained attached, and even beholden, to his family all his life. They had coddled him as their youngest. This was especially so after he lost the sight in one eye when, as a three-year-old, he had taken a hammer to a glass.

In Turkey the independent Elfriede appeared to be in control of every situation. His glass eye was never an issue. Her heart was essentially compassionate. She focused on his good qualities. Worldly sophistication was of secondary value. And what could a pregnant woman in a foreign land do on her own?

All their lives, despite their temperamental ups and downs, the couple were to retain a genuine attachment to each other. Their happiest years, however, came at the beginning.

Elfriede gave her consent to becoming a Catholic to the papal legate in Turkey, Cardinal Roncalli, a man of 'such magisterial bearing, charisma and genuine modesty' that he removed all her scruples about the Catholic Church and its beliefs. She fell on her knees in true acceptance.

Elfriede Bittnar and Rudolf Girschik were married in the chapel of the Austrian boys' high school in Stamboul. That same day, in late February 1935, they travelled by steam train across the snow-bound plain of Anatolia. In the next few months their places of residence followed Rudolf's work, beyond Çankiri and back. They settled in the village in a narrow valley. Their home was the top floor of a stone house beside the poplar-lined railway line. It was here that I was born, at home, at the height of summer. Rudolf delivered me himself.

Photographs attest to the bliss of my parents. They gave me the double-barrelled name of Helga-Maria, with Christine to follow. For a long time I was simply Hasi (little rabbit). The long name also shrank in common usage. Not only his mother, but several men in Rudolf's family, had Maria as a second name. Mother said that Maria was her choice after her favourite (male) poet, Rainer Maria Rilke. I know that Hasi was for my long legs and protruding ears, which my parents tried to tame for a while with sticking plaster. Maria also soon fell out of use and was offered only when I earned special merit.

Rudolf's twenty-eight-year-old wife became an innovative homemaker, with few resources. She cooked cakes in the lids of saucepans for the bachelor engineers Rudolf kept bringing to their modest table. One of his wedding gifts for her had been a huge Austrian cookery book, a gastronome's delight from middle-class Vienna. But she preferred simple things.

Bonded perhaps by their love of the earth, Elfriede won the friendship of Turkish women in the neighbourhood. She learned respect for their customs. But she used to speak of amusing misunderstandings. When a man suddenly appeared, the women would grab the hem of her dress and throw it over her face. They then would cover their own faces with their veils, as etiquette demanded. Elfriede was thus displayed with her underpants exposed, far ruder than her face according to Western custom. Was it then that she began to construct one of her favourite sayings, that 'manners are morals'?

Well into winter, and nine months after the couple's arrival in Çankiri, Rudolf followed the promise of work in Iran. He drove my mother and me in an open car through Iraq and Syria. In Mosul I became so ill that my parents hurried to a Dominican monastery to have me baptised a Catholic. The incident illustrates that Rudolf's Catholic obligations, and his devotion to the beliefs of his family, ensured that no child of his was to be deprived of the spiritual consolation promised to all Catholics who receive the Sacrament. I survived to enjoy the Turkish name *Yildiz* (star, or Stella in English) given me by the Christian stranger, the Turkish godmother who was called in off the street to act as witness.

Rudolf and Elfriede otherwise did not attend church in the Middle East. Perhaps there were few Catholic churches in Iran. After their arrival in Tehran, we began life in the upper floor of a rented apartment.

My parents associated at first with Austrian and German expatriates who lived in the city, and observed with them the unfolding of events in German politics. Like most German-speakers of their generation, both my parents initially commended Hitler's social programs, aiming to bring everyone in Germany employment during the deep, disastrous Depression after World War I. I cannot recall that either of them ever subscribed to Hitler's aggressive nationalism, to his hijacking of government, to his theories of the superiority of the 'Aryan race' and that the future belonged to Germany. They came to Iran for Rudolf's work and immersed themselves in that country and its cosmopolitan work force with great energy.

Caring mostly alone for an inquisitive young child in a foreign country, and entertaining her husband's many guests kept Elfriede well employed. At that period of their marriage Rudolf from Vienna was proud of his talented wife from Breslau. His admiration for her never died, although he was to express it less and less openly over time. I loved my father with unbridled enthusiasm in my early years.

We could not know then how profoundly the coming War would affect our lives.

5
Meeting the Relatives

My mother filled in some of the gaps in my earliest memories. What are now just a few shards of memory in my mind belong to the larger story of my family. My father was trying to support a pregnant wife and child in Iran, on a contract fixed to a project. When that project was completed, there was no certainty that other work would follow. What is missing from the retrospective accounts of their early years in Iran, and the enthusiasm both my parents felt for the country, is the insecurity of my father's paid work. It was subject to vulnerable contracts in a country attempting to modernise itself in a climate of world Depression.

When Rudolf's Tehran project was approaching completion in late 1937, he sent Elfriede and me home. At the same time, he was making preparations to go to Sao Paulo in Brazil to work on harbour construction.

Mother and I were to take a boat across the Caspian Sea, then continue our journey by rail to Breslau. She was then expecting her second child, and was to live with her mother in Breslau until the baby was born the following June. Father expected to be settled in Brazil by then and was to call us to join him when mother and baby were strong enough to travel such a long distance.

The day that we left Iran, she told me the Caspian Sea was extremely rough. I do not recall that I was upset at having to leave my father, and had thrown a tantrum in protest. Nor do I remember trying to jump the ship's railing to return to him.

During the subsequent storm at sea, my mother received burns to her arm when she was thrown against a ship's oven. The long journey by rail was taken in an atmosphere that seemed somewhat ominous. At railway stations in Poland, soldiers with bayonets pierced bundles of cloth in search, it was said, of fugitives from Russia. The Russian Revolution had left a huge legacy of fear. But in the sleeping compartment next to ours, a Russian general travelled with his daughter, his maid and his samovar. He sent the maid to invite me to play with his child, and offered cups of tea to the elegant German woman.

I do not remember any of these details. Previously I have clung stubbornly to my own memories, not wanting to lay claim to what others have told me. But there is a kind of imperceptible osmosis at work, and one hungers to know *what really happened*. Our imaginations grow to embrace the stories of others and absorb them as our own. Perhaps I have done that more than I know.

I do know that my mother's family in Breslau welcomed us with open arms. Every morning Omi, my great-grandmother, Bertha Friebe, brought warm milk to me in my cot. I am now surprised by how much I welcomed this milk.

We had none in Iran and later in life I disliked milk on its own intensely, especially the skin on top as the heated liquid cools.

Photographs from that time show that the German Christmas was a wondrous experience, with a decorated spruce, silver 'angel's hair' and real candles dripping wax into the little metal dishes that were clipped to the fragrant branches. My little eyes are shown as wide with astonishment. Mother's brother made me a wooden doll's pram and I was given my own 'child', a doll named Käthe.

There was a visit to Berlin and more relatives. The glass-sided department store escalators proved irresistible. A visit to the famous *Berliner Tiergarten* (park and zoo) ought to have topped the popularity stakes, but I have no recollection of that either.

Then Rudolf sent one of his urgent telegrams: 'Come back, wife. We are staying in Iran.' It must have been February 1938, about three weeks before Hitler moved his army into Vienna to bring his native land back into Greater Germany.

On our way back to Iran, our way back 'home' to Pappi, we visited my father's people in Vienna. They received us in their inner-city apartment near the Danube Canal with generous-hearted hospitality. They kept to themselves their view that they found my mother too opinionated and assertive. I was only to hear that view decades later. In her turn, Mother never felt entirely at ease with them after their first dismissal of her. But her dour father-in-law fell in love with me, his first grandchild. He surprised his family when he became all Viennese charm, dancing with me with abandon. I warmed even more to my aunt's singing. At the end of Bach's loving tribute, *Willst Du Dein Herz mir Schenken* (If you want to give me your heart), I walked over to her, curtsied as I had been taught to do, and kissed her hand, with the plea: 'Please Tante Annie, sing me that lovely song again.'

At this point my own recollections and my mother's stories leave a gap. My father's fine photographs have us in a townhouse in Tehran. It is Easter, because I am carrying a large chocolate egg wrapped in shiny paper. There is a small walled garden and a little pool in which my mother's naked, swollen body is relaxing. Later that day she sits with her arm lovingly around my neck, her stomach bulging under her tailored dress. We are sitting on a verandah behind a garden of roses. We are both laughing. Later, my smiling father and mother stand in loving embrace.

Then, on the day that my brother is born, I was packed off to stay with Herr Baumgärtel and his Iranian wife. They were kind to me but I had never been separated from my mother. My third birthday would be in four days. But mother would be away!

It was very hot, late in June. On the first night away from my mother, I had my first-ever, memorable nightmare. It was a simple childish story about my family becoming hostages to the Turkish pilot of a flying house. He disappeared, and we managed to jump out of a first-floor window and hop into cars, crossing many bridges that kept on collapsing behind us, repetitively, a theme without end.

I wake up. Herr Baumgärtel and his wife are bending over me, having heard my screams of fear. But I do not want them. I want my mother.

I tell the incident here because it begins a constant theme in my life. In the simple Arabian Nights–type dream, we do not come to any real harm. In other dreams, and in real life, I may be frightened out of my wits, but optimism always ends up outstripping fear and loss. In dreams in later life I am occasionally threatened by a massive avalanche of water towering above me like a tidal wave. I am on a simple raft, threatened with drowning. But my raft rises, like a lift going up many floors, to the top of the wave. It then slides down gently to calm waters beyond.

I remain a creature of hope. The sense of security imparted by my loving parents keeps at bay the terrors that fly through the night. I never became a victim of annihilation. Of course, one may argue that such simple faith demands less intellectual energy. Scepticism and doubt require real courage and, in later life, I came to admire people who challenge received knowledge for the sake of correct information.

But in June 1938, my life was simple. I did not warm immediately to my new brother, Peter Michael. He was red and wrinkled and ugly at first. But, day by day, he grew ever more handsome until he grew into my ever-better playfellow, my only constant child companion. As he grew and walked and talked, it was he who rescued my neglected dolls, he who wanted to dress like me, and play my games. Mother was a sufficiently free spirit to allow him to wear dresses, to grow his hair long and tie ribbons in it, until this urge disappeared. He remained a nurturing person but did not become ostensibly effeminate. I was a bossy older child, but I probably loved him even more than he loved me. His loyal friendship I was to take for granted.

6

For the Love of Iran

People say that it must have been tricky being a girl in repressive Iran. That was mostly not true for us in my childhood. What I remember when we lived there after the birth of my brother in 1938, right up until 1941, is that we were foreigners. We lived on the periphery of the real Iran, and usually on the fringes of the desert.

Those were still feudal times, with little in common with the ruling theocracy of today. Foreigners like my father had come to modernise the country. There was no organised opposition to the changes which Reza Shah himself was sponsoring. The ruler of Iran was sympathetic to German-speaking professionals. My father worked for Danish companies staffed by foreigners who supervised Iranian labourers. What I know about Iran is coloured by the sense I have of my father's itinerant work and the homes we lived in along the expanding railways.

I have many generalised memories and can recall a few anecdotes. Few of them are focused on people. Instead, they reflect how isolated we often were. They are obviously tinted with my mother's romantic love of the place, 'her spiritual home', as she was to remind us over and over again long after we had left the country.

'Nowhere are the cherries so plump and the apricots so delicious,' she would opine later, in middle age. She once put her hand through a flimsy wooden door in frustration when we as teenagers teased her over what we saw as her rose-coloured view of a place we had taken for granted.

In Iran father relished the various engineering challenges that confronted him. There was too much salt in the soil; there were obstacles in tunnels; there were bridges washed away by floods. Under his command worked large teams of locals whose varied dialects he could hardly hope to learn. It was work on a grand scale.

My mother was a true believer in the spiritual beauty of ordinary Iranians in their rural environment. That love she held to her heart. It had been born in the years spanning 1936–41, and was confirmed when she went back for a year in the late 1950s and again during the 1960s. Since then Iran, with much else in the rest of the world, has undergone irreversible change. It is easy to romanticise the past, or to understand it in the light of present-day conditions. But what my brother and I lovingly stored as happy memories must have been influenced by the way both our parents spoke about their time there. What follows is the vintage that I have laid down from a blending of observations gathered in the years between 1938 and 1941.

Except for a number of enduring images, oases of the mind, my recollections of Iran have become generalised impressions, like the shifting skies and the scenes of mountains and desert which, my mother remembered, were like a stage set. You drove towards the mountains and they fanned out as another range appeared. The vast stretches of desert, which we crossed so often by car on poor roads, were dotted with oases. These were stable and coherent places of habitation: perhaps a mud-baked wall, surrounding date palms, flat-roofed houses, a spring. Perhaps there was simply a set of terraced gardens with elaborate irrigation, supporting crops of watermelons and cucumbers.

One place was simply a small field. We came across it by chance, but the feeling of excitement associated with it has remained. We walked through a waterless riverbed, stepping on smooth stones and boulders, and climbed up a steep embankment. It was so steep that I had to be lifted up. But once at the top I stepped into a forest of sunflowers in bloom. At their feet sprawled cucumbers, with their clumps of leaves and tendrils. I cannot explain why suddenly my life seemed full and satisfying. I wanted to stay there forever.

Listening to me talk once again of that special place, my parents asked: 'Don't you remember that we could not get home? That a flash flood suddenly rushed down the riverbed and carried away the car and our driver?' I was astonished that I remembered none of this. But I do recall another late afternoon when we came to a flooded river and we could not cross. We were rescued in the twilight by a bus full of people.

My mother confirmed that this was on the very same day, and that the people on the bus were all pilgrims travelling to Mecca. They stank horribly of stale garlic, enough to make us want to faint, she remembered. 'But they were so happy to help us.' My parents had obviously concealed from me the tragic death of the driver who had parked father's car in the dry riverbed.

Some oases were large cities. Beyond, across the stark land the engineers laid roads on difficult layers of salt-impregnated soil. Their workers burrowed tunnels through mountain ranges, and laid railway tracks to open the country to modern ideas. Meanwhile, nomads moved about with their tents, carpets and flocks. Occasionally they set up barriers to progress, creating problems which Rudolf had to solve.

Father adored his work. Mother fell in love with Iran. Nowhere else did the poor accept their fate with such dignity, she thought. 'Nowhere else could peasants recite the words of their great poets by heart,' she used to say. Nowhere was silence so large a frame for the sounds of people at work, for hyenas crying like babies, for the bells on the necks of camels that moved in procession from one depot to another.

My own recollections merge with my mother's deep attachment. Hers was a poetic response, springing from the sense of liberation she felt as a foreigner in this wonderful land. She was not bound by other people's strictures or any need to conform. Unable to do anything about the terrible feudal situation in which rich landlords ground down the poor, she focused her mind instead on noble peasants whose religion enabled them to live with dignity and hope.

She often repeated these lines from the Iranian poet Hafiz:

> If of your worldly goods you are bereft,
> And in your store two loaves are left,
> Sell one and, for the dole
> Buy hyacinths to feed your soul.

This is, of course, a defence of the stoic resignation of the Iranian poor. My mother also sometimes grew melancholy as the wife of a busy engineer, making do on her own during workdays with only young children for company. Poetic romanticism compensated for that loneliness. It was her way of coping.

My brother's and my boredom at being confined in cars for hours on poor roads was made easier by the security we always felt, knowing that we were safe with our confident and loving parents.

One day I was alone with my beloved father. He often took me to work with him in his car because I so much enjoyed climbing and balancing on low scaffolding and riding in the Dressine, the little wagon that ran along railway lines under construction, to check on completed work. Once as we drove down a mountain range, we saw from a distance what we thought was a lake. Then, as we approached and passed it, the mirage turned into an abandoned garden where grape hyacinths competed with grass between crumbling clay walls.

My early childhood was like that surprise: simple and refreshing.

My brother Peter, often with domestic staff, grew up Iranian. I am ashamed now to remember that, on one occasion, I was uppity about them. 'They are only servants, after all!' was my self-defence for some naughtiness. Mother reminded me of my comment years later. Who had given me that patronising impression? Surely not my parents, who allowed Peter to mingle freely. He sat in the kitchen with the cook tasting *sabse polo* (vegetables with rice)—especially if they were shelled broad beans—*baddenyan* (aubergine) or yoghurt. He babbled away in Farsi, as much as German, his first language.

The earth and plants of Iran provide some of my most vivid memories. No nursery-bred beauty has ever surpassed for me the little bright red tulips with black hearts that flowered so briefly in the stony mountains. As an adult I can interpret my fascination. They flowered so well in so many places where no one could see them, buffeted by the wind, in soil too poor for most plants. There was independence and strength in their brief display. This has its corollary in the noble side of the human condition, when people do the right thing without expecting to be noticed.

6. For the Love of Iran

After rain in Iran, patches of green and tiny scented blooms covered the harsh desert in which nothing soft survived, spread out like a vast carpet. You might suddenly come across desert dwellers, hard as scorpions or, as you rounded the bend of a hill on the back of a donkey, catch the sweet-bitter scent of stands of wild thyme and rosemary growing along the track. Those few shrubs thriving on stony ground still survive in a corner of my mind, beyond a vllage where the track would spring into life as a creek during the wet season.

In my memories, old Tehran lives, with its cobbled streets and the smell of urine in the gutters, a mixture of poverty and neglect and classy hotels. We sat in these on warm nights in rose gardens beside fountains, and ate delicious pink and white ice-creams from glass goblets on long stems. After one such outing, I became feverish and mother rubbed down my body with pure alcohol.

The Bazaar in Tehran was huge. Its arcades supported moulded ceilings that swept up to an opening through which light entered in shafts. Galleries ran in different directions. The place was always crowded, loud with people's talk and the noises of animals, smelly and very mushy underfoot. Mother bought vegetables and brass, bronze or silver utensils, as well as fabrics. But she also bought her produce from travelling vendors who announced themselves at the house door. Their donkeys were laden with *polo* (rice), *bamia* (okra) or *baddenyan*. I also saw fleet-footed carriers moving down the lane where we lived, delivering whole meals in stacks of white interlocking enamel pots. We ate sheep's milk yoghurt which had been set and was sold in little baked day ramekins. No milkman came and no milk was for sale.

There was one shop with special appeal to me, near our house. It stood on the corner of a wide dusty street and in its window were huge closed glass bowls with sweet cordials that tempted children with their colours: green, yellow, orange, red and even blue. This shopkeeper also sold delicious little bars of nougat with pistachios and the pollen of a lily. And oh, the smell of nan, the flat bread cooked on top of hot stones above glowing charcoal! We caught a whiff of that here and there wherever we travelled, but years later, after we had left, that fragrance drifted unexpectedly, seemingly from nowhere to my nostrils, long before flat bread was sold in our next homeland. Along with the smell of freshly cooked bread I immediately see clay ovens.

Then there were the *Droschken* (horse-drawn carriages), with their animals tapping along the road. We would stop to go inside a shop, where a man on the ground would unwrap the purple paper from a pyramid of compressed sugar and tap it with a little hammer to free the granules. The loose sugar would be carefully weighed on a set of balanced copper scales.

From Tehran we spent an occasional summer holiday at Schimaran in the foothills of the local mountains visible beyond the town. The tallest was Mount Demavend with its pointed, snowy cone.

My father rented a house in a large garden behind a high wall. There were rows of zinnias and a pond from which spotted frogs suddenly appeared. 'You were so worried their colour would wash off,' mother laughed later. Our parents had problems with plagues of cats. These feral animals used to take possession of vacant holiday houses, leaping through air vents into cool rooms when no one was there.

Out in the sun my mother prepared bottles full to the brim with cherries and sugar. These fermented into cherry liqueur. Most wonderful, however, was the very old and gnarled sacred tree at the end of the lane. Every Thursday people came to light candles at the base of its trunk.

My brother was by now taking his first steps in grey home-made felt shoes. 'Soldier boots' my mother called them. She had sewn them with leather soles. She was justly proud of her improvisation, since she had no patterns. She must have made them in the summer of 1939–40.

About that time I saw an airman fall out of the sky.

It was afternoon in Schimaran. Alone in the garden, I looked up to see a bi-plane doing acrobatics high up above our vacation house. The engine was purring as the plane looped. Now he was flying upside down, lying on his back. I watched with fascination, anxious for his safety way up there, but slightly cross at his stupidity. I felt how hard it would be to turn that metal bird back to its normal position.

Then I saw that he could not do it. Silence. A rattle. Deathly silence. The engine had cut out. Then smoke began to pour from the tail as the plane dived rapidly, making an eerie, whining sound. Would it fall into our garden and smash everything to pieces? I ran into the house, calling out. My parents were puzzled. They had heard the sound but had not associated it with an accident.

6. For the Love of Iran

I pestered them to take me to the wreckage. But no one was permitted to go to the site of the crash for three days. Father said that the man had been in the Iranian Air Force. Practising. When we were allowed to visit the site, we saw only bits of silver metal, too bright in the sun to look at. They were strewn far beyond our house, across a patch of scorched earth. The rest had been carefully cleared away.

I had waited with uneasy curiosity, thinking perhaps I might see the charred corpse. I had never seen anyone dead. I hoped *madly* I would see him. People were forever dying in children's stories, and I wanted to know what it was like.

Some memories lie inside glass cases like objects from past times. Others are like plasticine, to be kneaded into different shapes. Years later I became acquainted with the legend of Icarus, who fell from the sky when his waxen wings melted after he flew too close to the sun. The poet Auden wrote on the theme, describing the oil painting by Pieter Breughel the Elder. The various strands of these interlinked stories and memories are hard to separate. But my father brought my imagination bumping down to earth. The dead man was an Iranian military pilot who had failed to complete a training exercise, he repeated.

During this period in Iran we lived in a number of houses on the fringes of towns or settlements, at Khaladabad, Sharifabad and Karind. Our houses were usually made of mud bricks or adobe given a wash of mud or lime. They were flat-roofed, with large air vents down which the wind whistled. Sometimes these block-like houses had stairs to the roof, for sleeping under nets on a stinking hot night. There was usually a courtyard behind the front wall or behind the house, with plants and some kind of pool.

We were living in Khaladabad when my father celebrated his thirtieth birthday on 3 March 1940. His professional colleagues were invited for the day. Previously they had successfully hunted game, and we ate the delectable meat of gazelle and wild donkey. Our L-shaped house was cooled by a gallery of openings along the patio, serving as both windows and doors.

The sweet whitish meat of wild donkey was served with deliciously roasted potatoes. It was a festive banquet, but I found the adults boring. They drank so much alcohol that my father's Bulgarian colleague slumped across the table and remained immobile. I feared my father would do the same. This spectacle gave me an unpleasant sensation. My father's spirits always picked up with a few drinks. Of stocky build, he held his alcohol well. But on that occasion I remember he was taken off to bed before me.

Some days Peter and I shared a tin tub masquerading as a boat, and were pushed around in the fetid water of the courtyard pool (*basign*) by grown-ups using long thin poles. I could not swim and feared the boat would overturn.

Behind the orderly house with its pomegranate trees sprawled a neglected orchard, gone completely wild. In this safe domestic jungle I could become an explorer on my own: the call of the wild.

At Sharifabad, in our house on the desolate outskirts of town, we had an orchard of fruit trees and a small vineyard. The best eating fruit was on hand if you climbed an apple tree and bit into green apples that were just beginning to ripen. That walled garden was our shelter. The greenery was so lush I could keep a tortoise as a pet, until one day, after I left it on a table with a bunch of clover before going for my own lunch, it ran away.

In creeks all over Iran we came across huge wrinkled tortoises of great age. Perhaps it was forbidden to slaughter them. If a Muslim man intended to cut down a tree, our mother said, the Koran obliged him first to ask its forgiveness.

We travelled so much. My parents were always exploring, driven by their endless curiosity. Sometimes by the roadside on an open plain, Peter and I would press our ears against telegraph poles, to hear the wires hum. The vegetation on the ranges near the Caspian Sea was so thick it was said tigers could be found there.

We stopped at night wherever we had arrived, never seeking the luxury of a proper destination. Perhaps it was a caravanserai, a hotel or a *chai hane* (a men's tea-house) where special arrangements had to be made for 'mixed' company.

During one long journey we stopped at cotton fields. We had seen the white woolly tufts from afar as we descended towards the mud houses of the town of Natanz. On that same journey we stopped to watch carpet-weaving families in Esphahan and saw the lines on which bundles of burgundy and dark blue wool were hung out to dry, above vats of dye. Pottery was also drying in the sun, and ornate carpets were draped unguarded over rocks. They had been cleaned with black tea.

6. For the Love of Iran

We also had holidays when we were transported by donkeys and lived in tents, up high in the mountains at Thame, a place not found on foreign maps. I saw butter wrapped in paper lowered by string into a *kanat* (underground irrigation channel) for cooling, deep down where sunlight barely touched the watercress. I heard that a daring thief once stole some by crawling along the subterranean canal.

In northern Iran it was not unusual, after crossing a mountain on a perilous road, to follow a stream down into one of the valleys. I can still see through the windows of my mind a pristine stream, lined with poplars, gurgling over smooth pebbles.

I acquired a special fondness for camels. They bore my adoration generously even when I would leap noisily around them at watering stations. It worried my parents when they saw these bubble-blowing mad things, in sexual heat, but no camel ever harmed me. I was more at risk from humans.

I did not tell my mother for many years how one of her domestic servants, Ibrahim, an Iranian father of twelve children, had one day in the garden tried to get me to massage his erect and naked penis. I was five. I did not even know what that very long sausage sticking out of his trousers was, but I knew instinctively not to do as he asked. I pulled my hand away from it with assertive words: 'No. I don't want to do that!'

He panicked, threatening me with *shaitan* (the Devil) if I told *Hannum* (the woman). Perhaps that is why, among a handful of remembered Farsi words, there lingers the word for Devil. Did this episode cause me to dream of black snakes, over and over again? For a while, later in life, they turned green, before disappearing completely.

Had my parents made me a prude? I recall feeling shame when my father wanted to photograph Peter sitting naked on a chair. I stood between the chair and the camera. I am the only one who remembers why I stood just there. It was not because I wanted to be the star of the picture.

Peter followed Ibrahim, the occasional cook who understood the local dialect, everywhere. I meanwhile listened to endless repetitions of the music records my parents had acquired from a departing Scandinavian engineer. I was enchanted by the picture of the dog on the label listening through a trumpet-shaped ear-piece, labelled His Master's Voice.

A grown-up would wind the gramophone by turning a handle, while a needle on the record magically made music pour forth. Mother was surprised when one night I asked her to send me to sleep by playing again 'that piece of music in which God walks through the room in silver slippers'. At first she did not know what I meant but, by process of elimination, found that I had paid J.S. Bach this supreme compliment.

Classical music was to remain my faithful companion. Since those early days it has re-energised me whenever I am tired, filling me in turn with admiration and joy. I can also argue that my mistake in music in early childhood cut across the anti-Jewish propaganda that was to mark the coming years.

This is how the argument goes. One of the children's songs which I used to like singing when young was Mozart's *Frühlingslied*:

> *Komm lieber Mai und mache*
> *Die Bäume wieder grün …*

And so on. It is a simple song in honour of Spring. I was already an adult when I discovered that one of the lines which I sang, *ein schönes Judenlied* (a beautiful Jewish song), is really *ein schönes Jubellied* (a song of jubilation). Anti-Jewish propaganda never took proper root in my head later on. My parents did not encourage it and besides, I knew that Jewish Germans sang lovely songs, because Mozart had told me so.

My mother carried some of the stock prejudices of her upbringing but my father always corrected her if she ever uttered the misguided statement that Jewish financiers had contributed to Germany's woes and therefore helped the ascent of Nazism. I remember my parents as being cosmopolitan: civil towards and tolerant of strangers.

The Iranian climate and physical environment could present problems for those not used to them. I nearly lost my sight from sandy blight after my father was forced to drive us through a sandstorm. A Russian specialist visiting Tehran saved my sight after I had lived for a terrifying period in total darkness and was put for safety back into a baby's cot.

Peter was intermittently sickly. At one period, all his teeth turned black and began to crumble; he had rickets. Occasionally both of us were infested with parasitic worms. They lay in wait in the dust and on the food we ate in public places. I had yellow jaundice for which my mother's prescribed cure was vitamins from grapes and the exposure of the naked body to sunlight, accompanied by buckets of cold water poured over you in the open air, if in the privacy of the garden. Mother told me that the cure for tapeworm was to lure it out by pouring warm milk into a chamber pot. When this did not work, she was told to swallow a couple of tablespoons of petrol. Fortunately, our children's worms were less threatening.

One doctor commented that we were particularly susceptible to infections because mother kept us too clean.

Some of the best times at Sharifabad were our visits to the dunes where our mother took us to play, while father worked his long hours. Dunes were everywhere in Iran. They moved imperceptively, leaving wave-like patterns behind them. Sometimes a set of dunes completely covered an *imamsadeh* (holy man's grave), until the wind carried them away. We played at making little houses: the holy man's mausoleum, a mosque, village houses, a tea-house, a caravanserai. They were usually just mounds of sand decorated with bits of wood and stones, but mother's imagination transformed them.

One day a caravan suddenly appeared over the dunes. Mother heard the bells approaching, graduated in tone according to the camels' rank. As the long line of beasts and their keepers passed, laden with goods, she heard in the ringing of these foreign bells something more. She realised that it was Pentecost Sunday at home in Germany, and she began to cry. Pentecost fell in the middle of Spring.

She remembered that the laziest donkey in her homeland would kick his heels in the air when violets appeared in clumps and when fruit trees bloomed all over the land. She had by this time been an expatriate for several years, and had only been back to Germany once since her marriage. The sadness at the core of her happiness as the expatriate wife of a busy engineer may be summed up in an image that has stayed with me. We are walking along a track, probably at Sharifabad, beyond the settlement. It is a mild but grey day, hinting at rain. We children notice pairs of dung beetles with their shimmering green and brown backs pushing huge lumps of sheep dung to their shelter. We follow the track to a weathered wall, stepping through a broken slab and finding ourselves inside a walled orchard, full of high grass. Several trees are covered in white blossoms. They are almonds.

'A group of brides in white,' says my mother.

I approach what I think are blossoms scattered on the grass. As I draw near I see that they are feathers stained with fresh blood. It was probably a fox, the adults explain, that ate a duck.

Later in life that scene in Iran was to find resonance in other metaphors. There was John Shaw Neilson's celebration of the light in the orange tree. And in one of William Blake's *Songs of Experience*, the worm that flies in the night devours with its fierce possessive love the crimson heart of joy of a rose.

Years later, when I was lonely in a foreign boarding school where there was no one with whom I could communicate in my language, I used to bring out these recollections of Iran as one would shuffle a pack of cards. My memories became my friendly ghosts, the companions of my heart. There was little to disturb their pleasurable innocence. Like the faces of people whom I have truly loved in my life, the memory of them is deep and comforting.

These memories of childhood are of a simple, happy day-to-day life. At that early time, life was not about serious human striving, about mental development, the growth of awareness, identity, sexuality, ideals, politics—all those preoccupations of the lives of adults. I had no knowledge of government or of war, no awareness of nationality or politics, nor even a sense of organised religion. My parents had not entered a church with me since my baptism.

7

To the Bottom of the World

I was just over six years old and my brother three when World War II caught up with us in Iran. We were living in the north-west of the country quite close to its border with Iraq. My father was building a railway and upgrading the road through a mountain pass. We were based in a company-owned house at the edge of the Kurdish village of Karind.

I remember it very well: the mud-baked houses with their flat roofs, clinging to the slopes of the valley; the nearby cemetery with its tombstones engraved with the goats owned and cherished for a life-time; the fast-flowing stream moving through a dense thicket beyond the village. Above it, black-and-white butterflies as large as your hand floated in filtered light.

I remember also the wind-up gramophone which mother used to place on the table on the back verandah. Perhaps it would be a movement from Mendelssohn's first piano trio floating towards the mountains and mingling with mother's feelings of melancholy. I still have the record.

Elfriede had followed Rudolf to this remote region with two young children and a large dog. When she arrived she was nursing a wound from dental surgery in Tehran. One of her cheeks was bloated, and she disguised it under a scarf.

Her toothache added to her feelings of unease. How safe was the family in this Kurdish settlement? The European War had already moved beyond Europe's boundaries. I, of course, was oblivious to all this. In later life my mother occasionally berated Rudolf with her tongue for his impulsive, impractical ways. Although I always knew him as a responsible breadwinner, considerations of practicality and indeed of family safety sometimes ended up well behind his passion for his profession. The more remote the location and the more challenging the work, the better he liked it.

Mother had lived with this since her marriage. It gave us our adventurous life. His exploits, such as the car and driver being swept away, or the road through the mountains at night ending in a ravine without a bridge, became grounds for recrimination. They grew into dragons' teeth.

The War appeared as a single aeroplane with circles on its wings. On that fateful day, my mother had scrubbed my head and was brushing out my tangled hair. We were in the lane outside our front door, and I was protesting angrily.

My mother was an intelligent parent who paid attention to new scientific ideas about vitamins, including the healing powers of sunshine. She had taken me outside to catch some morning sun. I spotted the pale aeroplane rumbling towards us over the mountains. It began to descend and fly low over the village.

Mother dropped the brush and rushed out of the lane to see better. When she saw that the plane was British, she burst into tears. 'That's the end of us,' she cried. She came and held me close.

The plane circled a couple of times, then disappeared. It was obviously on a reconnaissance mission. An invasion was clearly imminent, even though Karind lay in difficult terrain.

Before this day, my parents had been wondering what to do with me. Within the year I was to turn seven, the age at which children were sent to school in Germany. Although I had not been told, my parents had arranged that I should lodge in Tehran with an Iranian doctor and his German wife. The doctor had studied in Germany. I was to attend the International School while living in their house.

Had the War not intervened, our family may well have remained in Iran. I might even have married there and now be living surrounded by modern Iran's religious communities. But the hand of fate moved us in another direction on life's chessboard.

If I had been sent to school, of course, I would have been separated for years from my parents. I was to be saved this trauma.

7. To the Bottom of the World

Next day, as I was playing with the local Kurdish children in the lane outside our house, I heard a loud rattle and saw a green metal vehicle with a long gun in front rolling towards us. Its bulk took up most of the space between the houses. I pressed myself against the wall and watched with trembling fascination. This engine of war did not stop at our house, but moved beyond the settlement. Village children swarmed behind it. I stayed close to home.

Later, as my family was lunching on the verandah at the back of the house, facing a derelict garden and a sluggish creek, soldiers in khaki climbed through an opening in the baked mud wall. They kept on coming until there seemed to be about a dozen. They immediately surrounded us, standing in a wide circle, each aggressively pointing at us the bayonet tied to his rifle.

'Don't move. Stay where you are,' an English officer commanded, in most peculiar German. We immediately put our cutlery down on the table. Turning to my father, he shouted: 'Hands up above your head!', then led him away like a thief. We did not see our father again for two days.

I was told in later years that the person in charge of the soldiers' camp was Sir William Slim and that the day of this momentous happening was 30 August 1941.

In May, British troops had entered Iraq to protect their oil interests. When Hitler's forces attacked the Soviet Union in June, it joined Britain in an invasion of neutral Iran, to protect landlines for their war supplies. Reza Shah abdicated, and his son ascended the Peacock Throne as Mohammad Reza Shah Pahlavi.

The villagers had been asked by the soldiers who found us if any foreigners lived nearby. It was many years before I learned anything about my father's interrogation, about how he was offered no food for those two days, but was obliged to come home for his meals under military surveillance. Over those days, he tried in vain to convince the soldiers that he was not in the pay of the German government. No, he told them, he was not a German spy.

The British papers of the time told stories of several thousand agents of the Third Reich in Iran, thinly disguised as German professionals. A list of the names of seventy allegedly active agents was leaked. Rudolf's name was not among them.

My father's captors offered him a car and protection for his family if he was willing to become a secret agent for the British government. He was one of twenty civilian internees deemed to have considerable knowledge of Iran and Iranian grassroots politics. 'No,' he was supposed to have said, 'I am not prepared to spy for any government.'

This was the wrong response. On 1 September, my mother was told to pack everything up, at once. Each family member was to be assigned no more than a certain weight—I think thirty kilos. We were to leave in a few days.

A group of soldiers guarded our house around the clock. In the tent where he was a prisoner, my father became more and more anxious about what was happening to his family. What was going on: rape, plunder, bribery, blackmail, theft? He also brooded on the insensitivity of his removal. Dragged away from his loved ones, he had been treated like a criminal. According to my mother, who only read it fifty years later, after he died, he recorded in his diary that on a visit home for food two days after his imprisonment, he had glimpsed through a window his wife in a compromising position with a British officer.

Why did he write this? A projection of his fear? A fantasy of his captivity? Anger with his wife over a marriage that was under threat? Perhaps my mother had later accused him of landing us in this mess. And she always admired the English.

I doubt that there was any truth to this story. Indeed, Elfriede would not have told me such an incriminating tale against herself had it been true. She never confided intimate details of her life to me. She was a stickler for a repressive form of sexual morality in conversation with the children. It was also unlikely that Rudolf, under military guard, had the opportunity to spy on his own house.

My mother told me she had destroyed the offending page. She probably destroyed the diary itself, since I have never seen it. For me, this distasteful incident illustrates how confusing and alarming were the circumstances of our abrupt capture.

Elfriede was then forced to make nervous decisions about what to pack, without Rudolf's advice. A military doctor came to check our health. He reproached my mother rudely for 'burning' my scalp with kerosene

7. To the Bottom of the World

in her attempt to rid me of the lice I had acquired from associating with the village children. He advised her to apply soothing black tea to the wounded skin.

I was annoyed with him for the belittling tone with which he addressed my mother. But I could not grasp his position as an 'enemy'.

The larger body of William Slim's group then moved on, leaving us in the charge of a few armed Gurkhas. The doors and windows of our house were boarded with wood, and many of our possessions were left inside.

Our dog was given to the Iranian police. I saw him leave in chains in the back of a van. He howled and I fretted. At times I had felt I loved him more than my family. He had always fussily protected Peter and me and risked his own safety for us, walking on the side where danger might lurk. My father was informed years later by a Danish neighbour that Fram had kept escaping from police custody and returning to the house after we had gone, looking for us and kicking up a terrible racket.

According to family memory, we left Karind on 16 September. We and the possessions we were permitted to take with us, in a few suitcases and crates, were loaded on to military lorries. My mother and I sat in front beside the driver, with my father and brother behind in the back, under olive green canvas.

Several military jeeps drove in convoy to Basrah in the south. What possessions had my mother packed? Much later I discovered that they were more than such a hurried departure warranted. They included valuables like carpets and silver, possibly to sell in an emergency; practical things like clothes and her Singer sewing machine; items of great sentimental value, like photograph albums and the HMV gramophone; and exotica from Iran such as a samovar.

The military convoy made several stops, the first at the town of Kermanshah, where my father was separated from us. We did not see him again for several weeks. The British did not want to take wives and children into custody, and encouraged internees from Iran to send their families 'home'. I do not know who insisted that our family not be divided. In an emergency my wiser, practical mother usually took the lead. She could be a tigress in our defence.

At the Basrah detention camp in which we were placed until our departure by ship could be arranged, our parents were interrogated separately and continuously, as if they were harbouring deep secrets which they were unwilling to divulge. My father was forced to live away from us the whole time.

My mother told me much later, dramatising her forcefulness and character, how British intelligence officers had asked her, in German, about her political affiliations. 'Rudolf and I have never been members of any political party,' she told them. 'We don't know in any detail what's going on in Germany. But if you put us into a prison camp with a bunch of Nazis we may not have much choice but to join them. They seem to put huge pressure on other people. That's what they may do to us, and that's the risk you take,' she threatened, hoping to reverse the decision to remove us from Iran.

But it was all in vain. Rudolf was unable to convince his interrogators that he was simply an engineer doing his job, not an agent of the Third Reich.

I was to read as an adult in William Slim's *Unofficial History* that he was convinced that the 3,000 or so citizens of Germany working in Iran were in the service of the Nazi government. According to Iranian sources, there were only a few hundred Germans in the country with their families. I was also to discover that when Britain entered the War, Winston Churchill gave the order that all German and Italian citizens in countries with a British sphere of influence were to be interned: 'Collar the lot' was the order given. Although Iran was not a British possession, the country had a share in its oilfields. Citizens from nations of the Axis alliance were seen as a danger to its interests.

In our compound at the Basrah camp, Peter and I played carefree games. From the shell-grit paths we took the larger bi-valve and smaller spiral shells and made tea sets for imaginary little companions. Peter turned shells into cars, aeroplanes and trains. Our concentrated attention on our games distracted us from our mother's hours of absence as she was questioned.

The Gurkha guards in their camouflage uniforms indulged our games good-humouredly. After a day's intense heat, with other women, they took my mother and us—but not the men—for walks along the banks of the wide Shatt-al-Arab. Or was it one of its canals? Tall palms grew at

7. To the Bottom of the World

intervals. The water shimmered a lustrous black. Shafts of light crossed it from bank to bank. A hint of swamps and of sea salt hung in the air. The river suggested voyages, trade, leisure for the local inhabitants.

When the Gurkha garrison left us, formidable, grim Sikh guards in white turbans replaced them. Generally taller than our friendly Gurkhas, they stared down on us severely. They commanded us with brisk words. They stopped Peter and me from plucking shells from the paths. They stopped our walks. They were uncompromising. They made us uncomfortable.

One day we were put on a British ship called the *Rona*. The men were separated from their families. This was the first time we saw our father again after his long absence. He stood in the open part of the hull, waving to us from the huge group of dispirited men.

The ship was not comfortable. Conditions for the men were terrible. Bitter complaints arose about their crowded sleeping quarters and the few toilets that were meant to serve everyone. To shouted questions, women's voices replied reassuringly from the deck overlooking the men's quarters.

The ship made a slow passage along the swampy, meandering river cluttered with small obstacles. Years on, once in a while, that river appears again in dreams. In one such dream, I stretch my hands over the railing to pull at a branch, so close seems the land. In another I call in vain to people on the shore to help us get off that ship.

On that real day in October 1941, however, we children felt no real dread. It was exciting for us to move along to who knows where.

Then suddenly our vessel reached the river's mouth and the Persian Gulf. There was no stopping us now. The wind was blowing strongly, and waves heaved the ship forward into the ocean. She gathered speed. A frothy trail behind the *Rona* showed we were moving ever further from the groves of palm. Impulsively we waved goodbye to no one but the land which had nourished us. We watched the shore as it grew ever fainter, until it disappeared altogether.

We travelled to our destination, Bombay, with father mostly hidden below and mother with us in our cabin above. We were to be interned in India. At Bombay Harbour, with the hand luggage and cases that our mother had packed, we waited for the signal to disembark. We also waited to meet up with Rudolf.

Instead, without warning, everybody was ordered to board the *Rangitiki*, a large New Zealand ship which had appeared beside the *Rona*. A gangplank was placed between the two vessels. As Bombay vendors jostled with each other for trade in a congestion of small boats, we walked the plank from ship to ship, above thick rope netting. It was a terrifying moment.

When we found the cabins that had been assigned to us, we were delighted to be reunited with our father. The few families now had the first-class cabins, while nearly 500 men on their own remained crowded together. Perhaps the *Rangitiki* was a larger ship, perhaps the fathers had been well-behaved and could now be trusted to join their families. The adults were told that a famine in India had caused the change of plans.

Arrangements had been made to send us to Australia. 'Australia?' my parents exclaimed, never having contemplated such a move. They knew little about the country except from coloured calendars that presented rolling plains and Aborigines with spears hunting kangaroos. Our parents were not pleased to be on the way to 'the bottom of the world', to a land without big cities and, as they saw it, without history or civilisation.

At the time no one mentioned the change of plan as perhaps determined by anti-colonial sentiments in India. It would not have been wise to have enemy aliens among people agitating to throw out their British masters.

Many years after these events I was to learn how our British captors, in an arrangement with the Australian authorities, were able to send us there. Officially we were prisoners of the British government, but Britain was prepared to repay Australia for the cost of our internment to get us out of the Middle East, where we were simply in the way. A military garrison would receive us in Australia.

As we awaited departure, some trading took place. Father had been allowed to keep a small amount of money from a larger sum that had been taken from him in Kermanshah, with a promise (not fulfilled) of its return. He bartered for a hand of bananas and some coconuts. Peter and I watched as a delightful family of three ebony elephants rose up to us in a basket. They were ceremonially received, one by one. Then our indulgent parent sent the money down to an eager face in a canoe below.

7. To the Bottom of the World

We made the crossing from India via Colombo to Singapore, and from there down to Australia, with a Scottish military garrison. An armed warship steamed in front, others followed behind. We children took daily interest in the grey convoy of military ships as we moved through the Indian Ocean.

Every afternoon before sunset, soldiers in kilts marched up and down the deck playing Scottish tunes on their *Dudelsäcke* (bagpipes). At sunset a bugler performed the Last Post. On one such occasion the Cocos Islands lay in the distance to the south of the ship as Scottish warriors strode up and down with their pipes. I was to recognise some of the tunes and words years later in my Australian school, especially the refrain *Will ye no' come back again?* and *Speed bonnie boat like a bird on the wing.*

Fond relationships have been known to grow between captors and captives. During the journey we attached ourselves to some members of this Scottish garrison. They were men with families at home and our presence was a reminder of what they were missing. I recall especially a Captain John, who treated the women with attentive civility, who joked with us children and gave us a number of privileges.

One evening, somewhere in the Indian Ocean, a loudspeaker sounded the alarm and declared a submarine alert. I heard the word 'Japanese'. The whole ship was suddenly blacked out for about two hours. But what if it was a German submarine come to destroy the British ships, not knowing we were on board? Although we had been reassured that we were probably safe, the strictest precautions were imposed. An explosion, fire, or a sinking ship hovered uneasily in the realm of possibility.

The ship remained in darkness for some time after the emergency had passed. We were then permitted to walk on deck, still in the dark. Between curtains of mist, stars had gathered in great shoals. Below us, against the iron sides of the ship, waves broke. Marine 'glow-worms' flashed in the foam, like tiny torches chasing one another.

When the ship's lights came on again, I was ordered into bed. Even a War on the horizon made no difference to the domestic rules that governed our lives. When there was no emergency, bedtime was always seven o'clock.

We had been prepared for the possibility of an attack at sea. Periodically, we were ordered to carry our life jackets up the steep iron steps. Children staggered under these awkward bundles. Younger children were carried by their parents. Everyone was ordered to go through the drill, gathering by the lifeboat assigned to them. One day we might really have to jump into the sea. This was too terrible to contemplate. The ship was so tall and the sea so far below! I had never liked heights. They made me dizzy. 'What if we really had to jump?' I thought. 'I'd rather turn into a stone or die on the spot.'

Every day there was also an ordinary routine, as our time was measured out by the bells that summoned us to meals. Then there were other routines imposed by our parents, like the time to get out of bed or to put out the lights over our bunks in the evening.

These routines were enlivened by getting to know others on the ship. I remember a Jewish doctor, Dr Fuchs, telling me a sequence of gripping fables he had improvised. My brother and I were cast as the white good sheep (myself) and the black naughty sheep (Peter). Then there was the wily, wicked wolf playing his clever games. I well remember my growing sense of disquiet that I should be favoured over Peter. 'Surely we should change parts occasionally?' I demanded, confronting Dr Fuchs with my mother's sense of justice. But my protest displeased him and he stopped the game.

He did, however, know others. He gave me a pair of his blackened surgical scissors, which I used to make paper cut-outs. I used the scissors so much that he eventually gave them to me as a souvenir of our voyage.

The few privileged adults assigned the cabins on the ship interacted with mutual gracious concern. My parents spoke of them with respect. There was Franz Zubeck, who told us he was the Professor of Music at the Tehran Conservatorium. Then it was noticed that he was mentally disturbed. Nevertheless, I was fascinated by his virtuoso performances of Tartini's *The Devil's Trill*, since my father had plans that I should learn the violin myself one day. I secretly came up with the view that a man who plays for the Devil is a shady character.

Zubeck's wife, his sixth, was quite different. A fashion designer, she made me a cut-out paper doll to clothe. She added, piece by piece, a wardrobe of paper clothes for different occasions: tennis, skating and hunting outfits, party dresses, a night-gown, a bridal gown, a riding jacket. These paper ensembles were cunningly made, decorated in pencil with fabric patterns, trimmings of fur, bows and laces. Madame Zubeck painted the doll's lips with real lipstick.

7. To the Bottom of the World

I noticed that my mother, who had been stylish in urban Iran, gave up wearing cosmetics from the day that she was imprisoned. Madame Zubeck, however, still painted her face. Mother's appearance was to continue to change over the next five years, turning a once-elegant woman into a dowdy Hausfrau. She acquired the look of deprivation seen in many prisoners. She suffered her fate with apparent resignation, but I could sense how disturbed she was in spirit.

The Zubecks and Dr Fuchs, because they befriended me so graciously, impressed me most. I have no recollection of the other families who travelled with us, not even the other two children.

Peter and I shared cabin space and a double bunk, his underneath mine. One day, although I was six years old and ought to have been better informed, I tested whether humans could really fly. I took the risk of leaping off the top bunk with outstretched arms. I crashed on my head. Although I was not injured, I never doubted my frail mortality again.

My moments of arrogance never got me far. The lesson of my tiny presence in the vast universe was reinforced as I watched the sea washing past our port-hole, sometimes covering it altogether. What wild beasts, what monsters of the deep, lurked in these depths, I wondered?

Before Singapore we entered a thick fog. We stayed blindly in it for a long time. To a young child it seemed like two or three days. Then one morning we woke up to a harbour full of trading boats, just as we had seen in Bombay.

No one then knew that Singapore would soon be captured by Japanese soldiers. Father again bought a hand of bananas and some coconuts. By the time our convoy sailed on, the mists and fogs had dispersed. We sailed past islands where groups of figures, dressed in long white robes, waved to us. They could not have known that we had become undesirables. We returned the greeting. I was sad when we left the friendly world of islands and entered the open sea once more. In later years I imagined that Shakespeare's *Tempest* had taken place in such a world.

Most days the horizon moved up as the ship tilted on one side, and down as she rose again on the other. Motion was constant, water squelching below, streaming past, frothing. On calmer days, the ship's wake amused me and my brother. We watched fish flying in arcs of silver. Several times a group of dolphins adopted the *Rangitiki* and swam alongside with playful purpose. We acquired sea legs which scampered up and down the steep iron stairs. These were bonded, bolted, riveted, a reminder of tough work and tough times. Then there were the more domesticated wooden kind, for tamed travellers. We children became knowledgeable about our floating carrier. But we knew some areas were out of bounds.

At the end of our journey, we berthed in Adelaide harbour. I do not remember leaving the ship, although the pain of being parted from Captain John had us children, and some of the women, in tears. He cried as well.

I do not recall angry shouts of 'Nazis!' at the wharf from the crowd of Australians who had gathered there. That incident I heard of later, from someone else, not my family. My brother Peter stresses the civility with which my mother was helped to disembark by an Australian soldier. He carried her case to the wharf and welcomed her to Australia. This makes me wonder whether there was an angry crowd at all.

Electric light poles were silhouetted against a dark red November sunset as we boarded the train that took us to the railway station in central Adelaide. Children do not take in much information when adults are looking after the packing, unloading and re-stacking of luggage. Nor do they understand much of those formalities that are adult concerns during such a heavily guarded journey. So the sunset remains in my mind at the end of the long journey, not the inflexible rules that were propelling us into a prison camp.

We boarded the steam train that ran between Adelaide and Melbourne. Sitting up all night, we stared out and wondered what this Australia was like outside. But we saw only our own reflections in the windows.

Later someone told me that the windows of the train had in fact been covered with newspaper. Could that have been true?

From Melbourne we were taken by bus on a very long ride to the rural district of Tatura, in northern Victoria. We arrived in daylight. In late November 1941, with the onset of the early summer heat, it seemed a desolate place. A few dull trees stood in dry, cleared land. We saw before us the corrugated iron huts and the barbed wire of Prison Camp No. 3, the civilian family camp. Much later in life I learned that the land belonged to the pastoralist-politician, 'Black Jack' McEwan. The Army had requisitioned it from him, supposedly for a substantial sum.

8
Das Lager

I cannot now remember how we were received by the Australian military authorities. I know that we had to leave the bus and were vetted by the reception committee of commandant and officers outside the military huts that housed the garrison supervising the prison camp. There were checklists of numbers of people per family and of the possessions that went into the camp with them in their suitcases and bundles of cloth. There were dockets for confiscated property such as radios and cameras. These were to be held in trust until the end of the War.

Somewhere on that journey to the camp, family documents and the money my father had confiscated from him at Kermanshah went missing. And Wartime confusion affected even Army discipline. My father's expensive Leica camera, his pride and joy, with which he had illustrated his travels as a young man, his courtship and his six years of marriage, was never returned. Despite repeated letters, he was never able to retrieve from Australian or British authorities the money, documents and camera that had been taken from him. But stacks of his photographs came with us into the camp.

The whole camp sat on six hectares of land, and was surrounded by two widely spaced high fences of spiked wire. Coils of barbed wire sprawled in the space between to discourage potential escapees. Whenever anyone wanted to enter, a large gate was opened by military guards. The person or vehicle would then move through a broad cage of wire to another secured gate, and from there into a wide fenced-off carriageway. Four gates in the carriageway gave entry to the four compounds.

Our family was assigned two rooms in a military-style barrack in Compound A. Only one other couple from Iran, with their son, came with us into this compound. The contingent from Iran was only twelve people in all. This included four children. We were a tiny minority among the huge number of Palestinian Germans who had arrived a few months earlier.

Once we were installed in our new quarters, my parents shooed Peter and me outside to play. Then they unpacked and started to settle into this strange variation on married life. No more privacy. From now on they were surrounded by inquisitive ears behind thin walls and multitudes of eyes at close quarters. There was to be no escape from communal living except into those two tiny rooms with their flimsy fibro walls. Our family did not know—no one did—that my father's confinement would last four-and-a-half years and my mother's and ours exactly five.

Every time I think of our arrival in the Tatura Camp, there is a particular place where my memory lands, like a glider. I see the same dusty, barren land. A number of huts are on the periphery of my vision. My eyes rest on a bare yard where soil and gravel are compacted. I hold my brother's hand. I am six-and-a-half. He is three years younger. His platinum blond hair and grey-blue eyes contrast with my brown hair, brown eyes and olive skin. Clinging to me as if I were his second mother, he accompanies me to the building site. 'Come on, Peterle,' I coax him, 'let's see what they are doing.'

I perceive a hazy afternoon with a faint suggestion of rain. But the place is so dusty.

Children are playing around the wooden skeleton of a hut under construction. They swing in the window frames like monkeys, strut like wading birds on boards above the ground, play chasey around the posts. Sawn-off bits of timber have become cars in the hands of young boys negotiating an obstacle course. Some hands are flying timber planes into the air, carrying imaginary pilots. The children have taken possession of the site.

Peter and I stand on the boundary of happiness. We wait to be invited inside. Although schooled to use formal manners on special occasions, we are awkward in company, having been brought up in virtual isolation from other children. We always wait to be invited in by strangers.

8. *Das Lager*

Eventually a pert girl of about my own age with fair plaits strolls up and looks us over. 'What are you doing here?' she asks. 'Your parents are spies.' Her accent is a broad German I have never before heard, and which I later learn is Swabian dialect.

'Excuse me,' I reply politely in my usual Hochdeutsch, my mother's preferred 'correct' style of speaking, 'can you please tell me what are spies?' 'Oh, I don't know,' she says with a trace of irritation, flicking her plaits. 'You better ask my parents.'

So ends this awkward exchange. I expect, by her tone, that my parents have been accused of something bad, something sinister. The playground is not to be shared with the likes of us. Then, without further ado, she takes my hand and drags me into the middle of the games. Bliss descends like a velvet glove stroking my skin.

Peter is permitted to follow me, but remains shy, because others are clearly in charge here. When my father comes looking for us, he is surprised to find us climbing on the scaffolding, surprised how quickly we have managed to make friends. It is for him a reassuring sign that his children will not suffer too much.

After that introduction, we explored more of the surroundings of our new home each day. We became increasingly familiar with them. We discovered that the camp was divided into four diamond-shaped compounds, named Compounds A, B, C and D, and that D was shut off from the others because that's where most of the Jewish people were housed. This was because other Germans were said to hate them.

Later, some Lutheran missionaries from New Guinea also came into Compound D.

For a while (or was it always?), the gates that were closed between the other three compounds were locked in the evening. Was there a curfew? I do not recall. Between A and B and between C and D ran a wire-edged strip of land which was soon named No Man's Land.

We discovered over time that Tatura was a dusty, hot place in summer and that winters were unpleasantly cold. In spring the countryside was ordered by its own hidden impulse to turn a green seldom seen in Iran. We only saw this transformation in a restricted way, because the camp lay in a hollow.

Every late afternoon in the warmer months, residents took the air outside the huts, walking along the wire fencing. It was a way of meeting others once it became a habit. Some women also had designated washdays and gathered in the laundry as the coppers were fuelled and a concrete trough was cleared for use. During this meeting of women at the wells, there was much talk, and confidences were exchanged. I loved to get together with the mothers and daughters and very young sons in the warm steamy washhouse. Once I saw my mother cry into her washing while Mrs Wennagel tried to comfort her.

Other, more formal ways of meeting were ordained. The self-appointed administration of the community through the commanding voice of the *Lagerleiter* (camp leader), organised everyone into duty rosters. I recall the word *Ordnungsdienst* (work roster). I did not know then that it could be a cover for other kinds of service beyond the monthly lists for cooking in the kitchen, setting tables, distributing food, loading wood, stacking furnaces, cleaning shower blocks and removing rubbish. This camp ran like clockwork, with good German precision and attention to detail. Nevertheless, there was a lot of squabbling among the adults.

I do not know what constitution the internees in Camp 3 adopted, except that it was in sympathy with Nazi politics. I was too young to understand government and politics. My impression is that there were rather loosely constituted committees that made major decisions, each with a leader at the head. I think most of their members and the overall camp leader were drawn from the dominant majority of prisoners who had been brought to the camp from Palestine. That they had come on the enormous ocean liner *Queen Elizabeth* says something about their numbers.

Most of them had been interned in Palestine from where they had arrived some months before us. I heard the word 'Haifa' mentioned a lot as a kind of lost paradise, and the people who came from there described as *die Palestinanser* or *die Templer*, an abbreviation of members of the Temple Society.

The Templers had left Germany's Swabia region some generations back, but still spoke the Swabian dialect. They had settled in Palestine as a commune, attempting to live a purer form of basic Christianity as outlined by Jesus in the New Testament. They longed to live close to the places where Jesus had lived. They established orchards with exemplary irrigation systems which, some say, became a model for the Israeli *kibbutzim*. The Templers in Palestine had insulated their communes so as to avoid the corrupting influences of modern liberal secular thought on the one hand, and the worldly bureaucratic structures of established Christianity on the other. They were Christian fundamentalists.

It was the compulsions of fundamentalist Templer beliefs, rather than the pluralism which would have worked better among so large a collection of different people, that became a good match for the Nazi ideology of some of the other inmates. Under the pressures of internment, the authoritarian, compulsive nature of both came to the fore. Templer Christianity became entangled with national pride, so that Templer and Nazi ideology together waged war on toleration and rational liberal thought. This may account for the apparent contradiction of Templer Christianity adding fuel to racial intolerance.

As far as I could tell, the youth leaders in the camp had no critical decision-making powers. They stood over those younger than themselves but were quite subordinate to the adult administration. Some of them expressed fanatical enthusiasm for Nazi ideology.

The Australian authorities had their own roster of duties in relation to the inmates. The camp was under surveillance twenty-four hours a day by guards who worked shifts on the observation towers. We called out to tease them now and again, but often they did not seem to be there at all. Perhaps they had nodded off in the noonday sun. At night their watchful eyes and companion rifles were helped by fiercely bright searchlights that could move over the four compounds to cover every exposed area.

The Australian guards were not, however, ogres. Some young children crept through the barbed wire to prove that they could tunnel their way out. My brother did so with some mates and I did the same at another time, with my own accomplices. With the guard sleeping, or more likely turning a blind eye, each group of children daring to challenge the instructions of their parents leapt briefly around like little rabbits in the long grass, then decided to make their way back through the dangerous wires. It had seemed easy enough to get out, but the one time I tried this adventure, on return I found it most troublesome to avoid the barbed coils of wire between the two tall fences. I feared my scratches would show how I had disobeyed my father.

Every morning, and later in the day before dinner while it was still light, all the men had to line up for a rollcall to check that no one had escaped. During the early period of our internment, every morning every resident of every hut had to assemble outside their doors to be ticked off a list by two men and one woman from the Australian Army. They wore khaki uniforms.

Sick people were also noted, and the interiors of huts checked for hygiene and safety, and to ensure that nothing forbidden was being kept. The hygiene inspections were important under such crowded conditions. Bed-bugs were to become an occasional irritant. When the plague of bugs became too bad, all beds had to be carried outside to be fumigated with DDT, then scrubbed down. In time the vermin grew fat and resistant. I can still see my mother ringing her hands: 'For God's sake, what is one to do?'

Communal gifts such as books, sheet music, toys, sporting equipment and musical instruments arrived from abroad, courtesy of the German Red Cross. Handcrafted items were lovingly made for us children in the officers' camp, sited nearby in the Tatura district. We soon learned that Camp 3 was only one of several camps in the region. Tatura, Rushworth, Murchison, Moroopna and Waranga became familiar names. We heard that one camp was for military officers and one for lower-rank military men. Officers always got special treatment under international military agreements. We also heard that single civilian men lived separately. When a young man turned seventeen in the family camp, the authorities removed him to the single men's camp. I can imagine (but not remember) the wailing complaints of a mother and her family at the prospect of losing a son to an all-male camp that was out of bounds to Camp 3.

It took some time before we familiarised ourselves with our everyday circumstances, assessing what was significant (or not) in our interaction with others, and how we might manage to establish a decent existence. I remember almost nothing of our first two unlined rooms in Hut 7, under metal sheets of corrugated iron. My parents found, when a stinking hot Christmas was suddenly upon us, that our quarters were too hot as well as full of fungus left over from winter.

What disappointment that Christmas brought! Since people had only fairly recently arrived, no one had organised it properly. 'It's all wrong. It shouldn't be like this. It doesn't feel right!' I heard grumbled around me.

8. Das Lager

A pine tree was brought in, a tree of open structure with thin needles which seemed to be suffering from the mange. 'This is not a real Christmas *Tannenbaum* (spruce, or fir tree)!' they complained. But there were a number of humorists in the camp who lifted our spirits. They provided catharsis when too much gossip and verbal muck washed around. They dissolved glumness with laughter.

Depression hit the most sensitive adults. That Christmas of 1941, carols were sung half-heartedly, since nostalgia for home weighed heavily. Those who attended church, which my parents usually did not, were able to give thanks to God and pray for deliverance, in the hall near the kitchen. This served also as *Kindergarten* and meeting room.

On subsequent Christmases the German Red Cross sent real decorations: coloured glass baubles, candles in holders and silver *Lametta*, plus appropriate Advent calendars with windows to open. It also sent sheet music for choral singing.

I do not know why and when we moved into Hut 1 in Compound A. It was not long after our arrival, and we stayed there for three years. My brother and I thus acquired a new neighbourhood, with its barrage of do's and don't's from the new set of adults around us.

On one side of our *Baracke* (Army hut) lived a family with two daughters of roughly our ages, the Schnerrings from Palestine. Mrs Schnerring was Tabitha, a marvellous Biblical name (in German the stress is on the 'i'), while two of her three children had truly German names: Heidi and Ingrid. Behind us lived one of the many Wagner families. A ten-year-old girl, Leni, used to report on her precocious observations of private adult activities. Pastor Schneller, a gracious elder of the Lutheran Church who lived on the corner, encouraged my love of music. And there was also a certain Frau Kroening, a 'coloured woman' I heard it said, from the South Sea Islands, a niece of the legendary Queen Emma of Samoa and New Britain. She was interned with her doctor husband.

Diagonally opposite us lived the Streckers, whose plump daughter, affectionately nicknamed Pampel, offered us lessons on a descant recorder. A couple of huts from ours were the Wennagel family, whom my brother treated like a second family. Behind the latticed arbour they had built and under their hut he pretended to be deaf to my calls for him to come home.

Neighbourhood groups banded together because that was how to get along. People were categorised, however, both by the places from which they had come, and by their region of birth in Germany. We were classified with *die Iranier* (the Iranians), while those Germans who had come from Palestine were *die Palestinanser* (the Palestinians), and people interned from Australia were often grouped as *die Australier* (the Australians), even though they had German citizenship. Italians tended to be *die Italiener* (the Italians) even when they were interned from the Straits Settlements of Singapore, while people of Jewish ethnicity were always *die Juden* (the Jews), even if their sense of being German was a strongly held part of their personal identity and history.

Neighbourhood solidarity did not dissuade people from quarrelling. I remember my father having a terrible falling out with Mr Schnerring because my brother was squabbling with his younger daughter. This was in spite of the fact that at the age of four he was enamoured of her. The quarrels were short-lived, however. This one did not stop Mr Schnerring from allowing me to join his daughter Heidi for violin lessons in one of his rooms, once I had turned ten. Mr Tietz provided the lessons. I think he was a relative of Mrs Schnerring.

Once I saw my father rolling in the dirt in a punch-up with someone who had insulted him. I was horrified and deeply ashamed, hoping only that my father would win and both men stop their quarrel unharmed. It was so passionate an engagement that the assailants had to be separated before serious injury was inflicted, for Rudolf was strong as an ox. He had not, however, been a labourer like many of the internees.

This is just one example of how people became degraded by the atmosphere in the camp. Mother did not find out about this until I told her forty years later. Or so she said. Had she deliberately closed her mind to it, like so much else? It is more likely that she had forgotten it.

Our neighbourhood with its too-close living quarters had serious drawbacks. At night I used to hear moaning and groaning sounds and the thumping rhythm of movements in the room behind mine. 'What is going on in your room at night?' I asked Leni, the daughter of that family. 'Oh that,' she said airily, 'is dad peeing into mum.' She said it nonchalantly, as if the activity was no different from watering a plant. When I was told that she was slightly retarded and took an interest in things that were none of her business, I tried to dismiss the matter from my mind and to avoid her company, as my mother had told me. But that was impossible. And I remained curious. Since my mother never corrected my mistaken notion that at birth puppies came 'out of a bitch's bottom'—and was proud that I had seen this for myself—I think she was negligent in my sexual education. But parents behaved differently then.

Beyond our immediate neighbourhood lived the Beinssens, who had been interned from Australia, and who came with a nanny of noble background, a certain Fräulein von Koch. She often volunteered to sing solo at concerts, but her high-toned performances were not to everyone's taste.

My parents got on well with the Zachens, their original neighbours from Hut 1. They had also been interned from Australia. They were a straight-talking husband and wife team from Berlin who had married in Australia, and had no children. They livened up the place with their *Berliner* humour and, although they had become acculturated to Australian ways, remained German citizens. Although Lydia suffered from the heat, I never heard the couple complain about being interned, except as a joke. They could see that it was politically reasonable.

We all got on well with the keeper of the washhouse and our compound's shower furnaces, Mr Wiedt, one of many families of Wiedts. He had a wife with the charming name of Nellie and a daughter my age.

For a short while my parents were friendly with a part-Jewish German couple. I loved to play with their only son who was older than me, because he owned a marvellous fleet of individually named miniature steamships with pointed hulls, pennants and flags. He and I played harbour masters, making a large port on the floor and moving the vessels out from their wharves and beyond the harbour's breakwater, to the lighthouse and the buoys. I did not know for many years why contact between our families suddenly ceased.

The truth is that my father soon noted vicious anti-Jewish feelings and prejudices in the camp community. Abuse was directed at the mother and her son. He was jeered at and treated so badly that he was sent off to school in Melbourne. His mother was referred to as 'that Jewish bitch' who had given birth to a 'Jew bastard'.

In secret my father apparently excused himself to the couple, with whom he had been on the friendliest terms. He had to tell them that he could no longer be seen in public with them. Upsetting as this was to me when I heard of it years later, I know that he did it for our sake. From then on in public he ignored the couple completely.

I cannot recall if he instructed us to keep away from the family. Nor did I find out why the man had been thrown at the camp's barbed wire fence by German fanatics. Why had he not taken his Jewish wife and child into the safety of Compound D? I subsequently heard through gossip that he did not want to be locked up with a lot of Jews! He was known as a German nationalist.

My father must have known the delicacy of the situation. He had neither the wisdom nor the courage to handle the pressure, and so caved in. When I asked my mother once why contact between our families had ceased, she was evasive. 'The wife was clever and a true lady,' she said, 'but he—he was an arrogant pig.' And then, shaking her head, added almost as an afterthought: 'You wouldn't believe that she lent those dreadful people her sewing machine, after the disgraceful way they treated her!' Sewing machines were rare in the camp.

I wanted to know more, but my mother's lips were sealed. There is so much sadness and pain in these anecdotes, and so much we will never entirely know about the dynamics between the groups. This is just an example. Later, people did not want to talk about such shameful goings-on.

There were stories about informers in the Camp 3 community. My own family had come under suspicion as British spies the moment we arrived. My mother told me late in life, some months before she died, about one allegation, not one directed at her. Apparently precise information about German shipping traffic in the Persian Gulf had been leaked to enemy intelligence by someone in the camp. As a consequence, three German merchant vessels were sunk, with huge loss of life.

Under the uncertain conditions of War, and knowing of the terrible Nazi reprisals in Germany for national disloyalty, those in the Tatura camp behaved in circumspect ways which may have been uncharacteristic.

Although my childhood memories are rather hazy as to dates, I now know that it was in February 1942—shortly after we had arrived in the camp—that excited rumours suggested the Japanese were attacking north

8. *Das Lager*

Australia. This was regarded as a mixed blessing. People were desperate for liberation, but were also afraid of a Japanese rescue. There was desire to be freed by an ally together with real fear of the Japanese. I sensed at the time that many adults thought they would be worse off under Japanese control.

I don't know how such news came through from outside. Mail was censored. My brother tells me that at some stage forbidden newspapers were smuggled in. It is not unusual for outside threats to bring warring factions of a community together. While there were distinct ideological divisions in people's minds, the confusions of War led to collusion between them.

A precise ideological divide would have been hard for an outsider, looking in, to discern. And it is difficult to fathom human complexity by studying an interrupted set of documents and exploring memories which often have huge gaps. Interactions in a prison are subtle. There is the waxing and waning of opinions, strong values on the one hand, temporary or lasting compromises on the other. Expedient behaviour alternates with altruistic non-conformism.

When the hut that was being built on our arrival was completed, the Drude family moved there with their daughter, my sometime friend Gabriele. She was a well-grown, fairly stable girl. Like myself, she was on the outer from time to time and dependent on the kindness of others for admission to other children's gangs.

Her brother Michael practised childish deceptions in the face of strict controls to such a degree that their father was forever chasing us for misdemeanours we had not committed. Dr Drude, a physicist, was much respected as a great intellectual achiever, something important to Germans. Maria Dannenberg, who lived in the same hut, was a sweet-tempered and rather fragile child. I took a great liking to her, so much so that when it came time to be photographed in our neighbourhood, I once placed myself with Peter in a photo of the Drude and Dannenberg families, then with our own.

My mother also became friendly with one of the Lutheran missionary wives from that hut, Frau Zimmerman. She was not bothered about people's religious or political affiliations when they did not put pressure on a friendship. That's why she later corresponded with a Lutheran pastor, a Nazi sympathiser, who shared her love of Silesian literature.

My father, who had travelled so much as a youth, was singularly lacking in ill-feeling towards people different from himself and his family. He had previously shown not the slightest trace of anti-Jewish feeling. Peter and I inherited that attitude from him more so than from our mother. However, she so rarely expressed the residual prejudices of her background that I was shocked when, many years later, she asked me to name one of my favourite famous men. Unhesitatingly, I said 'Yehudi Menuhin, because he is a marvellous musical ambassador and humanitarian.' She looked at me with surprise and blurted out, instinctively, it seems: 'But he is a Jew!' I was shocked and said: 'So what?' She immediately withdrew.

She never entirely shed some of the stock prejudices of the time and place in which she had grown up. I remember this incident because it contradicted my comfortable view of the person I thought she was. But it is hard to generalise. Some years after our release, my mother placed no obstacle in the way of her younger sister when she wanted to marry into a part-Jewish family.

The camp did have a demoralising effect on many of the inmates. There were ambiguities in inter-relationships which a child observer is not in a position to describe accurately. The same may be said of modern researchers who never set foot in the place. Most of the adults who were interned have died. They took their silence to the grave. Those still alive were not mature enough at the time to understand some of the deeper personal histories and relationships of older people.

Our once-loving father became excessively strict with us in the camp, and often extremely threatening. He no longer hugged us, and avoided physical affection of any kind. This meant we shrank from embracing him.

When he was angry, he sometimes roared until he turned red in the face, and he whacked us across our heads with alarming strength. 'Like a frog, blowing himself up,' someone commented. 'You can see his rage coming.' I was furious that anyone should so malign my father. The engineer from Iran whom I had loved had, however, become rather remote. I feared him. I also thought his blows would damage my head.

Camp life was so petty, so boring, that his energies were dammed up. They were only released in an occasional furious rage.

8. *Das Lager*

His marriage also suffered from his confinement. Our parents discovered, and transmitted to us, that to be locked up in such close confinement with some people they found extremely disagreeable added insult to injury.

My first encounter with adult suspicions occurred on my very first day in the camp. The 'in' group struck at 'outsiders' in our little community, warning even children to be wary. We could see that cliques of Nazis had already engineered favourable conditions for themselves, choosing the best available living quarters. They built on an ideology of paranoia which rejected Jews and all others not of the 'correct' blood lines. Those who had come from Palestine spoke a hybrid German-Arabic language which excluded all others.

I myself did not fit the stereotype of the blonde, blue-eyed Aryan, but I somehow merged with the crowd. We children sometimes formed the impression that things were going wrong for our parents. They did not participate in Nazi activities. Having come from Iran further isolated them. Mostly they said very little. My parents never included us in their discussions about adult problems in their world. They had far too much discretion to invite further trouble by possible inadvertent revelations in the playground.

Some of their discomforts were of course shared by others. No one knew exactly how the War was going, when it was likely to end, or what was to happen to them when it did.

People had relatives in War zones, but no one knew then the horrors of the Holocaust for Jewish people. The camp was just nasty, lonely and unpleasant for our parents.

It was also a hotbed of discontent. There was too little structured work and too much talk, including gossip, whispering campaigns behind cupped hands, and eyes over-engaged by the movements of others, often from a strategic position behind a window. Here were the ingredients of an explosion spawned of boredom.

I gathered that my parents loathed much of what went on, as obviously did many others. We caught the flavour of our parents' reactions, as if wearing their cast-off clothes. In this insecure life, gossip was probably a safety valve, preventing many more fisticuffs than the sordid few we witnessed.

With few really well-educated people in Camp 3, there was little opportunity of transforming our unfortunate imprisonment into fruitful intellectual and morally purposeful activity. Rather, the opportunity was seized to impose Nazi-style political organisation. The first and largest group of internees to arrive in the camp further commandeered resources and saw themselves as the rightful rulers, elected by so-called democratic processes, by virtue of their early arrival, strength of numbers and 'correct' ideological allegiance. They set up the make-shift internal administration. The Australian authorities left much of the control of the camp in the hands of these self-appointed leaders and their stooges. Their administration took a laissez-faire approach. They did not interfere too much in our day-to-day lives.

'A crop of little Hitlers sprang up over the years,' my mother commented later, with disdain. She explained that a man without much education or experience, perhaps a grocer in ordinary life, suddenly had responsibilities of leadership heaped on his shoulders out of all proportion to his abilities.

His megalomania prevented him seeing that his zealous ineptitude had damaging consequences. Those in the minority who disapproved became targets of malice.

These self-appointed leaders, and the group from which they were drawn, quickly entrenched a 'national socialist democracy' without much real opposition. It gave individuals little breathing space.

Amongst its interned community, Camp 3 at Tatura was usually referred to as *Das Lager*. The description has an old lineage. It is essentially a nomadic term. In English it means a camp, a resting or staging place. Tatura camp, however, was just a prison without any particular purpose except to keep us locked up out of harm's way, and out of the reach of Australians.

9
His Majesty's Guests

The camp was still being built when we arrived and the building program went on for as long as two years. The huts were in the temporary military style, with fibro and masonite walls. They were built above the ground, with room underneath for ventilation, and to discourage vermin. Each was roofed with corrugated iron, on which we wished the infrequent rain would drum more often, in soothing, regenerating downpour. When it did rain and puddles lay about, we children could leap into them, splash one another—and then get into trouble for our mischief.

My mother had a talent for transforming any ordinary place into a charming home. During the course of the War we moved four times. In Hut 1, our second home, she turned two rooms into a suite of bed and living room, with a colourful woven curtain as the internal doorway. Our sleeping quarters consisted of two double bunks squeezed into one room. She disguised the ugly furniture in the sitting room with Iranian *kelims*, set up the brightly polished brass samovar on a stand, and decorated the bare walls with hanging cloths and pictures of Iran, as well as with German Fine Arts calendars. Our father, urged on by her, made frames for these from the strips of timber which could be found lying round the camp.

So comfortable and home-like did our mother make our living space that I once ordered Peter to wipe his shoes well before entering the *salon*. This so amused our parents that the sitting area was thereafter referred to as *unser Salon* (our *salon*).

Other people displayed pictures of Hitler in their huts, but not my family. The inspection teams must have been amazed when they saw the way my mother had transformed the ugly rooms into a charming home. There is a word in German which describes an environment in which people feel really welcome. It is *gemütlich* and means cosy, relaxing, convivial all in one. My mother always managed to create a *gemütliche Stube* (room) wherever we lived.

Mother also transformed the bedroom, in a different way, with a game she played every week. Reclining on the top bunk on Sunday mornings, she would produce a jar of transparent boiled lollies, a jar of gems, their many colours flashing in the light of the window beside her. She told us she had collected the sweets from Arabia, where a magic carpet had taken her the night before. She then distributed the lollies as rewards for good behaviour during the week, or exacted promises from us to do better in future.

When I later reminded her of this game, she did not remember it. Our father had subsidised it from his small earnings. He worked in the camp vegetable garden beyond the wires, under armed guard. He quickly acquired gardening skills from the Templer vegetable-growing teams.

I half-wondered how my mother's stories of Arabia could be true, at the same time I began to question *der Weihnachtsman* (Father Christmas), whom my Austrian father insisted on calling *Sankt Nickolaus*. My mother helped our imaginations through periods of boredom by drawing a German cemetery with its church on the hill and sheep grazing among the tombstones, that simplified impression of her own birth village. But she always insisted that she could not draw. We copied her designs, which sometimes included incongruous rows of palms and camels.

In the camp, each compound ate communally, in its own designated hut. Each had its own shower blocks. We shared makeshift bucket toilets before something more permanent was provided. Would the sheets of toilet paper allowed each day last the distance? We were often scolded for our prodigality.

We were fascinated by the construction of four sets of pit latrines. The digging of two very deep trenches caused great excitement. When the trenches, like hugely oversized graves, were completed, carpenters mounted over them wooden seats with circular holes for average-sized adult bottoms. There were a few concessionally smaller ones for children. Each hole with its seat-lid was then given the privacy of a cubicle, entered through a door of planks on hinges.

9. His Majesty's Guests

The camp stood in fly-ridden pastoral country and personal hygiene was difficult to maintain among a community of over 800 prisoners, about 200 in each compound. Adults and children were fascinated and somewhat frightened by the pits and wondered how much of what they contained was alive. One heard the occasional threat: 'If you don't do X, I'll see that you get thrown into the pit!' Curious children lifted the lids to examine what lay below. Disinfectants were added to neutralise the stench.

The pit latrines came to be associated with what was foulest in the camp. Once someone scrawled the initials of Winston Churchill, WC (for water closet, although water was only for washing hands). They became synonymous with the arch-enemy. 'I'm going to the Churchill,' children called, to inform their parents.

Every day, the toilet blocks were hosed out. We knew this had been done thoroughly when a white residue of Dettol filmed the concrete floors and culverts. Adults turned a wary eye on what children might be getting up to in private cubicles. When I told my mother one day that a slightly older girl had told me to insert a knitting needle up my *Pinkel* (my father's word for urinary tract, although my mother knew I meant the vagina), she panicked. Thereafter she performed a series of intrusive inspections of my body in case I had been molested, but was too frightened to report it.

This was an embarrassing exercise for both of us. She was doing what she thought a responsible parent ought.

We had been taught never to directly question the authority of our parents.

Fear of seduction, molestation or rape of their children added yet another burden on parents in the camp. Because the subject of sex was taboo, problems could flourish in secret. I had never told my mother about Ibrahim's attempt, but I never forgot it.

Parents' fears left impressions on sensitive children. Girls were of course more at risk. Sometimes we badly wanted a wall of privacy to rise around us, rendering us invisible to all but ourselves.

There were probably some pregnancies in the camp. Attempts to disguise them must have been futile. We children heard whispers on the grapevine. I heard my parents comment many years later how one adolescent girl was seduced by a married man, but her morning sickness was described by her parents as amoebic dysentery. After she gave birth, her child—which I think must have been adopted out—was referred to as *das Amobenkind* (the amoeba child), one of the cruel camp jokes.

Long after it had taken place, we heard that some of the young women in the camp from the Templer group had somehow arranged to meet up with their boyfriends by planning a rendezvous with them out of sight of the guards' surveillance posts. Apparently both men and women escaped through the wires of their respective camps. This was one of the camp rumours, later substantiated, but I never heard any of the details. How was this arranged and what was the outcome? Could letters pass between compounds? Surely families that had been separated on arrival were at least allowed to correspond with each other by letter?

Despite the mixed and just plain wrong messages our parents so often transmitted to us, I never held my body in contempt. I relished its strength and flexibility in sport, and the 'Oh joy!' feeling of being truly alive. And yet I took such long showers—as if to wash away pollution—that adults got impatient waiting in the queue for their turn.

Over 40 years later, a family friend mentioned my long camp showers. One cannot jump to the conclusion that cleaning away imaginary stains was my obsession. As a teenager, my father was to scold me for not washing enough. In the camp, we showered in the wooden clogs that were our summer footwear. Clogs were turned out in great numbers to fit all sizes of feet. My mother no doubt warned against the dirt of the shower floors. She loathed clogs. My father thought they were sluttish.

Other children were permitted to run wild, to play outside until well past our bedtime, which my parents observed for years as seven o'clock. We could hear the alluring sounds of laughter, shouts and taunts, but Peter and I never attempted to escape into the inviting night. The beatings of our strong father put paid to those fantasies.

We soon learned to read the messages of the playground, to note the gangs that were formed, and who played with whom when. Often we were excluded, but when a gang did adopt us briefly, we wallowed in happiness, hoping fervently that our luck would continue. Certain children were invariably the centre of such gangs. How could they know what it felt like to be excluded? It was obvious to me that not letting someone in made them suffer. Peter and I learned early in life to loathe the tyranny of gangs.

9. His Majesty's Guests

We often experienced the playground as mean and threatening. Boys, especially, would roll in the dust punching each other, sometimes playfully but often in earnest. A crowd of onlookers would gather to barrack until older relatives came to extricate the antagonists.

'No, we are not playing with you today,' was a rejection Peter and I feared daily. Most children's play was in groups, 'we' against individuals. The atmosphere was generally very competitive. Hitler's ideology reinforced it. Loving one's neighbour as oneself was not a precept I learned until several years later, although most of the internees claimed to be Christians.

It was lucky that we could attend school, because there relationships were more equitably structured. In the classroom we were secure from those alliances which got their momentum from excluding others. In two of the official photos taken in the camp, I see a once-charming child becoming increasingly rat-faced from the competitive ethos, and seeming to grow ever-longer legs. To win was the goal set.

Physical illnesses in the camp were dealt with in the Medical Clinic in Compound C, presided over by a doctor and his nurse. The married doctor and single nurse formed what was commonly thought to be more than a professional alliance so that, according to gossip, a terrible incident had occurred. She had poured boiling water over her feet out of jealousy, and so she would have to live at the clinic.

Some women gave birth outside the camp at Waranga Military Hospital. My mother was one of them. My brother Herbert Friedrich was born not long before the end of the War, when my mother was 37 years old. Why did she not give birth in the camp? The Australian doctor who attended the ambulance that came to fetch her injected her with morphine, a highly irresponsible action, she later claimed, because it could have killed her. I did not hear her say that this may have contributed to Herbert's later heart problem which, when it was diagnosed, meant predictions that he would live for only 25 years unless there was surgical intervention. In 1960 Herbert had the 100th heart bypass operation in Melbourne's Alfred Hospital.

I was once taken from the camp to the Mooroopna Hospital with suspected scarlet fever and kept under quarantine there until it was discovered that I did not have the disease after all. Among the beautiful Australian nurses in their white dresses with their Queen of Hearts–red capes, was a Sister Anne. I remember her leaning over me tenderly and making me comfortable in a language I could not understand, her copper-coloured hair peeping from its starched veil. Other young patients also spoke only German and the nurses made an effort to communicate with all of them. My brother Peter was next door, recovering from surgery. He had both his tonsils and appendix out at different times.

Although I was well treated, I feared being away from my parents. It felt peculiar being out of the camp.

As children of foreign parents who had lived in the Middle East our teeth were not like those of indigenous children in Iran. But Peter had developed something akin to trench-mouth disease there. In the camp I needed dental attention and acquired a number of Dr Xilo's durable metal fillings. An obstetrician who had qualified in Yugoslavia, and who was assisted by her husband as dental nurse, Dr Xilo had turned to dentistry after finding that working as a female doctor in the snows of winter in the rural areas of her homeland was far too dangerous. While drilling my teeth she entertained me with stories of wolves prowling the forests through which she had to pass in a horse-drawn sleigh to attend births. She was a perfectionist, so her fillings outlived some of the newer substances introduced by dentists after the War.

Those of us who had arrived at the camp in late 1941 were permitted to leave it only to go to hospital, to gaol or, for men only, to work in the vegetable garden. Military guards accompanied us on each occasion. I heard years later that the original policy was not to have families imprisoned so completely. The Templers had apparently been taken for an excursion to the Waranga Basin some time after their arrival in August 1941. Instructions were given that no one was to swim to the other side of the lake—and there was more than discipline at stake. The lake was full of dead trees and broken stumps hidden under the water.

A few older girls, apparently, had kept on swimming until they reached the opposite shore, despite repeated calls from the guards for them to stop. Were they setting out to reach the single men's camps? Is this the same story as the one about the lovers' rendezvous? Stories do get confused. According to this version, a regulation was then introduced that because the internees could not be trusted to do as they were told, outings from the camp were from then on forbidden.

After the War with Hitler was over, we were in fact taken on monthly outings to the Waranga Basin.

The camp gaol was near the garrison's administration offices. Although it was occasionally inhabited, I do not recall what the offences were. Joy Hammond, in her book *Walls of Wire* (1990), refers to a Court of Honour inside the camp organised by the internees themselves. The academic Christine Winter has confirmed that there was an internal law-enforcement mechanism. She suggests rather sinister implications, and that this could have threatened individuals beyond official scrutiny.

Alternative mechanisms of law enforcement are not necessarily bad or evil. Of course, in the wrong hands, they can have terrible effects. Our camp was operating in Wartime. In peacetime, secret societies with the ability to punish should never be permitted to function. Public scrutiny is necessary. During War, however, they may have a de facto role in doing work a government is unable to perform but might forbid if it knew what was going on.

In our camp, where not everyone favoured Nazi-style internal administration, if a kangaroo court was being run by a group of bullies with secret police–like support (aping what was happening in Hitler's Germany), then it was obviously remiss of the Australian garrison to allow it to function. The Australians may or may not have known of its existence. There were certainly inmates who would have complained to the authorities if they had known of such a thing.

If they knew, why didn't the Australian authorities intervene? They may have been relieved at being saved the bother of punishing people themselves. And they had to be careful of how they treated German inmates so as to avoid retaliation against Australian prisoners in Germany.

One small incident illustrates my suspicions. My mother was taken to task late in 1946, after my father had left the camp, scolded because her infant son constantly entered other families' rooms uninvited. Hauled before a committee, she was told to keep her children under better control. But she never made much of that incident, then or later. Should she have? Did she think of it as being called before a Court of Honour? There were things she refused to discuss about our time in the camp, or felt that it was pointless to raise.

Alcohol was forbidden to internees, although I thought I remembered my father assisting his Italian friend to distil *grappa* from dried fruit like raisins. A cellar had been lined with bricks under a pergola this man built, and the distillery and bottles hidden there. Years later father told me he had not been involved. Perhaps he was only an innocent bystander. I can certainly vouch for the hiding place's existence, because I was there when it was discovered by a military inspection. I saw the bricks being kicked away by an angry officer's leather boots.

People brought their own clothes into the camp and these can be seen in the few surviving official photographs. They have a German look about them. People now laugh about the military-style woollen clothes, dyed burgundy. 'His Majesty's Clothes', they joke.

Some of these garments would have been made by hand, stitched laboriously without a machine. Clothes were rationed during the War. Blankets were not supposed to be cut into pieces, but perhaps the regulations were relaxed after a while, because my mother tailored some smart outfits for us: trousers, skirts and vests. She was one of the few people in the camp with a sewing machine. And because she was a hoarder, a result of her World War I experiences, she had no doubt brought some lengths of cloth into the camp.

She made me a sky-blue linen frock with exquisitely embroidered motifs of ladybirds and sprigs of flowers. Peter, who sought always to copy me, pestered her for a similar dress. She made him a tie with the same embroidered design. Although I took for granted much of what mother did for us, my little hand smoothing the embroidery, over and over again, was an instinctively loving gesture of gratitude. I was appreciative of the beauty she brought into our lives. Years later I gave the embroidered section of the dress to the museum at Tatura.

Our mother's sewing machine, the table model Singer, she operated by hand, with great technical finesse. She also produced magnificent outfits for us from doctor's flannel and striped mattress covers that were slightly damaged. She sewed little bags with shoulder straps from linen, and from cut-down hessian bags, embroidered in cross-stitch with different motifs for each of us: a rocking horse with rider for my brother, and a couple holding hands for me.

My mother often courted trouble by refusing to follow the styles of fashion prescribed in the camp. She did not like the preferred use of either Bavarian or Swabian regional costumes on festive occasions, and despised the Nazi uniforms which were worn during the many remembrance feasts. Who made these? Were they sent in or handmade in the camp? My mother often wore a Dirndl, a basic dress in modern folkloric style, without exclusive ethnic signature.

For better occasions she used to dress us in smart tailored clothes. But we objected. We wanted to be dressed like everyone else. Children used to throw stones at those who were different. I never liked to see stones being thrown at anyone. Throwing stones, I gathered, is a common practice in the Middle East. I cannot swear, however, that I did not occasionally join others in the practice. Peter and I no doubt got carried away with children's games, surrendering to what was expected of us.

By no means model children, we certainly joined others in raiding the communal cucumber patch. We climbed the castor oil trees to pelt each other with their spiky poisonous fruits. We probably joined other children in jeering at some unfortunate individual. I do not recall doing so, since we were very carefully nurtured to have respect for others.

Nevertheless, my brother and I were often disobedient, leading to terrible thrashings from our father. This was usually out of all proportion to the offence. Beatings, however, did not make us tough. They made us frightened. But they were part of the way many parents behaved in those days.

At the age of 10, German girls were pressured to join the *Jungmädl* (young maiden) association, a younger version of the BDM, the union of older German girls which was an adjunct of the *Hitlerjugend*. This gave access to marvellous sports programs and a variety of social and political activities. In June 1945 I had a tearful argument with my mother, who did not want me to join. My father must have told her to let me be. 'What harm is there in it now?' he would have asked, adding, 'The War with Germany is over.'

Only Japan fought on. On reflection now, it is odd that all this political activity went on in the camp for a few more months. So I was permitted to participate.

Every morning at seven o'clock we were primed with a run around the camp. Sports uniforms were obligatory. Mother, who thought them ugly, tailored me a smart pair of black shorts. When I turned up in my different outfit, I was pelted with a shower of stones, and ran home crying. Mother then modified my shorts into bloomers so I could avoid further pain.

As well as these black bloomers for sport, girls were expected to wear a white shirt and a Berchtesgaden cardigan with a knotted leather ornament, rather like a serviette holder. My mother refused to knit me the traditional cardigan Hitler had adopted as a youth costume or get me a leather tie-holder. I suffered intensely for this. I begged her to let me wear one of those pretty black Berchtesgaden cardigans with red and green borders. '*Nein!*' She was adamant.

I eventually inherited a hand-me-down cardigan and mother changed the 'uniform' with Iranian buttons of silver. Frequently there were tensions between what my parents insisted on and the unwritten rules of camp society or the playground. Such differences of opinion are, of course, a universal feature of childhood, but within an institution they are magnified into conflict.

I also suffered stoning for my religious beliefs.

My parents had not instructed us in any particular religion, although in Iran when we were very small, my mother had prayed with us every night before we went to sleep. We used a rhyme from her childhood: *Lieber Gott, mach mich fromm, dass ich in den Himmel komm* (Dear God, make me pious, that I may enter Heaven). For that reason, perhaps, I did have some notion of God. When a group of children who had absorbed a good measure of anti-Christian Nazi mythology once asked me: 'Do you believe in God?' I hesitated, then said 'Yes'. A shower of stones—some quite large—descended on me. Beware the honest truth! Such incidents taught me to be more circumspect—and that was a pity.

Looking back, I am now extremely pleased that my mother taught us that it isn't necessary to please other people simply by following their views or actions. She helped us acquire some backbone and prepared us to be intellectually independent of conformity for its own sake, including unquestioning ideological conformity. But it took many years for that message to filter down into my actions.

We children nevertheless became acquiescent in day-to-day relationships because of the pressure of family life and the severity of our father's rod. As for belief in God, I later learned that it must be tested with occasional challenges. This helps to focus on what is valuable in one's relationship with an unknown deity. It also provides insights into secular moral realities, and supports relationships with non-believers.

Although the various groups in the camp held their own religious services once a week, my family did not attend the Catholic Masses. There may have been a tension between my father's agnostic version of his Catholicism and my mother's acculturation into the Lutheran faith which she had given up in order to marry her Catholic husband. When the Catholic Relief Agency brought comfort parcels for interned Catholics, my father stood proudly on his principles. 'I have not practised the Catholic religion. I have no right to accept favours from them now that I am in distress,' he said.

He may have taken a different position when small amounts of money appeared from the German government. After all, his country owed him something for depriving him of his professional earnings and of the future he had planned for his family. Germany had taken over Austria, and had prepared the way politically for the *Anschluss*. I'm sure he would have thought that the German government, which had taken over his official papers from Austrian embassies, and whose War had landed him in this mess, owed him quite a lot. He may have registered himself as loyal to his own government rather than voice criticism of it, to be branded a traitor. The official policy of the Third Reich was that Austrian nationalists, his preferred position, were secessionists, a treasonable offence.

There was a Capuchin monk in Compound A who lived in one of two or three large white tents near the boundary. My parents thought that we children ought to get some religious instruction from him in order to offset the secular and immoral influences that were affecting us. We went there for instruction a few times, but then the man was moved from Camp 3. So my parents' religious plan for us came to nothing.

How did that mixture of people in the camp, with its various religious affiliations, function as a community? Long periods of truce between people were interrupted with squabbles of various kinds. Children could find themselves scapegoated if they proved immoderate or disobedient, sometimes thrashed by someone else's parent for no good reason.

Even adults were observed to punch one another for insulting someone else's children. Nevertheless, there was a set of rules which were made clear to adults, about which we knew little. In them, religion was mixed up with German politics and the aspirations of the Third Reich.

Perhaps I have overstated the differences of behaviour between those who were fundamentalists and others. I was a simple child who saw things in black and white. I viewed my parents as nuisances as far as my need to belong was concerned. Our parents weren't the only ones in the minority who were not from Palestine. There were also the Italians from Singapore and others from Malaya who had worked on the rubber plantations, as well as the Lutheran missionaries from New Guinea. Our parents seemed to associate more with people who had not come from Palestine. But every group must have had members who were political fellow-travellers with Germany's and Italy's governments, as well as those who clung on sceptically as citizens, hoping for a change. There were also those who refused to be associated with Fascist regimes.

My parents did not take a conspicuous, public anti-Fascist stance. Would I as an adult have had the courage under such cramped conditions with belligerent people to do so? I somehow doubt it—with regret. But who knows?

10

The Imaginary Homeland

My memory of these years is like pools of thought which are sometimes connected to other pools. The only sense I acquired of the passing of time was from the birthdays that were celebrated around me, my own changes of age, and my schooling, in which each year was straddled by classes from September (according to the school year in Germany) to approximately June the following year.

I recall being really bewildered by the slow passage of time. I used to ask myself: 'How much longer will we be here? How much longer?' One day, asking that unanswerable question, I shinned my way up the smooth flagpole in Compound A in order to see beyond the camp. I had tried this before, but had only ever managed to get half-way up before losing my grip and sliding back down.

I stared out gloomily at the red dust of a sandstorm, from the direction where the town of Murchison was said to be. Once, in late summer, the smoke of bushfires had drifted over the camp, making us feel even more anxious and vulnerable.

During these seemingly endless five years, I passed from the *Kindergarten*, which volunteers had set up, through to the beginning of the fourth year of schooling. At first I was sent to *Kindergarten* for six months, delighting in the toy shop there provided by the German Red Cross. I enthusiastically sewed card pictures, threaded beads, and made puzzles and plasticine shapes in many colours. Some children preferred to play with soft toys or to dress dolls and take them walking in little prams. In the German way, we were taught that everything was to be treated with respect, not to be handled with sticky fingers and, at the end of play, stored back in their allocated containers.

As the original German name implies, the *Kindergarten* is somewhere for children to be treated like plants, nurtured and domesticated. I started school at the age of seven in September 1942, again following the German educational calendar.

While we were at school, the adults were trying to transform their drab environment. Some of their creations were really wonderful. The arid surroundings of the huts were soon blooming with gardens and arbours. I can still see the feathery foliage of the tall stands of white and pink cosmos which our father planted outside Hut 1. We snapped open the mouths of snapdragons (*Levkeuen/Löwen Mäuler*, lions' mouths) without picking them. Rows of bright portulaccas grew on low banks, responding well to the sunny position. We collected their seeds in matchboxes and sowed them out again, eagerly awaiting any colours that might appear. Then there was the silvery-grey foliage of a bush known as *Wermut* (wormwood), which we young ones used to roll up in bits of newspaper and secretly smoke.

I sometimes lay stretched out on patches of grass in No Man's Land with my ear to the ground, listening for the earth's heartbeat. I would watch little insects in a world all their own, a layer below ours.

Our Army rations for our communal meals were delivered in trucks, and included tinned fish, corned beef and cheese and butter in low round tins. On some of them was a picture of a life-belt and a sailor in blue, who also appeared on Capstan cigarette packets. We caressed the shapes and coveted the colourful labels from tins of preserved fruit and jam. If we were lucky enough to acquire a few labels in so competitive a field, we cut out the pictures and pasted them up into new arrangements: a bowl of fruit, for instance, with pineapple, plums, apricots and strawberries, or a parrot on a branch gazing out at a sailor at sea.

Mother did not encourage this practice. She thought it uncreative and encouraged us instead to draw our own pictures. I was told that the camp had regular deliveries of 'bread enough to burn'—large rectangular loaves made from over-refined white flour which offended many a German palate. We longed to sink our teeth into earthy, crusty rye bread, liberally dusted with baked caraway seeds.

Plentiful fresh vegetables came in from the camp market-garden in which men like my father could work for a token wage. The money was enough to feed my parents' habit of cigarette smoking and to buy sweets for us from the tiny canteen that sold a very limited stock.

On winter mornings, on the bare wooden tables in the dining hall enamel bowls were lined up. They were filled with steaming, lumpy porridge. In summer we got the Weet-Bix I much preferred. The hot milk we children were given in the Army's tin mugs tasted so metallic that I subsequently shunned milk for most of my life. And many years later, during my first pregnancy, I suffered a nauseated reaction to the smell of aluminium inside cupboards. It was a whiff of the past, of those metal cups filled with that breakfast milk topped with the inevitable skin which I found so disgusting.

Between meals when it was cold, we children sometimes melted blobs of cheese in jam tins on top of the small wood heater in the dining room and singed bread with toasting forks over the glowing coals through its open door. When it rained, between meals, we sometimes made cubby houses under tables and benches. These games depended on a lenient supervisor being on duty, because playing in the dining hall was usually forbidden.

When I think back on it, we were an ungrateful, critical lot. Generous Army rations were a privilege during the War, when Australian civilians were given the more restrictive civilian ration coupons. People in the camp also grumbled about styles of cooking. The roster ensured that there was a turnover of talent. Boiled cabbage cooked with a ring of oil on top of the boiler was subject to periodic attack from everyone but the Italian cooks, who liked it that way and refused to change. I loathed finding the odd boiled grub in my cabbage but my father was unsympathetic. 'It's an excellent supply of essential nutrition,' he said, encouraging me to eat it up. But I refused. After mother's intervention, he would relent.

There were many productive forms of entertainment in the camp. The younger girls and young unmarried women attended regular evening knitting bees. These *Heimabende* ('at homes') produced scarves and socks for German soldiers. During these evenings, older participants took it in turns to read a chapter from a book. Since we children were often present, I particularly remember a saga about a German coffee planter's family in East Africa, living at the foot of Mount Kilimanjaro and plagued by locusts and marauding lions.

Part of these evenings was spent singing folk songs in harmony. Someone might lead with a guitar or piano-accordion. Mouth-organs and recorders were also frequently played. There was at least one piano in the hall in Compound C in which most of the communal gatherings and entertainments took place. There was also an older woman who gave readings in her own hut to well-behaved children. She read us fairy tales like those of the Brothers Grimm, which underpinned the social order, and those by Hans Christian Andersen which nourished our nostalgia.

At first, our school was conducted in the dining hall. I attended *Kindergarten* in Compound A. The first two grades of primary school were held in Compound C. I remember the excitement of learning to read and write there.

School was conducted in the German language, and followed a German syllabus. Trained teachers conducted the classes, helped by university students and educated adults who had some teaching experience. Starting school at seven, I was old enough to find this adventure one of the great experiences of my life. Literacy provides confidence, independence and entertainment. It is a door through which one discovers a whole new world.

The first element of that experience is lodged in my mind as a small angular mark, the letter 'i'. It was a symbol which stood for *Igel* (hedgehog) and was the first letter I ever learnt, before even 'a' for *Apfel* (apple). Like one of the beasts chalked in the prehistoric caves of Lascaux, the drawing of a hedgehog in my schoolbook reminded me what sound it was that the little scribbled 'i' represented, when we were asked to 'drill' the vowels: I, E, A, O, U.

That was the way we learned them, for simplicity. Later the sequence was replaced by a standard convention, following the alphabet.

The guiding idea of the camp was that learning was not simply a mechanical progression but a mixture of adventure and standard classical conventions. We were taught holistically, all subjects shown as being interconnected. My exercise books were soon filled up with writing and drawing. There was another one with numbers associated with problems to be solved from real life situations. Under the kindly and patient supervision of Tante Gudrun, our teacher, we were set solidly on the path of learning.

10. The Imaginary Homeland

The excitement of being at school in the camp outshone the schooling I received later, when we were freed. It was as if in captivity our minds were released to fly like birds. This is a great tribute to my teachers.

The dining hall in Compound B was used for school years 3 and 4, and 10 was the magic age when we were permitted to take part in sporting programs. The attendant political endurance ceremonies, however, I found arduous. The schoolbooks I still have from that later period, 1945–46, after the War had ended, reveal how foreign we were to the country in which we were stranded. Even those teachers who had come from Palestine, in their lessons known as *Heimatkunde* (social/heritage studies, or knowledge of the homeland) taught us about Germany and things German, even though no one in the camp had actually lived there for any significant period.

Our structured learning was also very competitive. As soon as a child had completed her 'mathematical' problems, she was permitted to leave the room and go out to play. I suffered because of my lack of commitment to another lesson, the art of embroidery, which annoyed that queen of all seamstresses, my mother.

One of our marvellous teachers, the enthusiast Tante Lilo (Aunty Liselotte Wagner) introduced parent guest lecturers into the classroom. Lilo admired learned men and my father accepted her invitation to tell us about engineering. How unexpectedly proud I was to discover that my father had a genial rapport with other people's children! I had always thought that my parents were different, something a number of inmates from Palestine had told me, with some distaste. How my heart glowed when my father came one day to explain to us in class how red and green railway signals were used to regulate the safety of trains and their cargo. He also described some of his adventures supervising the construction of tunnels and bridges. He dramatised the big questions: would the two sides meet in the middle? He made these boring technical matters fascinating. My father became a hero to the fourth-grade boys and I was treated with deference for a few days by those who otherwise would tease me by pulling my plaits.

Both our schooling and our social life turned our minds to a *Heimat* (homeland), which most of us had scarcely visited and were perhaps never to see. Perhaps the exaggerated nostalgia of the people in the camp can be explained by the need to preserve an identity at odds with a foreign land, especially as we had no idea what lay beyond our prison.

In later years I found a text from the Bible which brought inward tears to my eyes: *By the waters of Babylon I sat down and wept, and thought of thee, Oh Sion.*

When I later reached out to a Jerusalem that was the spiritual home of both Christians and Jews, I realised I was revisiting an emotional experience, travelling over the same road but through a different country. In the camp, my *Heimweh* (longing for home) was directed at Germany, a place I had only visited for the briefest few weeks. I knew it was a green and pleasant land. My mother's stories of home were reinforced by the rhetoric of our teachers. An imaginary Germany pushed my vivid experience of Iran into the background.

In the school exercise books still in my possession are long German narrative poems copied in the fine, elongated Gothic script I learned. On those pages are depicted deciduous trees like birches, beeches, elms and linden, together with a family of evergreen pines. Each separate genus of tree is defined by leaves, flowers and fruit, and by the basic architecture of stem and branches, while a tree in leaf has a canopy that is peculiar to its own family. Thus we absorbed the basic principles of science without being consciously 'scientific'.

In a drawing that has sat for 50 years in my exercise book, a German fox sits by a lake ready to pounce on a family of ducks. On another page, wild strawberries grow in clusters of decorative leaves. An eagle, a hawk, a swallow, a woodpecker and other birds from the northern hemisphere are caught scanning the horizon of their future. Another page about Germany's mythological past depicts an earth wrought from fire. There stands the great Tree of Life, with the three *Nornen*, the women who spin the web of life, the past, the present and the future.

Elsewhere, the names of each day of the week are given their Norse derivation. My classmates are listed one by one and explained. Herbert = leader of the *Heer* (army), Irene = lover of peace, Helga = supervisor of healing, are three samples. We were taught to admire rather horrid Nordic heroes of the military caste, with morals no better than the devious and aggressive Greek gods.

In one of these exercise books I have kept there is some evidence of political indoctrination. But there is more about German identity in a general sense than about its specific Nazi affiliation. And that's the way I remember it. Our school was not a vehicle for indoctrination. Rather, that took place through the youth movements, at political rallies and in the playground, where what the parents of some told their children acted on the others by a kind of osmosis.

In school, the swastika symbol of the Nazis nevertheless appeared on the front of textbooks and in the corner of our school reports. For us as children it had no sinister connotation. It was as free of taint as the flag to the Australian children of the time, who saluted it every morning before going into their state school classrooms.

I can still read in my nine-year-old hand that 'Words that make us brave' are *flag, hero, Hitler* and *Hitlerjugend*. Anti-Jewish and pro-Aryan sentiments, if they figured at all in school, have escaped my memory. I probably suppressed them after the War.

I was told then that anti-Semitism was a force to be reckoned with in the camp. I had developed a habit of explaining my conduct with excuses—probably in self-defence, since I was beaten so often—so it is likely that I was as much a participant as others. But I do not recall it. Since I do not make a habit of forgetting unpleasant things I have experienced, I either had no conscience about such villainy or I was not engaged by it.

In the sandpit we made relief maps of geographical features, naming the ranges and the rivers flowing into the sea. Sometimes they demonstrated an exact place on a map of Germany. Meanwhile in class we were asked to recite, word-perfect, one of the long poems we had transcribed and committed to memory. Among the ones we were given were those by Schiller characterised by his concern with liberty and justice and the notion that hope springs eternal: *Noch im Grabe baut er die Hoffnung auf* (Even in the grave he still builds up hope). Heroic words these, well suited to military goals and an attendant sense of civic pride.

Well after the War had ended, and not long before we were released, at the beginning my fifth year in school, in September 1946, my Lutheran missionary teacher, Mr Streicher, taught us about prehistory. He spoke of the great *Völkerwanderung* during the first millennium. It was a way of introducing us to the German tribes and the origins of their societies. But he also extolled the movement of nomads as exemplifying the energy for which Germans are noted.

From another perspective, I might have learned—but not from him—that the wandering tribes were a pack of vandals, looting and pillaging as they went. Nowadays one can make a comparison between the rampages of Vandals, Goths and Huns and the thuggish looting and killing that was perpetrated by Nazi gangs in a so-called 'civilised' society.

Herr Streicher was fervent about the German past, but he also talked about God. This may or may not have been forbidden earlier at the school. His experiences in New Guinea gave him a keen sense of the lives of the swamp dwellers of prehistoric Heidelberg and for 'primitive customs'. He had us enthralled with his tales from New Guinea, such as the cunning ambushes of the Kukukukus (Highlander 'pygmies') and their repulsive mortuary customs, which, according to him, obliged a close relative of a dead person to drink his juices.

Herr Streicher no doubt exaggerated to gain our attention. A Kukukuku custom related to this story was, however, around 1954 identified by scholar doctors as a cause of *kuru*, the deadly laughing disease. Streicher had not invented the whole thing.

The word *Vaterland* (fatherland) was used a lot in the camp. It has the connotation of a strong base for the roots of an oak tree, of a land defended by one's people, the place from which one's paternal lineage comes. It is a much colder word than the one preferred in the English language: motherland, the land of my mothers. Ironically, of course, Britain at that time was the country most associated with the use of nannies to raise children in well-to-do homes. But then, one has to be careful of giving words too much weight. Sometimes they merely present an aspiration.

The associations with motherland are of nurture, empathy, soulfulness. Nazi ideology was forever praising the *Vaterland* and we were supposed to build up an attachment. Something of that hard-edged, competitively thrusting energy certainly clung to us Germans as a habit of behaviour. We took it into the future and had to curb it in situations in which it was of little use.

I see my personal background as determined more by the women of my mother's family, from whom I gained my basic direction in life. 'You and your cursed romanticism, with which you have afflicted your children!' I once accused my mother. For if romanticism nourishes the soul, it goes along with a need to discover 'the absolute source' of all things, as mystics have taught us. My mother's traditions and the German fairy tales share this need for certitude. The classic British children's stories, like the stories of Alice in her Wonderland and Winnie the Pooh, are more like games to a child nourished on continental romanticism. They are too cerebral, too detached from our nostalgia. They appeal to a child's reason.

The stories of the Brothers Grimm that we were told in school have been passed down through the generations. They are like crucibles of the traditional values of western European societies, tested over the centuries by trial and error. Many of them have a strong ethical and moral base. They extol the virtue of hard work and describe the conflict between good and evil. They speak of belief in the supernatural, and the power of witches, giants and trolls, which may be friendly or hostile to humans. They deal in in transcendental possibilities: that lives are not tied to ordinary experiences and ordinary time and that death is not necessarily the end of life. Some stories support a notion of a correct blood line. Stepmothers, for instance, are inevitably hostile.

The other stories we were told were Hans Andersen's. From them, one gets an overall impression that life is fragile and brief, pleasure passes and nothing really lasts. The poor are not compensated on this earth. Such realism has its valuable messages. Life cannot be depended upon to provide security. One must focus one's mind on why we are here on earth.

These tales come from a period in which monarchical government and the arbitrary rights of an aristocracy were the established political order. They nevertheless present strong themes: standards of justice and concern for the poor, for instance.

Tante Lilo's teaching turned us into enthusiastic students. Nothing in my later schooling matched her ability to enthrall me. She showed us the joy of knowledge acquired purely for its own sake. She always provided a context to render meaningful what she taught.

My brother Peter hated being separated from our parents, and at first used to run away rather than go to kindergarden. We always knew where to find him, however, carefully hidden under the dangerous communal wood heap. He was bright, we said, but preferred to hide his talent under a pile of timber. Christianity was systematically ignored in our school syllabus. Music was not. Tante Lilo taught us all to sight-read music towards the end of our fourth year. Musical talent was displayed in a number of performing groups. The German Red Cross supplied recorders, some string instruments and piano-accordions. Some instruments may also have been brought into the camp.

Children also performed in plays, often with the adults. There was special children's drama using favourite Grimm's fairytales presented as shadow plays, behind large white sheets (*Leinenwand Theater*). Once we performed for the wedding of another teacher, Tante Gudrun. We wore wreaths of russet chrysanthemums in our hair, formed a guard of honour and danced during a performance in German of Shakespeare's *Midsummer Night's Dream*. We were Puck's elves to the music of *Anitra's Dance* from Grieg's *Peer Gynt*.

I relished this artistic life. I used to run to the hall for orchestral and chamber music performances. My parents encouraged my interest. When my mother asked me what attracted me so much, I once answered with natural simplicity: 'Oh, I do love it when the trumpeters pour out the spit from their trumpets!'

Nationalist ambitions, I think, inspired the vigorous school sporting program. Tante Lilo's partner in this was Eva Ruff, a youth leader in love with folklore, who was a skilled player of the piano-accordion. She taught us folk dancing and gymnastic exercises to music. We performed these during the celebration of commemorative feasts.

It was obvious to the authorities that an interest in sport kept us healthy, and a sports ground was eventually added to Compound C. It was securely fenced. Towards the end of our imprisonment, upper primary and high-school classes became permanent fixtures in the new huts erected in this sports ground annex.

Everyone from the age of 10 who had real athletic ability was recruited to be trained as if they might become a future Olympic champion. Every day we set out on our long early morning runs, boys and girls at separate times. We ran several times around the barbed wire fence when the gates between the three sections were open. This was followed by calisthenics and gymnastics.

We participated in every kind of competitive running, pitting ourselves against imaginary world records for our age for sprinting, hurdles, broad-jumping into sandpits and high-jumping over a pole between sticks, with the intervals marked with nails. I learned to rattle off the names of German

10. The Imaginary Homeland

Olympic champions and the records they had broken. I was to learn later that children in other places, like the Australia beyond the fence, had similar sporting ambitions. So competitive were we that the *Palestinänser* camp leader once wanted to show off his 10-year-old daughter to the Australian camp commandant by having her sprint against me.

The imaginary backdrops to our efforts were the great German sporting festivals of Nazi inspiration, a mixture of Greek Olympic and Nordic mythology. They were full of gods and goddesses with burnished spears and impenetrable shields, their fair hair braided, and their banners flying.

Three young men came briefly to the camp. One of them, an accomplished sportsman who had trained German runners for the 1936 Olympics, offered to coach me as a hurdler. My parents thought better of it. They had me taught the violin instead.

In those times in Germany, emphasis was placed on art and craft education in schools. I still have a craft teacher-training book which my mother was able to take when the camp library was broken up at the end of the War. It shows how women were encouraged to do woodwork of all kinds, making wood-cuts for printing, cake moulds, dolls' houses, small theatres, flower presses, picture frames, book-ends. They were encouraged to learn how to weave, work in leather and bind books.

Such skills were all tried out in the camp, and some in the school. I'm sure they helped to make imprisonment much more bearable. Today in the Tatura Museum you can find a collection of handwoven clothes, leather bags, wooden clogs, bound books and journals, posters for theatrical performances, handmade toys, scale models of camp huts and much more. They are displayed with the many written records from the camps.

Our children's games sometimes arrived like seasons. Someone would decide that it was the time for kites. Then every child got out an old kite or pestered their parents to produce one. When one child played with a top, everyone suddenly had to have one. These were carefully carved tops with nail-head tips, which we propelled along with leather-strip whips. We also had stilts on which we raced, jumping over puddles and culverts.

Out-of-bounds places were secretly explored in games of Hide and Seek and Cowboys and Indians, often under the huts, known by us in children's dialect as *Dach-dacherle* (rat tat tat). Crawling under there was dangerous, for poisonous red-back spiders clung to the wooden boards and props.

We played hopscotch, the German version of Oranges and Lemons and dug small pits for games of marbles 'for keeps', wearing our thumbnails down. Peter and I made earth-mounded alley slides, into which we poured water. Near my father's garden at Hut 4, he and I constructed an elaborate canal system around miniature settlements in which resided stick figure people. We knew not to intrude upon his fine stand of sunflowers.

Skipping-rope games were popular with girls, as was rounders played with a strong stick and jam tins as markers. We performed flamboyantly in the hope that our parents would pass by and witness a victorious home run.

Our children's adventure playground was also responsible for a lot of wounds and painful gravel rashes, which became infected.

While we played, the adults lived their own mysterious lives. In January 1945 my mother gave birth to my brother Herbert after that dangerous journey to Waranga Hospital.

Because it might have seemed strange to have another child during such insecure times, the boy was lovingly nicknamed *das Kriegskind* (the War child). He was such a beautiful baby that he became the focus of much admiration. Peter and I did not resent this. We delighted in the amusement Herbert afforded us, with his quaint and bright-minded ways. *Das Kriegskind* brought a new interest to our family. He lightened our minds. My parents also made some strong new friends through the attention people paid him.

A childless couple, Lydia and Fred Zachen, were prominent in the Herbert admiration society. Things became much more relaxed in Hut 4. The addition to our family may have entitled my parents to a third room, because we got one somewhere in late 1944 or early 1945. Our new living quarters seemed spacious.

My mother asked if she could introduce *Kinderküche* (infant meals) on a roster in the dining room. The answer from the camp leadership was an emphatic 'no'. Later, when other mothers of infants saw the wisdom of her case, she refused to join in. 'They can keep their stupid, cussed pig-headedness!' she exclaimed. But they begged her to show the way. She participated, she said, for the sake of her child.

10. The Imaginary Homeland

My mother did not forgive easily and harboured grievances, a trait she has passed on to me. The opposition to her extremely sensible suggestion still rankled long after the way had been cleared for her project. She expected others to be as uncompromising as she was. It was an aspect of her puritan upbringing. My father, by contrast, never bore lingering grudges. You knew exactly where you stood with him. His fuse was short, but he soon forgave.

When Herbert was five months old, keeping my mother extremely busy with the daily washing of his cloth nappies, my parents nevertheless stood by their promise to me of a 10th birthday party. This raised problems. Which of my playmates would we invite?

Instead of allowing this to arise every year, my parents had always promised just one party, for the important 10th birthday. A large number of children could then be invited. Our usually strict father provided jolly leadership. He was full of surprises, even producing an impressive kite. Somehow my mother managed access to the communal kitchen and amazed us with her chocolate cakes decorated with elaborate, Austrian-style butter-cream piping.

Other children also had parties. The Schnerring family produced animals carved from carrots, capsicums, tomatoes and cucumbers. The games we played at these affairs are familiar across many lands. They included Blind Man's Buff, Pin the Tail on the Donkey and treasure hunts. Leap-frog and tunnel ball were also played during school sports classes, along with the usual individual competitions.

On ordinary days, when we were forbidden to play outside, we made our own cardboard-box puppet theatres. I recall devising stage sets and a string pulley-system by which the sun and moon rose and went down behind trees and mountains. There was also a spider which moved down its web on a thread, then up again.

As well as Christmas and Easter, nationalistic feasts of Nazi inspiration were celebrated. When the German officer POWs made gifts by hand for many of the inmates of Camp 3, I do not know what we sent them in return. One of the feasts we celebrated now seems sinister and frightening. During the winter solstice, bonfires were heaped with books and burnt. I think the books included those by Jewish authors.

Since I was a good jumper, I leapt over the flames with the older ones. Sometimes I thought: 'What if I fall into the burning coals?'

Reading material for every age group was sent by the German Red Cross to the camp library. I often had my head buried in a saga of adventure describing the migration of reindeers along the Baltic Sea, the life cycles of bears, the adventures of sea captains, or the gold rush that emptied Melbourne town of its population in the 1850s. One book stands out. It made me very uncomfortable with its spiteful, anti-Czech story. I shrank from its obvious manipulation of hatred. I knew what it felt like to be excluded from power.

Father had grown up with a love of brass music. The ceremonial Nazi parades were often redeemed for him by the music that accompanied them. Both my parents enjoyed the pomp of the colourful ceremonial processions of an older monarchical order. Mother also had a compassionate heart for what soldiering meant in defence of home and hearth, and for the self-sacrifice of men who gave their lives for the sake of their country. Father was a pragmatist. Some happenings one simply had to accept. That was life. At the time, I found a certain nobility in such fatalism. Later it was to irritate and worry me constantly.

At the age of 10, I saw my parents as an obstacle to my personal choices. My father was stern, and my mother often placated him on our behalf. Perhaps that way she also introduced a wedge between him and us. We regarded her as much more 'on our side' in most disputes. However, she could also be extremely obstinate. That's how I felt when I wanted to be with my peers in the Union of German Girls *Jungmädl* group.

At political gatherings we were obliged to stand perfectly still, nearly everyone rigged out in the prescribed costumes. Once we stood still for almost two hours while our leaders harangued us with torrents of words extolling the virtues of Hitler and his followers. Sometimes on these occasions one of us would faint from sheer exhaustion. Did they not know that Hitler was dead? Had the news not entered the camp? I recall a particularly well-attended and showy ceremony, at night in the open air in Compound C. There were flags and political emblems and people in uniform singing an anthem of which I remember the melody and the opening lines:

10. The Imaginary Homeland

In München sind viele gefallen,
In München war'n viele dabei …

(In Munich many have fallen
In Munich many were there …)

This ceremony was staged on 9 November 1945. Why that date? For years afterwards, I did not bother to inform myself of the so-called 'Nazi martyrdom' it celebrated.

These events were part of a situation that in retrospect I consider dangerous and politically evil. I now know that this special ceremony was staged when the Australian authorities decreed that all emblems and symbols of significance to the Nazis were to be destroyed. I remember that ceremony as long, solemn and well-attended.

My need as a child to belong with my peers is a cautionary tale about the human condition. I am now wryly amused, not only by my 10-year-old innocence, but also by the respectful attendance of the Australian garrison. If our 'enemy' masters did not know, how could young children have understood its true meaning?

The pomp and bravura were of course a ridiculous mimicking of Hitler's performances and rallies 'at home'. All this one lacked was the presiding criminals. There may well have been bullying to force people in the camp to attend. I know nothing of any such goings-on. The nostalgia expressed for Germany by so many internees gave me a mental construct of a very green and artistic 'home' which I shared with them, and for which I longed with a burning heart. It was derived mainly from books and folk songs. So I suffered with the others the intense *Heimweh* (homesickness, a word which in its English translation does not catch the emotional yearning associated with the German). Religious literature speaks of the soul yearning for God. Our yearning for a Germany we had not known was a non-religious, but nevertheless overwhelmingly emotional equivalent; a pining of the heart.

At that ceremony, the atrocities perpetrated by the Nazi regime had yet to sink in—if indeed they were then widely known in Australia. People were wary of War propaganda from either side. All mail both ways had to move through military censors. The degree of ignorance during War-time confusion and secrecy is now difficult to imagine.

After the marriage of Rudolf and Elfriede in the chapel of the Austrian Secondary Boys' School, Istanbul, Turkey, 2 February 1935. The celebrant, Father Dvorak, is centre back.

The house in Çankiri Village, Turkey, in which Helga was born.

Grandmother Emma Bittnar and Helga entering the door to her first-floor apartment in Breslau before Christmas 1937.

Four generations of Elfriede's family in Breslau: Bertha Friebe, Emma Bittnar, Elfriede and Helga Girschik.

Elfriede and her children in Tehran, 1938.

Iranians with Peter among dunes, with holy man Ali Agah Abass' grave and shrine in the background, 1938.

The first train out of Tehran Central Railway Station, which Rudolf helped to build, late August 1938.

Christmas at home in Khaladabad, south of Kashan, Iran, 1939.

Picnic on Nowruz, March 1941, by Figtree Creek beyond Sharifabad in the Mashad neighbourhood with Elfriede and Rudolf's Armenian colleague friends.

Cliffs by the road outside Karind, Iran, July 1941.

Elfriede with face bound because of the abscess on her tooth. Armenian engineer friend Mkhitar Miramian, Peter, Helga and the dog Fram, on the way to Karind, Iran, July 1941.

In the Australian internment camp in Compound A with the Drude family, from left: Helga's friend Maria Dannenberg with her father, Mrs Müller and her children. Peter and Helga are second and third from the right.

The Girschik and Strecker families in Compound A, Camp 3, Tatura.

At Mornington beach, the family visit Peter at the Mercy nun's boarding school, Star of the Sea or Padua College, 1947. Helga is wearing her black Hitler cardigan which Elfriede transformed with Persian silver buttons.

Forms 7 and 8 were taught in one room by Mercy nuns in 1947 at the Academy of Mary Immaculate, Fitzroy, Melbourne. Helga is extreme left, second row from front. Her friend Frances Hendriksen is in the top row, second from right.

Elfriede with Herbert dreaming of her homeland among the ships at Williamstown port in Melbourne, winter 1947.

In Blackburn, Melbourne, the Girschik family welcome Willi Zapf's children Erika and Peter to Australia, August 1949.

The Matriculation class, Academy of Mary Immaculate, late 1952. From left top row: Judith Wilson, Pamela Poynton, Mary White; front row: Pamela Brady, Helga Grischik, Kathleen Kehoe.

Example of Rudolf's engineering work in Iran. Date unknown, most likely during one of his several post-war engagements, in 1951 or during 1958–60. This is the work of an engineer whose qualifications during this period were not accepted in Australia.

Helga and Jim with their small wedding party in Rome, 1956. On Helga's right is Des O'Grady, an Australian journalist, and on her left is bridegroom Jim. [The group is named on p. 255 of this book].

Jim and Helga visit Melchior ('Mel') Togolo, at his home, Rorovana Village, Bougainville, Papua New Guinea in mid-1973.

Helga and Jim Griffin with their grown-up children in Canberra, from left: Justin carrying his son Julian, Denis, Gerald, Anthea, Cathleen (Cathie), Gabrielle (Gabi), c. mid-1988.

11

Shadows and Flames

Our future was frighteningly uncertain. Would all internees be repatriated? Was a watch kept on people in the camp by the authorities in Germany? What reprisals would there be if Germany won the War, or lost it? The degree of community ignorance may be demonstrated in that it took many years to convince my mother that the Holocaust had happened, even though she despised Nazi ideology, Nazi thugs, who claimed that 'the future belongs to us'. My parents were not deceived by this rhetoric of exclusion.

'I felt very troubled on my visit home with you in 1937,' my mother used to say, 'when "*Grüss Gott*" (God be with you) was replaced by that idiotic "*Heil Hitler*" greeting.' The old monarchical order in Germany, with Kaiser Wilhelm at the head, was a political order with which she could identify. She accepted the old-world militarism of Prussia for its defence of hearth and homeland. My father's family still clung emotionally to a monarchical political order 11 years after the War had ended. Father himself did not. He was a social democrat. My mother was to become one as well, though always a little more to the Left than he. Yet she always retained her admiration for Kaiser Wilhelm, acquired from her local community in childhood.

My parents realised, I suppose, that I would be ostracised if I opted out of the political youth union which all 10-year-olds in the camp were pressured to join. In those days the uniforms in which people dressed, the swastika, the many flags, emblems and other ceremonial paraphernalia just seemed to me a great novelty. It had no sinister associations for us. Many Germans admired the ceremonial occasions staged by British royalty. The military flavour of the German version of pomp and circumstance in the late 1930s and early '40s did not leave the nasty taste in the mouth it did after 1945. It is amazing how innocent one can be in a familiar setting, then so disgusted by later awareness of it, or its stereotypes.

Perhaps my parents permitted me to belong to the youth league at that eleventh hour of German nationalism because it separated the sexes and afforded some protection from free-running male teenagers. Keeping us safe and obedient was a burden to them. I once got the most hideous thrashing from my father for running barefoot against his wishes in a game of skill and speed.

He may have had good reasons for insisting that my clogs stay on. Hookworm was no doubt prevalent and difficult to treat. Thirty lashes was what he threatened and that's what he stuck to, despite my mother's protests.

In my mind's eye is a second hut that was never there.

It stands at one end of the parade ground, and I am at the opposite end. I hear the screams of a girl across the empty space. I am the girl, but the observer too. The horror and the pain of this are muted now, but the experience has never left me. It has become a symbol of all the beatings of children in the camp.

When the birch broke, my father took his belt to complete the task. I could not sit down for three days. After that my blistered buttocks turned black. That was the worst beating he ever gave me. That was sadism, Nazi style. And yet, someone who found such treatment of us abhorrent, who had reason to think the worst of him, informed me that my father was never a Nazi. Internment brought out the worst in some parents.

This beating cast a long shadow over my relationship with my father.

At times the approval of my peers was more important than obeying my parents, despite such consequences. That's exactly what they feared. Once we left the camp, my father stopped beating me with his rod. Only an occasional whack across my head relieved his anger with me, although Peter continued to be beaten and humiliated. Sometimes I wondered if we would end up with brain damage or defective ears. My father's authority was at this time more often expressed by his letting fly heavy clubs of words, centred on my stupidity. I had no weapons against him. I became more stubborn and obstinate.

11. Shadows and Flames

The Palestinian Germans who set the tone in the camp were not intrinsically bad. While my family had been used to a fairly nomadic lifestyle before the War, they had lived for generations in their settled communities in Palestine. Their communal culture was well formed. In the early 1940s, a homogeneous majority in a wretched situation, the Templers were ideally placed to protect their preferred manner of social organisation and ideology. As a group they redirected their festering frustrations against non-conformists and other vulnerable scapegoats, for instance by calling them 'spies'.

Their use of the patois of street Arabic and Swabian dialect demonstrates their need to communicate exclusively among themselves. It was a way of keeping unwelcome listeners out. That private language of course irritated 'outsiders'. We found out, for instance, that *Patie(a)ch* (German phonology) meant melon-head. Just as birds carry seeds that sprout elsewhere, their children carried their dialect across the frontier to evolve further.

Everyone was aware of tragedies in the camp. One Lutheran missionary family lost two out of four children in different accidents. One child died when a tip-truck emptied its load of wood where the little boy was playing. The other was burnt alive. I recall the day when my father foolishly put his head round the dining room door and yelled 'Fire! Fire!' People fell over each other in the rush to get out. Everyone thought: 'Is it my hut?' People used to make little ovens from large empty tins of preserves, with chimneys from smaller tins, to heat up the damp, cold huts in winter.

We saw the flames leap high and two brave men force their way into the burning building to save the two children who were sleeping inside. I overheard that the family had been drying napkins near the stove. We thronged around the burning hut and saw one child carried to safety. It was too late for the other.

One morning I heard some boys whispering about a shocking sight. They offered to take me into the men's showers which were out of bounds for girls. There, hanging naked from a wooden beam, a rope tied round his neck, was one of the camp's leaders. I wonder now whether this happened after the War had taken its fateful course against Nazi Germany's vain ambitions, and Hitler was known to be dead.

Once, earlier, I think and on a Good Friday, I saw Mr Zubeck parading naked in the camp carriageway, preaching atonement. He tied a crucifix high on a pole. A curious, baffled and mumbling crowd gathered.

Some jeered, while others took pity on Mr Zubeck. It was not the only 'madness' in the camp. Herr Rosenthal was seen one night trying to dig up the grave of the Biblical Abraham. Most of the rest of us were watching the amazing spectacle of the Aurora Australis sending up its flares of russet, orange and blue into the dark southern night sky.

We were forced early into close observation of bizarre adult behaviour. This tended to make us prematurely serious. Outsiders looking on may have found camp activities hilarious. The Australian garrison must have watched in a constant state of amazement. They were generally kindly men with a job to do, probably bored beyond endurance.

Some soldiers joined us for the films that were shown occasionally. Many of these were silent. A few, with a talking soundtrack, I remember well. There was *Heimat*, for instance, that evocation of the German homeland. Everybody cried nostalgically as a group of fair-haired children sang like angels the well-known German folk song *Weisst Du wie viel Sterne stehen an dem blauen Himmelsfeld?* (Do you know how many stars stand in the blue field of sky?). This goes on to speak of God's protective power. It is a simple song, often sung to reassure children.

I also recall a gripping epic of the American Wild West, with its ugly anti-Indian, pro-settler, pro-home-and-hearth message, rather like John Ford's *The Seekers*. I assume, sadly, that we sided with the settlers, but can't be sure. Then there was the film about girlish spite in a school, in which Deanna Durban acted the role of a whistling cyclist. This one was responsible for my terror at possibly becoming a victim at an Australian school after the War. Nasty English or Australian girls were one and the same. We knew no difference. How odd! How sensitive! It must have been a harmless enough film.

12

After the War

After the War, the camp began slowly to empty, and most residents of Compound D departed. Japanese families came to live in Compound A. We then moved into D, but spent a lot of time looking through the wire at the Japanese internees. I picked up from the adults around me that the Japanese did not value our civilised attitude to horticulture. I believed that when they came, the Japanese destroyed all our gardens. This was because I had not seen it was really the Germans who had done that, to deprive those who came to replace us of our produce. Whole families destroyed their gardens rather than let the Japanese have them.

My family and one other in Compound A had apparently left their vegetable patch undisturbed. Other vandals could not cope with this, so destroyed ours as well. My brother Peter told me how he watched through the wires an old Japanese man attempt to resuscitate a strawberry patch with a watering can.

Rules in the camp were relaxed at the end of the War. I presume the guards were as anxious as we were to get home to their families. After the armistice, we were permitted to leave the camp occasionally, under armed escort. We walked along dirt roads through the property of local farmers, opening and closing gates as we were commanded, and then along a public approach to the Waranga Basin. We explored the adjacent quarry for simple treasures and discovered rabbit holes, which we poked with sticks. When one emerged and shot off in fright, a wild chase ensued, accompanied by our shouts of delight, and always ending with our prey escaping.

Above the muddy bottom of the Waranga Basin, Peter and I made pathetic attempts to learn to swim. The water seemed to offer us no buoyancy. We sank like pieces of metal. The Basin presented a desolate scene, especially when the sky was overcast. The grey water lapped knee-deep against stands of dead eucalypts, a *pavane* on the death of trees.

Nevertheless, we loved these excursions, which included autumn mushrooming trips. We noticed the smallest things as the seasons changed. We caught the bitter fragrance of peppercorn tree fronds along the way, and noted colourful broken plates sticking out of rubbish piles under the dead oleander bushes deprived of water, in the ruins of someone's abandoned house.

Once as we returned home in the late afternoon, a soldier caught a silver snake as it slipped into a hole. Holding its tail, he pulled at it in a tug of war. He then whirled the body back through the air and cracked it like a whip. He broke its back. Then he dropped it unconcernedly on the ground.

The snake slithered into its hole as best it could. Our screams half froze in our mouths as we watched. A translator was on hand to report on the soldier's amused grunt: 'Of course she's poisonous, but don't fear. She'll only last until sundown. That'll finish her off.'

Peter and I and a couple of friends went on a yabbying expedition to a dam quite close to the camp. Arming ourselves with empty jam tins, a short piece of string and a bait of earthworms, we set our traps and sat like experienced anglers waiting for one of the denizens of the deep to enter and take the bait. We came home with one or two samples each. We waited hungrily as my mother quickly steamed them for us. Then while we turned our backs for a few minutes, waiting for the three tiny morsels to cool down inside their armoured shells, our little brother, swift as a waterbird, devoured the lot. This incident tickled mother's fancy.

My father told me years later that before the men were released from the camp each family was examined for its political status and therefore its fate. A Committee of Inquiry, presided over by Justice Simpson, a judge from Tasmania, was set up to examine possible deportations for Nazi die-hards, and what to do with those who wanted to be repatriated or to stay in Australia. People with contentious claims were released later, after investigation by another arbiter, Judge Hutchins.

12. After the War

Although our father was told that our family would make good migrants, he held out to have us repatriated to Iran. He knew that his own homeland was suffering after the War, and he had no professional connections there.

The official response was that no ships were going to the Persian Gulf. He did not know that the British government had pressured the Iranian authorities not to allow the former 'enemies of Britain' back into oil-rich Iran. When we missed out on repatriation to Europe, my father reluctantly sought release to Melbourne. We stayed behind in the camp until he had established himself. He was playing for time, hoping the Australian authorities would make future transport possible.

The suggestion of Melbourne as our future home was sensible, if daunting. My parents had left their homelands so long before that they had no assets there. My mother's family in Breslau had suffered terribly towards the end of the War, and had fled westwards to Zwickau.

People from the camp who wanted to stay in Australia could not leave it until their breadwinners had found work and accommodation for them. There were no migrant holding centres then, no English-language classes, no employment agencies designed to help immigrants or ex-prisoners find work.

So my father left the camp alone to look for work in Melbourne. At first he shovelled sugar at Melbourne's docks but was immediately told by unionists to 'Slow down, mate. What's the hurry?'

My mother had a terrible time after my father left us. We had by then moved into Compound D, to make room for the Japanese families awaiting deportation. She was in sole charge of three lively young children who were always getting under other people's feet. This was when she was hauled before the committee that supervised public order, and was strongly rebuked by it for her youngest son's habit of appearing in people's rooms uninvited. Herbert was not yet two years old. Without my father, my mother had no one to protect her from the bullies.

13

Stranded in Exile

The housing shortage in Melbourne after the War was critical, especially for families. Children were not usually made welcome, as if equated with cats and dogs. From the camp, my mother used to remonstrate with Rudolf by letter when he wrote to report yet another knockback. 'Tell these people that our children are well brought up, that they do what we tell them, and that they have good manners and will not tear the walls apart!'

The weeks dragged on as my mother and we children remained behind barbed wire while Rudolf lined up in the middle of the night with other hopefuls outside the offices of the Melbourne *Age*. These other homeless and unemployed people all wanted a newspaper 'hot off the press before the ink was dry'.

In search of a job or accommodation, my father caught the first available bus or train, anxious to be at the head of the queue. Usually, however, he found that others had beaten him. Then he had to wait, sometimes for a long time, for his turn to be interviewed. Although he spoke school English reasonably fluently, it was with a heavy accent, with gaps and awkward grammatical constructions. His imperfect language, after a bitter War when foreigners were not well accepted, was a problem for some landlords and employers. They wanted only those whose first language was English.

My father was caught in a vicious cycle: without a job, he had no means to pay for accommodation; with a job, there would be no time to look for it, except in the early mornings or late in the evenings.

Eventually, Rudolf was given a job as a draughtsman with Woodall Duckham, a construction company in the city which at the time was building gas storage cylinders in the Melbourne suburb of Highett. Their office was near Spencer Street Station, a blessing for someone who had constantly to travel by bus, tram or train seeking a home for his family.

Its director had no animosity towards ex-internees. His patience, however, did not stretch to my father's disappearances for a couple of hours through the day every week. He threatened him with dismissal if he did not put in his full time at work. Apart from the urgent need to find somewhere for us to live, Rudolf may also have been insensitive to such strict routine, never having experienced rigid timekeeping at work. In Iran he had worked on a grand scale and for very long hours. His five years in the camp, largely without paid work, and wearing whatever he pleased, also did not help him easily become an office cipher in a suit.

We were, however, enthusiastic that he had at last found paid work, and that we would soon be able to join him.

Suitable housing remained an obstacle. Finding space for a family of foreigners, three of whom were children, was much harder than finding a room to let for one single mature man, even one just out of prison. My father's letters became despondent again. He had not expected his wife to reproach him with such impatience. Her gloom became an affront to his exertions on our behalf.

Then at last came the telegram, urging her to 'pack up immediately'. She stored everything except some basic clothes in cardboard boxes ready for the signal to leave. Then another letter came, with a different message. In tears of rage she unpacked the stack of boxes containing virtually everything we possessed.

'That damned telegram!' she exclaimed. In a letter to him, she wrote: 'Don't you realise how much work was involved packing with three young children? And all for nothing! Why are you so impractical? So inconsiderate? I'll just resign myself to spending the rest of my life here in this camp while you have your freedom.'

She did not seem able to comprehend how difficult it was for him. Another adult from the camp later hinted to me that there were other problems between them, which had developed in the camp, and of which we knew nothing. Despite his short stature and glass eye, my father charmed women. That admirable person, my mother, carried formidable grudges for suspected wrongs. Her deep emotions made her very human to us. We loved her wholeheartedly, but ducked away from her anger, her tongue, her sulking.

As a youth in Europe, my father had been an adventurer. But in domestic life he was not a practical man. Perhaps he had begun to rely too much on his wife's management skills. After internment he could not find work appropriate to his qualifications, because they were not recognised in Australia. The War had destroyed his career and deprived him of professional standing.

His confidence was affected. Despite the tight rein he kept on Peter and me, we respected him, with love and a tinge of fear. His pure love for his infant son, Herbert, reminded us of the man we had known in early childhood. That man had not completely disappeared. But because he never hugged us, we were much emotionally closer to our mother.

Our family was well aware that many people like us were much worse off during and after the War. We might have ended up in a Siberian labour camp, or have been killed by bombs. Grim news from the homelands of my parents trickled in by mail. My own family had been spared the sufferings of their relatives.

Whether they had been directly implicated or not, a sense of guilt must have hung over much of Germany-Austria for that woeful catastrophe which German militarism and arrogance had spawned from its so-called civilisation. Post-internment depression also gnawed away at both my father and my mother. I can't speak for my brother, but I caught some of that feeling myself. We felt ourselves locked in by fears about the future.

As our father tried to solve the problem of working his full week while looking for family accommodation, he found temporary lodgings for himself with an old couple near St Kilda beach. Eventually he found some living quarters for us all in a boarding house in Park Street, not far from where he had been living.

At last we were able to join him. It was not long before Christmas 1946. I was then 11 years old. Peter was eight, and Herbert was almost two.

That Christmas of 1946 has been wiped from my mind. It has lost its importance in the queue of remembered experiences. The greatest of these was seeing our father again in early December. He blessed the ceremony of reunion by buying us our first ice-cream of freedom, a neat little sandwich of frozen vanilla cream with the label Sennitts on the packet. It was the most delicious food I had ever tasted. Not only was this truly exquisite vanilla cream melting on my tongue in the heat, but in my head it tasted of freedom and of a future near the sea.

Everything was new. So much space now, and so many noisy vehicles moving about! I felt the sea breeze on my bare arms and heard gulls calling to one another. We ate our ice-creams on a lawn under a date palm, one of a stately row. I looked at these symmetrical trees and found them strangely out of place after the landscape of scattered, twisted eucalypts at Tatura. 'How out of place they seem here!' I remarked to father. 'How they must miss their desert homeland. Why did people bring them here? They don't look as if they really belong.'

Then, without giving this another thought, I took off down the park, leaping over every seat. *Oh Freude! Und Freiheit!* (Oh joy! And freedom!).

My parents swiftly drew my attention to this now unseemly behaviour. 'Young girls do not behave like this in cities!' my father cautioned. I began to sense in myself the beginnings of a new kind of psychological unease that was to last for years. It partnered my sense of dislocation. We lacked the confidence of tourists. At the time we had an uneasy feeling that we were not supposed to be in Australia. I have heard other migrants and prisoners speak of this. The problem is particularly acute for those separated from loved ones—which of course we were not—but also when accompanied by the onset of puberty. We were now in a place where, apart from family talk, we children and our mother could not understand anything anyone was saying a lot of the time.

While mother sorted out our possessions, my father took us to see where he had been living on his own. It was only a few blocks away. Entering a single-fronted terrace house we walked down a dark passage into an equally dark sitting room at the back. All the blinds were drawn.

I later learned that this was the custom. Heat was kept out in summer and furnishings were protected from sunlight, producing what I always thought of as an atmosphere as depressing as funeral parlours which, of course, I had never entered.

13. Stranded in Exile

The radio was blaring. Often later on while passing someone's open window, I would hear the energetic voice of a racing or football commentator, slurring his words and shouting. I also caught a lingering whiff of gas, as if the stove was leaking. This was my introduction to domestic Australia.

The old couple were happy to meet Rudi's children. They took Peter and me to see their pets in their tiny backyard. There were two elegant greyhounds with wire cages over their dribbling mouths. Father explained that, apart from renting out his room, the couple raced the dogs for money.

St Kilda, that suburb with its large amusement park and pavilion by the sea, was then a sleazy haunt. Later I was to hear that numbers of foreign professionals and some quacks, without a licence to practise, found work there. Nor did I know that a network, by word of mouth, brought customers to prostitutes, patients to doctors and dentists, and anyone who needed them to backyard abortionists. Black market services were cheaper. All manner of trading was done via back stairs leading to unregistered businesses.

Perhaps that was how my mother was given a job sewing men's suits for a factory owner. She worked in the bedroom of the lodgings Rudolf had found for us. We were poor. We could not afford to buy the mouth-watering Continental cakes of Acland Street.

Our lodgings in Park Street were in a shared Federation house with gargoyle-like ornaments on the corners of a pitched roof. The front entrance was from a small angled verandah. A corridor ran down the middle of the house between rooms each side, ending in a kitchen at the back. The house belonged to a Communist who rented out several of its rooms. Mrs Hall was the landlady.

My parents took two adjoining bedrooms. They shared theirs with Herbert, and turned the other into a lounge. We shared the toilet, bathroom and kitchen with another couple, on a roster system. Peter and I shared a sleep-out in the small backyard under a well-grown tree with pendulous branches.

We lived like strangers on the margins of somebody else's life. The lounge and sleep-out were temporary retreats.

When Mrs Hall was in a benevolent mood, she would invite us into her lounge to listen to the pianola. It was a kind of magic. While someone pumped the pedal near the ground, the keys of the piano played themselves, without hands, while a thick beige paper with patterns of holes, the musical code, emerged at the back of the machine.

The Teddy Bears' Picnic and *My Canary Has Circles Under Its Eyes* were the names of two tunes we often heard clink-clonking across the keyboard. Without English, the strange names left an impression on us. And yes, that's where I heard Schubert's *Marche Militaire*, for four hands, for the first time.

Father went by train to work, and our mother cleaned up then spent the day on her Singer machine battling with the intricately tailored designs of men's suits in worsted woollen cloth. It was difficult to keep us occupied, since we had no toys. To entertain ourselves between meals, we had to wander the parks and streets.

Twice I had the disturbing experience of being shadowed by men. One loiterer followed me into the sea where I was wading and tried to fondle me. The other appeared several times in the park. From the swings on which I liked to go very high, I could see him positioned below, waiting.

I was oblivious to such dangers. I only realised that something was wrong when he tried to follow me into the public toilets. I outsmarted him by changing my mind at the last moment. I quickly hustled my brothers home, relieved I had them with me. I was too shy to tell my parents, even though I had to make excuses for staying home afterwards for days at a time. The man seemed not to have followed us home.

Our enforced walks, playing in the park or paddling along the beach were not always happy occasions. Once I was wading perhaps too deep when a sudden wave took me out of my depth. Not being a swimmer, I began to thrash about anxiously, struggling. I gulped down mouthfuls of salt water and thought that I must surely drown. Then, suddenly, a pair of strong hands pulled me out of the waves, and carried me back to the beach.

This episode must have lasted a mere few minutes although it seemed a long time. I don't know how I got home. Presumably we sat on the sand until I recovered. Mother was beside herself with anxiety when I reported the incident and forbade me from going into the water unless an adult was there. I did not venture into deep water again without remembering my fear.

One day, in late December 1946 or early January 1947, father read on the front page of his newspaper that two men and a woman had been caught robbing one of Melbourne's largest banks. He noted with amazement that two of the three were the couple renting the room next to ours. It was clearly time to move somewhere else.

By now my mother had lost her job as a seamstress. Her work was too slow for the factory, and too perfect, she was told, for proper payment. They didn't want a tailor. The agent could no longer use her.

The plight of our family touched the heart of an acquaintance who had been interned in Tatura in the single men's camp. He had also worked as an engineer in Iran. There was some solidarity among the internees from Iran. We used to meet them in city cafes or walk with them in the parks. Wilhelm Zapf, a fellow Austrian from Graz, had been associated with my father's work but, as an ex-officer of the Austrian Imperial Army in World War I and with university credentials as an engineer, he had held a higher position than my father. He became something of a patron to my parents. He offered them a lifeline.

Mr Zapf now lived in Williamstown, a Melbourne port suburb, where he rented a room in what had been a small private hospital. The building's owner, Sister Flower, had been the hospital's Matron. With a few simple alterations she had turned it into a boarding-house at this time when rented accommodation was scarce. A single woman all her life, she had little patience with children and refused to rent rooms to families.

She became very fond of the elegantly mannered Mr Zapf, and gave in to his strong recommendation that the Girschik family were reliable and of good character. Sister Flower thus took in my parents as tenants on condition that Peter and I were boarded out and only came 'home' for school holidays. Then we had to keep very quiet or make ourselves scarce.

Oddly enough, she fell in love with my brother Herbert at first sight. He was so cute and angelic as a two-year-old. But we were to negotiate our short time in Williamstown with considerable discretion. Appalled by her attitudes, Mr Zapf and my parents were to refer to her as the Dragon Flower Lady, or just Dragon Flower—always behind her back of course.

The school year was approaching fast. Father had already set in train a solution to the problem of our education. He did not wish us to attend state schools, he said, despite mother's argument that a public education was what we needed. She was much more of a socialist than he would ever be, although she retained a touch of snobbery.

Father argued that, as ex-enemy aliens, we would be more kindly treated by members of a religious order. Besides, state schools did not take boarders. My mother argued back, and they compromised over the Quakers. But the Quakers could not help us in any way, either with accommodation or with schooling.

Every educational institution seemed to have been impoverished by the War. My father tried to secure us separate boarding facilities in institutions run by people he could trust. He felt awkward about begging for charity, but saw this as the only way out.

His view had been that he did not deserve support from the Catholic Church he had abandoned years before. But now he felt he had no choice. Approaching the Catholic Education Office, he asked for a list of the addresses of all Catholic boarding schools. Someone might take pity on and take in his children for next to nothing, with the promise of remuneration when he could pay them back He wrote to secondary schools on my behalf, and to those who took in boarders at primary level for Peter.

He received many letters back from schools which told him they were too poor to dispense charity. Four schools did offer a place, three of them run by Mercy nuns. Peter was booked into Padua, or Star of the Sea Convent, with the Sisters of Mercy, on Mornington Peninsula. I was intended for the Mercy nuns in East Ballarat.

We were going through the list of items boarders were obliged to bring to this school, including a sports uniform, tennis racquet and hockey stick, when a letter arrived from the Mother Superior of the Convent of Mercy in Fitzroy in inner Melbourne. The school was the Academy of Mary Immaculate.

The requirements for a boarder there were far less demanding. Even the tennis racquet was optional. Having prepared myself for a school in the country with large playing fields, I was persuaded by father that it would be cheaper to send me to Fitzroy. He would also save the monthly train fare each way.

My mother brought some enthusiasm to purchasing two summer school uniforms with a loan she had procured. She would also save money by making the winter uniforms herself, using the summer ones as a model. Every item was marked with my name which she embroidered on tapes in case the indelible ink washed out. An inventory of my belongings was glued into the lid of my case.

The Academy's uniform was a dark blue pleated dress in light-weight material with a sewn-on tie and a detachable white collar that could be starched. 'That navy blazer is fine doctors' flannel,' my mother remarked. 'That's expensive quality cloth.' The breast pocket carried the school emblem. A shiny metal brooch with the same emblem had to be pinned onto the tie. A hat band with embroidery of the emblem ran around the cream panama summer hat and its dark velour winter twin.

This formal outfit made the school seem a very special kind of place. The emblem was a shield-like mirror flanked by fleurs-de-lis, above a scroll with the Latin motto *Speculum Sine Macula*. Father translated this for me as 'mirror without stain'. A sprig of wattle below the shield was obviously a reference to Australia. My parents were right in thinking that the shield-mirror stood for chivalry and refinement, although only my father would have known that the school motto had a specific moral and religious reference to the Virgin Mary of Catholic belief.

I wondered whether Mary Immaculate was the headmistress. 'No,' my father laughed, 'the school was named for Mary.' He did not go on to explain the theology of Mary, the virginal Mother of God whom Catholics believe was born without sin almost 2,000 years ago.

My mother was enthusiastic about my school. She herself had only had the simplest, shortest educational opportunities. She hoped for better for me. Apart from being somewhat possessive of my love, she never begrudged me anything.

There was now little time to lose. In a fit of panic, my mother suggested to my father that they drill me in the basics of the Catholic religion in which she was no expert and which my father had not practised for years. They did it together, so that my abysmal ignorance would not be too obvious to the nuns.

Had my father concealed my pagan state from them? Had he merely stated that I was a baptised Catholic, and that Iran had no churches to attend? 'For goodness sake, don't make it obvious how little you know,' advised my mother. 'They do realise you could not make your first Communion in Iran or in the camp.'

They fell over each other's sentences in their attempts to give me an intensive course on the basic teachings of the Catholic religion. 'Don't forget that God is a Trinity.' 'That means that he consists of the Father, the Son and the Holy Ghost.' 'Each with a separate personality, but actually united into one. It is said to be the great mystery of faith, that the Three are One!' 'And you must know something about the Last Supper: when Jesus, the Lord of our religion, met up with some of his Apostles for his last meal with them.' 'Before he was killed … ' '… by being nailed to a cross soon after.' 'And that he rose from the dead!' 'You better learn the names of the twelve apostles who followed Jesus around.' 'They were his helpers.' 'And don't forget that Judas was the bad one who betrayed Jesus,' said my father. ' … and that young John was the one he loved best,' my mother added.

'Now repeat to us what we have just told you.'

There was one last word of advice: 'Don't show your ignorance. Just keep quiet. Don't ask questions. Learn by listening carefully!' 'And, above all, Be Grateful.' 'Be grateful to them at all times.' 'We are in their debt.'

Peter was packed off to the convent school at Mornington at the end of a long train and bus journey. He was only eight and my heart bled for him as we said goodbye. Mother's sorrow at losing her little darling was deep and lasting. Father hid his feelings. 'It will make a man of him,' he used to say whenever Peter had to face situations that were overwhelming for a sensitive child.

The following day, I was to be dispatched to the Convent of Mercy boarding house in the grounds of the Academy of Mary Immaculate.

13. Stranded in Exile

It was for my brother and me a radical change to be removed from our parents so soon after the prison camp. It was particularly devastating for eight-year-old Peter who, I believe, was traumatised by the experience for many years after he left school. He did not complain, but it was obvious to me. It never occurred to me that I might have suffered some aspects of trauma as well. This concept had not become commonly understood.

Some years later, when I was 18, a friend was to describe me as 'like a shy doe that had suddenly reached the end of a dark forest and was worried about the open field'. Nowadays in crowds I see the occasional young girl from south-east Asia who has that all-too-sensitive shy look about her. It reminds me of what we once were.

My brother Herbert was also to absorb some trauma from his parents. As a child he never quite fitted in as an Australian. He, too, was lonely.

14

Swimming for the Eucharist

On the last Sunday of January 1947, when I was 11 and a half years old, my parents took me, my suitcase and small personal bag, off to school. We travelled on one of Melbourne's green-and-yellow trams that still rumble and clang in procession along the same routes out of the city centre.

The tram stop closest to the Academy was near the Exhibition Building, a huge Victorian complex with domes and parapets. In front of it were dry fountains in a state of neglect following years of Depression and War. The surrounding suburb had an equally faded appearance.

We stepped off the tram into a heavy shower of rain. The downpour soaked our clothes and made my white panama hat droop limply by the time we reached the convent. My father rang the bell on the high stone wall. It enclosed tall, dark stone buildings and a bell-tower.

This prison-like setting filled me with foreboding. I wanted to go back home with my parents, but I knew this was impossible. A heavily robed woman opened the wrought iron gates and ushered us into another enclosure which she had already opened up. I noticed several women in black veils with what looked like stiff white cardboard around their faces peering at us from windows inside the cloister. This was obviously a place where inhabitants were securely locked in, and the world kept out.

We were taken to 'the parlour'. This was a dark room stuffed with old-fashioned furniture. Seeing me wince, mother gently squeezed my hand for reassurance. My father patted my shoulder, as if to say: 'It will be all right. Just wait and see!'

My eyes began to wander. I looked up gloomily at the paintings in gilded frames, trying to understand this place I had come to live. I could hear the nuns hastening along the corridor, their long robes swishing, things on chains rattling as they moved. 'The holy women', as father called them, entered the room in procession. They surrounded us, jostling gently to get a glimpse of me. 'If only I could disappear!' I wished, in the knowledge that I was being bolted to the floor of this arrangement. But ever a child of my father's realism in the face of my mother's romantic influence, I remembered the manners both had taught me. I curtsied to the group of inspectors. They looked surprised, but smiled.

As the head women talked to my father in their English language and the others listened in, I examined the group more closely. I had never seen such strange costumes, except on stage. Each woman wore exactly the same peculiar style of soft black garment, with stiff white material framing the face under a black veil, and a large starched white collar below it. From the wide black leather belt around each waist hung long strands of black beads.

After the formalities had been agreed on between them in my father's basic, broken English (which I could not understand), my mother kissed me goodbye warmly and tearfully. My father patted me on the shoulder once more in his manly way, and cautioned me in German: 'Now be a good girl for the Sisters. We are in their debt, you know.'

Fear outpaced self-pity. Before this, I had only been parted from my mother for a couple of brief periods, lasting a few days. All these odd things kept happening to me. 'Here we go again,' I thought. It was a fateful voice. I saw the anxiety in my little brother Herbert's eyes. We had never been parted before.

A buxom and jolly woman, whose vitality bore little relationship to her creepy black-and-white disguise, introduced herself as Sister Beatrice. I cannot now separate my later knowledge of her Irish origins and the total vacuum from which I had to interpret my situation. I attempted to explore my new environment cautiously, by degrees, sticking out my feelers and then quickly withdrawing them again in fear, like a crab investigating if the coast is clear.

14. Swimming for the Eucharist

Taking my suitcase, Sister Beatrice beckoned me to carry the much smaller school case and my violin, which I had stuffed under my arm when she held out her hand to me. 'The quicker and brighter, the less painful the exercise,' she must have thought about taking me from my parents. For she walked quickly.

Her maternal warmth gave me some confidence. I understood nothing of her cheerful commentary as she pointed to this and that feature of a too-grey courtyard over which the bluestone buildings cast their remote shadow. I steeled myself to accept whatever was to happen, to float on a tide of unknowing. I had no choice so this was surely the best thing I could do.

The only patch of greenery was set into two large slabs of concrete. These made up the entire playing fields of the institution. They consisted of two small rose gardens connected by an arbour over a seat facing some sort of game with painted lines, which I was later to learn was a tennis court. A few small shrubs grew in pathetic isolation in front of a cave with a statue of a woman in a flowing blue dress and blue veil, obviously a holy shrine.

The building we entered loomed dark and forbidding, so huge was it compared with the tiny cramped huts of the camp.

We entered a cool foyer with a row of washbasins along one wall and hooks for clothes along the other. There were so many steel cabinets that they turned the corner and invaded a stately entrance hall full of the paraphernalia of a more opulent age. We climbed a broad staircase with thick polished wooden banisters past several landings, up and up, to the top of the building. So high was it that four floors could have sat comfortably above ground level.

We moved through a sparsely furnished living room with lots of chairs, some framed pictures and a decoration with a man in pain stuck on a cross, an emblem I was later to discover in every room. We then entered a quaint room reminiscent of the story of *Snow White and the Seven Dwarfs*. Along the walls and in the middle were ranged many small washstands with bowls and water jugs of enamel, with a little cupboard underneath, a mirror above, and one wooden stool beside them. This was part of the boarders' bathroom.

In the four terms I spent as a boarder, I rarely saw the inside of one of the two baths or two showers next door. Bathing had to be reserved for special occasions, like an approaching boarders' weekend. The school was too Spartan, too poor to afford the cost of heating such a huge amount of water. There was no lounge, no easy chairs for leisure. If we wanted to read, we had to sit in desks in a classroom.

Sister Beatrice left me with a senior supervising girl, a chubby 16-year-old. Every senior girl was in charge of younger ones. A group crowded around me as my surrogate older sister unpacked my things, an unavoidable invasion of my privacy which my mother had always observed so delicately.

She was helped by her chums who gestured in surprise at some items. The flannelette singlets my mother had made were singled out for inspection and hilarity. The girls nevertheless placed every item respectfully in the cupboards or the dormitory next door. Of this sleeping area I had only a fleeting impression as a kind of hospital row of beds on wheels, with white curtains and blue-and-white starched covers.

Despite my apprehensions, this first afternoon left no wounds. I was not treated as an 'enemy' at the mercy of bitchy English-speaking girls, but as just another girl. The sincere concern of these lovely older girls enfolded me so kindly that I was able to disguise my abject shame at the teasing of their clown, a girl named Maureen French. For she was most amused by how different I was, my manners and my muteness. She grabbed my recorder from its canvas pouch. 'What's this? A flute?' she asked, as she demonstrated. She imitated a hornpipe and pretended to play it, between comical grimaces.

I was so alert to coping that there was no room for self-pity to take hold. That emerged later in life.

It was with relief that I met the girls on common ground on the asphalt below our dormitory. The senior girls allowed me to join their game with a tennis ball before dinner. Each of these kind young women, well-developed with breasts and the restraint of maturity, took it in turns to give me 'a go'. They were suddenly like the sisters I had never had. They had accepted me into their community without exacting anything.

I leapt around, long-legged, in my bright red dress with the white polka dots and the wing-style sleeves which my mother had so lovingly made. They were pleased by my agility and delighted by my pretty dress. Here was

14. Swimming for the Eucharist

sportsmanship rather than rivalry. On that day Josie Brown, Kathleen Madden, Maureen French, Janice Callander, Cathleen Ryan, Lynette and Norma Keane and others showed how important the encouragement of others can be to a lonely child.

There were only about 20 boarders that year. It soon became evident that the nun into whose care I had been placed controlled the boarding house. They had never had a girl who was a foreigner, without English. Nuns and students must have been instructed to take special care not to upset me. Having no precedents, no models for action, all they could do was to treat me with kindness, but also just like everyone else. This suited me well, because the last thing I wanted was to be conspicuously different.

The boarders only sometimes forgot their good manners. This was most evident at Sunday dinner 'cake time', when a practice known as 'baggsing' broke the usual rules of politeness and Christian tolerance. The quickest 'I bags' got the cake she chose. Soft voices were drowned by loud yells. There was no order or fairness. With my mother's insistence during our upbringing to consider others, I only ever got the cakes that nobody else wanted—which did not bother me greatly. I was prepared to do without in order to fit in.

Another peculiarity of those early days was the routine of prayers. This remained a confounding mystery for several weeks. There was nothing in my life to compare it with. Long prayers were said beside one's bed at night and after getting up in the morning. We had prayers before, in the middle of, and at the end of school, before and after meals, and before and after homework time. Occasionally a birthday or feast or tragedy allowed for a change to the set routine.

My misguided interpretations of the English language and of religious rituals are retrospectively difficult to recreate. For some time I was bewildered, but I cannot now remember for how long and to what extent. Children adapt more quickly than adults.

In a corner of the end of the dormitory, an enclosure with two half-walls served as the supervising nun's bedroom. Some with lighter teaching loads took it in turns to be in charge of the boarding house. The half-enclosure was intended to prevent us from talking in bed, from staging the midnight feasts so popular in school stories, and, most of all, to stop us from talking through the windows with men from the 'bad' suburb in the street below.

We recited our long night prayers kneeling beside our beds, in chorus. Then we hopped under the sheets and were expected to meditate ourselves to sleep. The supervisor's strictures did not prevent the girls from whispering to each other or from secretly circulating bits of food sent in parcels from home. The nuns' forays from the cubicle used to interrupt these transgressions with the admonishment: 'Be quiet, girls!'

At quarter to seven in the morning the nun in charge would emerge from her cubicle ringing a heavy hand-bell. It made an ugly clanging sound. We crawled out of bed, flung on our dressing gowns and fell to our knees on the polished linoleum floor. Sister led the prayers. We followed or answered, depending on the convention. The girls rattled off long phrases without hesitation.

At first I listened carefully to all prayers, unable to catch any familiar words. I learned much of my English, both simple and complex, in tandem with the monastically inspired theology that was part of the very air we breathed in our Irish Catholic school. After a few days, a number of repeated sounds enabled me at least to mouth words, in imitation. Most evening prayers included a long evocation called The Litany of the Blessed Virgin. After every evocation of one of Mary's personas we replied what at the time I understood to be *pei fas* (correctly, pray for us). I never succeeded in memorising all the invocations, even after some understanding had dawned.

Here are a few of the mystifying fragments of the chant the nun in charge intoned. They can be found in prayer books of those days. 'Mystical Rose', 'Tower of David', 'Tower of Ivory', 'House of Gold', 'Gate of Heaven', 'Morning Star', 'Refuge of Sinners', 'Health of the Sick', 'Queen of Patriarchs', 'Queen of Prophets', 'Queen of Peace', 'Mirror of Justice ', 'Seat of Wisdom' and 'Ark of the Covenant'. Now I know these terms. At the time, I had no idea what was going on. After each such metaphor for Mary we chorused the ubiquitous *pei fas*.

Familiarity with the words came to me only after months of chanting. Even then, it was not only my linguistic ignorance that left me in limbo. We were all too young to understand most of the meanings of these words.

Imagine the ignorant humming, droning, mumbling 'pray for us' compressed into that phonetic reading: *pei fas ... pei fas ... pei fas ... pei fas*. I began to identify the meanings of words in association with repeated activities. I wondered why the evening ritual included a repeated

14. Swimming for the Eucharist

invocation of 'breakfast', still far away. 'Why is this religion so preoccupied with eating?' I thought. Indeed, when a few weeks later Sister Beatrice asked me to read the most common prayers, the Hail Mary and the Our Father, from our prayer book, I was astonished to see that the words printed on the page bore no resemblance to the sounds I had learned off by heart by listening carefully to the others repeating them.

Sister was as baffled as I. 'How could you get it so wrong?' she seemed to remonstrate. This makes me wonder now whether the name for the ancient nun who was initially in charge of the dormitory when I arrived was not Walpurga after all. 'Why that name?' I had thought at the time. In German legends *Walpurgis Nacht* was a witches' sabbath. The occasional rantings of Sister Walpurga (about what I later found to be people called Communists marching up Nicholson Street), gave the name Walpurga a poetic resonance, which I mistook for reality. Although the girls sometimes laughed about her out-of-date ways, they had been much better tutored than I in a religion of 'love thy neighbour'. Used to her ways, they were tolerant, while I feared her sharp chin and humped back that so quietly emerged from the cubicle and stealthily moved around the dormitory. I was horrified that her face might suddenly peer inside the curtains that enveloped my bed. Walpurga or Walburga (as I later learned) was of course protecting us from the evil that flies in the night.

The nuns knew all about the saints after whom they had been named during their novitiate, their training. This religious name separated them from their families and, presumably, worldly ways and vanities. Most of the Academy's nuns were named after early church saints. For a long time my understanding of them was meagre, driven by the need to survive from day to day. I found out soon enough that the other-worldliness of their vocation was not something we could share. We never saw a nun eating, sleeping, dressing or removing her veil. This added to their mystique and our interest in how they behaved 'behind the scenes'.

My weeks of confusion reached a climax during one of my attendances at early morning Mass. Every morning, after we had completed our wash at the hand basin, where we sponged down our naked bodies carefully concealed beneath the drapery of our dressing gowns, we put on our uniforms and the obligatory beige lisle stockings. These were fastened with suspenders. After being checked for dirty nails and lice, we made our beds in the manner of hospital nurses, tucking in each corner neatly, and were once more inspected for tidiness. Last of all we threw a white net veil over our heads, put a piece of elastic around the crown and pulled back the front veil from our faces. Grateful for my rescue by this fine community, I admired rather than coveted the veils of my peers, edged as they were with beautifully-embroidered seams and held in place with fine, decoratively ruffled elastic. They had come from a special shop. My poor ignorant mother had sewn me up a strip of mosquito net with a tough band of underpants elastic. But no one questioned my plain substitute.

For reasons I do not know, unlike my brothers who were temporarily to succumb to the Australian ethos of being just like everyone else, I was never ever ashamed of my mother. Perhaps boys faced greater pressure not to show evidence of their foreign origins, or feelings for women.

With my mosquito net and underpants elastic veil, missal in hand, I followed the other boarders as they quickly descended the stairs and entered the chapel. Every effort was made to get everyone there on time.

On festive occasions we entered the chapel two by two. The girls sat in two rows of pews in front, with the aisle down the middle. The Sisters in charge sat in separate pews, but each nun also had an appointed place in the splendidly carved polished wood choir stalls, facing each other across the back half of the chapel. The nuns assumed a variety of prayerful attitudes. We eventually learnt to distinguish a particular body even when its face was hidden in cupped hands.

The neo-Gothic bluestone chapel was taller than it was long. A big marble slab in front, with a lace cloth, supported a decorated marble structure, almost like an imitation of a church, with spires and a decorated golden door. The little door obviously concealed the greatest secret, although it took a long time for me to register why the golden cup that was filled with stiff round pieces of white paper was given the highest honour. Along the walls two white marble plaques were mounted, with inscriptions which I later came to identify. One of them honoured Mother Catherine McAuley, the Dublin founder of the Mercy nuns. The nun who established the Academy in 1857, Mother Ursula Frayne, was remembered with a tall, free-standing granite Celtic cross embossed with a sheaf of flowers.

The four school houses, into which all students were divided, paid tribute to McAuley (green), Frayne (red), the erstwhile Bishop-patron Goold (gold) and Carr (blue), after the current Archbishop of Melbourne. I was attached to green, Sister Beatrice's preferred team. Even when we were not engaged in competitive sport, the notion of what house we belonged to gave us a place in the school which cut vertically across classrooms, and created community.

Most of us younger ones fidgeted during the Mass. We studied the chapel's furniture and plaques, its arched and peaked windows of simple glass tiles tinted in soft shades of orange and green. A number of coloured statues stood on pedestals around the interior, while a set of moulded pictorial plaques in wooden frames, shaped like Gothic leaves of clover, were to become known to me later as the 14 Stations of the Cross, sites marking the journey of Jesus to his crucifixion at Calvary.

Light from the windows played on the brightly polished brass vases filled with flowers in front of the statues and on the main slab of marble. These offered themselves to my wandering attention, as did a light in the red glass bowl on the marble table. It flickered ever so slightly. I wondered what this red light signified. 'Obviously it does not mean that "help is given here", as by an ambulance,' I thought.

On my first day in the chapel I lacked any points of reference to enlighten me. I had never been in a church before. This was theatre and pagan ritual, my only comparisons. It did not help that the Jesuit priest from St Patrick's College, East Melbourne, was in his 80s and looked like Father Time. He wore a bright green cloth mantle over white lace sleeves, and engaged in a lot of mumbling, bowing and turning, bobbing up and down, sometimes kneeling, holding a disc of paper up in the air, as bells rang, then holding the golden cup up high as if he was asking the sun to give it life.

Wow, I thought, this is something secret, something from ancient Egypt, a priest of the temple come to make things right with nature, come to invoke the sun. 'What does this do? How does it work?' I strained for a rational response.

For the next few mornings I followed what was happening with some anxiety. Then during one session, I panicked. I thought I probably had not interpreted my duties correctly. I got up from my knees tentatively, then followed the other girls to the rails as if I knew what I was supposed to do. Sister Beatrice had previously tried to tell me not to go up. But had I understood her correctly? Why was everyone who went to the rails sucking the pieces of paper? Or quietly chewing them? I copied the others and put out my tongue. The priest placed a thin round object on it. I went back to my seat chewing it discreetly as I thought I was supposed to do. It was not paper after all. But what was it? It was more like a very thin tasteless biscuit.

Suddenly, two black veils descended over my head, and I was quickly ushered out of the chapel. 'Have you bitten the host?' they asked, miming it with their teeth. I was not sure what they meant, but I nodded my head. 'That's terrible, terrible' must have been the mumbled words of their obvious consternation.

In those days you were not permitted to chew 'the sacred species', that 'bread' which I later learned had miraculously turned into 'the body of Christ', 'truly His flesh and His blood', but invisibly so. You could swallow as the wafer dissolved, but you were not permitted to chew it. That was like biting the sacred body!

I learned to interpret it when the nuns worried about me. 'She has not yet made her first Holy Communion!' And: 'She cannot make her first Communion without having first made her first Confession.' But how could she confess her sins if she could not speak the language and did not know what the rules were?

The nuns did not, however, consider this a serious obstacle. A 'delegation' of two priests, including our chaplain, Father Conway, came from St Patrick's Cathedral to examine my conduct. Was chewing the host an innocent, ignorant action, a case of mistaken practice? Or had I been prompted by the Devil? I had a glimmer of understanding as I tried to work out, with shame, what the fuss was about. Unable to penetrate my confusion, the priests soon took themselves away.

I had a German-English dictionary in which I checked out new words and what I thought they meant. The Devil had been mentioned. The German word *Teufel* sounds similar. The Devil? I did not believe in the existence of a real Devil, although *shaitan* was one of the few Farsi words that had lingered on from Iran.

The need to have me prepared for my first Communion was now undertaken with vigour. The date was set for May Day, among Catholics everywhere the glorious feast of Our Lady. Sister Beatrice took note of my frown: 'Ask your guardian angel to help you,' she directed and gave me a 'holy picture', a card showing a stately angel with the wings of a large bird hovering over a kneeling girl. But how do I get to know 'him', I wondered. Or was it 'her'?

She took me through my preparation again. I tried to memorise a set of words. From that first formal confession, not having enough faith was something I confessed for years. The words were put into my mouth and subsequently became a convenient formula for my inability to understand 'the Truth' adequately. But on that first day I also tried to find words in the creepy secrecy of the confessional for the invisible man behind the grid. I mentioned my occasional quarrels with my younger brothers and not obeying my parents enough.

How did my poor English put that into words? I can no longer tell. Later, for some years, my wider social alienation insulated me from those rivalries that spawn bad feelings, from participating in peer group gossip, from pranks and forbidden explorations, the variations on the moral conduct prescribed to us on the basis of the Ten Commandments derived from the ancient tablets of Moses. For me to become 'pure of soul' I conceived as becoming spiritually like one of my mother's blindingly white starched sheets from which all stains had been removed.

In our Catechism, the tenets of our religion were set out in question-and-answer style, to be committed to memory. For example: Q: Who made the world? A: God made the world Q: Who made God? A: God always was. Rules for thought and behaviour fell into degrees of seriousness. Disobeying them meant you had committed 'sins', either 'venial' or 'mortal'. Appropriate 'penance' was directed by the 'confessor' and consisted mostly of certain prayers and the avoidance of temptation, for which the technical word was 'the occasion of sin'.

If we deliberately failed to attend Mass when we were obliged to go, we committed a mortal sin. If we stole small change from our mother's purse or told a minor lie, the sin was venial. We could only be forgiven if we truly regretted what we had done and sincerely intended not to repeat it.

Like other children, I got the general gist of a complex theology of good and evil. As Catholics we became familiar with strange words and phrases like 'indulgences', 'coveting the goods of others', 'the cleansing fires of Purgatory', 'to remain in Limbo', 'transubstantiation', 'atonement', 'to make a novena', 'ciborium', 'to receive the Eucharist', 'chasuble' and 'to attend Benediction'—to name only a few at random of the bewildering array I was offered. A small dictionary could be filled with words spoken to us beyond secular daily speech.

For May Day my parents had to provide a fine white dress, which they could ill afford. In view of our circumstances, the need for white shoes and white stockings was waived. I hoped fervently that some of my fellow boarders would also be first communicants, but alas, I was the only one, everyone else having made theirs in parishes at home when they were younger. I longed to be inconspicuous.

The nuns provided a wreath of white rosebuds for my veil, and an escort of younger girls threw pink rose petals out of baskets in my path while the whole community sang hymns. These included the First Holy Communion hymn, which had a waltz-time tune and referred to Baby Jesus, and hymns to Our Lady which I did not understand.

The whole community of nuns and boarders sang its declaration of faith and hope as I returned from the altar. Only years later did I discover how uninteresting some of that music was, and how banal the words attempting to deal with a great theological mystery:

> Oh Mother I could weep for mirth,
> Joy fills my heart so fast,
> My soul today is heaven on earth
> Oh, could that transport last!
> I think of thee and what thou art
> Thy majesty, thy state and grace
> And I keep singing in my heart
> Immaculate! Immaculate!

It is odd that, in view of the superb tradition of liturgical music in the Catholic Church, such doggerel appeared in our hymnals. At the time, when little was revealed to me and the word 'transport' meant going by tram, bus or train, the community of nuns was singing its hopes for my return to the faith of my Austrian family. They hoped that, in the mystery of God's will for each of us, the seed of my faith would now be nourished.

Many of the strange words and cliches endured by us without meaningful explanations hindered a deeper understanding of 'the faith'. As I became familiar with a number of its part-mysteries, I felt that I had to hang onto a steering wheel of information with grim determination on a rollercoaster not of my choice. Clever older people knew better and had

14. Swimming for the Eucharist

tested 'the faith' over centuries. We children were often told that faith does not require deep knowledge: it brings understanding, and 'the truth shall set you free'. This theme kept on being repeated, because Catholicism was too complex to learn easily.

Slowly some of these theological mysteries seeped into my mind and heart. I can now see that the more I understood, the more my heart was opened; the more I loved this invisible God, the more I was prepared to accept unexplained mysteries. I was becoming a true convert. I heard certain statements repeated over and over again: 'Faith defies understanding' or 'The mystery of an Infinite God' who 'always was' cannot be grasped by 'mere mortal intelligence'. We learned the precepts of our religion off by heart, like parrots.

I had not chosen to be Austrian or German. Nationality had claimed me as a member at birth. Religion was to become a further strong feature of my identity. Religion had chosen me. My intelligence was focused on responding. Religion became my lifeline in an alien world. It might also have been my escape from banality. My parents certainly thought so.

Faith began to surround my heart like perceptible radiance. It was expressed through my gratitude before my mind could describe it in terms reasonable to others. It is difficult to put a date on when that happened. Nor can I say whether I ever entirely got over the problem that to be 'chosen' did not explain why others were not.

Were the words and actions of my first Holy Communion to open Heaven to my soul? Whether yes or no, nothing observable happened on 1 May 1947 to mark the significance of the day, except perhaps a near-disaster later in the afternoon.

Instead of porridge for our breakfasts we had each been given a hard-boiled egg with our bread, a privilege usually reserved for Sundays or Holy Days of Obligation, on which all Catholics are obliged to attend Mass.

Later that day after school, as on every other Thursday in summer and autumn, we were taken to the City Baths for swimming lessons. Two nuns escorted us as we made our way, two by two, through the Exhibition Gardens, which were normally out of bounds. It was delightful to walk under the generous canopies of old elms and beeches. Our black leather shoes clicked along the paths in reassuring rhythm. The lawns were strewn with dry autumn leaves which our lady-like shoes were not permitted to kick about.

The female section of the baths was private. I can still see the tiled walls, smell the strong chlorine and hear the green water splashing as people dived from the low board. The splashing was accoustically magnified because the sound bounced off the tiled walls. I can also still see the black lines of tiles against the dominant white floor, under the water.

On that day, many of us were to try for our junior swimming certificate. Others, more advanced, would be examined for their bronze medallion, which showed they were proficient in life-saving techniques.

The junior certificate obliged us to swim the Australian crawl for three lengths of the baths. My swimming was poor, because I had grown up inland and seldom been near water. I could not get the breathing right. Choking for air as I struggled into the third length, I could not continue. I really feared I would drown.

I pulled myself to the hand-rail and climbed out, defeated. Everybody else had succeeded.

Miss Carey, our plump teacher, took me by the arm. 'Aren't you ashamed? This is the very day on which you made your first Communion. Ask God to give you strength,' she scolded. She threw me back into the pool.

I struggled like a drowning rat. The other girls having finished their swims now gathered along the side, yelled encouragement, screaming whenever I faltered. 'Oh God, what do people do when a ship goes down?' flashed across my mind. 'I'd rather drown! What agony. I can't last. I'll have to give up.'

I don't know how I mustered the will to persevere. I did, somehow, make that heroic effort, like a warrior, beyond imagining, although I could not attribute to God any intervention in so trite an exercise. I did not pray for help. This was a sign that belief was not as yet a habit of my mind.

The others felt differently. My mentors persuaded me that God had definitely given my courage the necessary edge. It was to be some months before I found I could fall into a more prayerful attitude, open to such convictions.

14. Swimming for the Eucharist

By forcing me immediately back into the water, our tyrannical coach had actually made me swim twice the statutory distance. God's help or not, I never wanted to swim that again. But I loved being in water, floating on my back or swimming backstroke, looking up. I was made to participate in relays on sports days, and I eventually became a reasonably fast backstroke swimmer. This was a way of avoiding having to 'breathe' in water. I could both be chosen for the team and protect my stubborn nature.

15

Ad Maiorem Dei Gloriam

Since the day after my arrival, I had been attending classes in Form 1. I was placed according to my age. No one asked my father what lessons I had done to date, or found out that I had received only a little over four years of schooling in the camp. Strictly speaking, I should have been put back two years. I badly needed to learn decimals and fractions in Maths, and a quite sophisticated list of English words.

There was no remedial education at that time. The teaching resources were far too stretched: too few teachers, too few books. Having to learn by trial and error, rather than through a pedagogically structured program meant that I picked up some unfortunate ways of learning, which were later difficult to undo. Later on, my cognitive patterns were to confuse even trained experts. In the later years of my schooling, my father tried to redirect the obstinate, fundamentalist direction I had chosen for my future. I felt I had chosen my path from everything rich and rare in religion that my convent education offered. His life I judged as being banal.

With the day students, we sat in twin wooden desks in rows. We boarders did not, however, mix socially with the day students. Our teacher, Sister Josepha, was a large woman with a square frame and a rugged face containing large, uneven teeth. These were used to great effect in correctly modelling French pronunciation. Although of Irish birth, Sister Josepha had been educated for a while in Belgium, so we assumed her parents were 'well off'. She had some understanding of what it is to be a foreigner, but she struggled to control her large class of two forms in one room. So after our honeymoon was over, I was as much the victim of her ruler across my knuckles or my head as anyone else.

I was not so much disturbed by her periodic anger as embarrassed on her behalf. In summer it was unpleasant to be in a sweaty class stinking of rotting fish, which it took until the following year to discover had to do with menstruation. Given her age, I now assume that Sister Josepha's intemperance was due to menopause. It must have been insufferable for her if she shared the acute sense of smell I had inherited from my mother.

These were the days before commercially available sanitary pads; and tampons were unheard of. We young women were a restless bunch. The discomfort of not knowing whether one was 'fish or fowl' was summed up by this saying which my mother often repeated. It so aptly describes the uncertainties and agonies of the threshold of adolescence.

I was safeguarded in my ignorance of the language of the classroom by the routines that were followed. The first thing I learned to do in class was to rule up the pages of my exercise books with margins, and to place above them in large print the abbreviation AM+DG (*Ad Maiorem Dei Gloriam*: All for the Greater Glory of God). Everything we did, thought and planned was subject to this command. Secular life was offered up to an invisible divinity and had a place in the divine scheme of things.

Classroom activity was predictable, and there was much rote learning. Both students and teachers read aloud in class and discussed set texts. The English language came to me in little pieces. Rhyming couplets from Lord Tennyson's *The Lady of Shalott* were among the earliest passages I remember, but most of the prose of *The Talisman*, by Sir Walter Scott, D.K. Broster's *The Flight of the Heron*, Mrs Aeneas Gunn's *The Little Black Princess*, and Frank Dalby Davison's *Manshy*, went completely over my head.

These texts were set by the Victorian Education Department curriculum, which also provided each of us with a monthly *School Paper* containing short illustrated stories, homilies, poems and puzzles.

A few times Sister Josepha's anger with the aid of a ruler was instrumental in releasing those awful nosebleeds to which I was susceptible. Mother took my nosebleeds for granted. Both she and her mother had suffered from them and outgrown the condition at about twenty. It did not occur to me that the vigorous ear cuffs German children were given at that time by their fathers may have contributed to my nasal weakness.

15. Ad Maiorem Dei Gloriam

My nosebleeds were especially bad. The medical cause was given as a weak capillary in one nostril. The problem could be cured, we were told, by cauterisation. My parents preferred to let me 'outgrow the condition'. My mother's patience with washing out blood-stained clothes was more than human. She also produced the plausible argument, perhaps based on traditional folk medicine, that nature's blood-letting held at bay much worse disorders, such as violent headaches.

When one of my dreadful nosebleeds suddenly spurted forth in class, I was rushed down to the school foyer and laid on the cold concrete floor. A wet cloth was placed on my forehead and the school gate's enormous iron key placed at the back of my neck to cool the blood. The horrid red flood ran down my throat uncomfortably, disgustingly, for a long time until, it seemed, I had run out of blood.

My nose, disturbed by the slightest pressure to my head, was a cautionary prompt to Sister Josepha to aim for more cushioned parts of our anatomy. Hands, however, are also delicate instruments. Backsides were taboo. That left her with a dilemma. Teachers reigned unsupervised in their own classrooms in many schools of the time. Her lack of self-control was an exception to what usually went on in my six years at the Academy. Poor woman!

Sister Josepha and I nevertheless struck up a friendship in the room next to the chapel where she and Sister Bernadine were in charge of polishing the ecclesiastical brassware. I was a willing recruit. To amuse myself in chapel during boring Mass, I beheld with some pride the light playing on highly polished tall-stemmed brass vases filled with flowers grown in the nuns' own garden, which was out of bounds to us.

By the time winter arrived, the rhythm of each day had become predictable. I had chilblains on my hands due to the inadequate heating. Daily Mass was habitual if not obligatory: we attended because it was seen to be reinforcing our faith. Although we were supposed to have a choice in the matter, who dared to be so conspicuous as not to attend? It was easy for me to obey. That was the way I had been brought up.

Since everybody went to Mass, there was no discrimination between the pious and the less pious children in the convent. We were all treated fairly and kindly. Only exasperation with indolence, cheeky words or immoral behaviour brought on retribution. In that sense, obligation to conform also broke down discrimination. There was no carrot for being good; there were no rewards for conforming. It was an unquestioning necessity, like the air we breathed. Thus, despite the hierarchical order of the Church and the champions of the faith, an egalitarian ethic was deeply ingrained in us. So too was the injunction not to judge others harshly. We had to learn to separate the people (whom God loved) from their actions (which might be sinful or reprehensible), to separate 'the dancer from the dance'.

As a young teenager, my alienation led me to become very serious. I began to reflect on the Christian ethic of fairness and consideration for others, as the humane ingredient in what was usually stereotyped by people like my father as Catholicism's arrogant and rule-bound intolerance. I regarded the humane aspects of my new religion as its most valuable gift, especially when I was able to contrast them with the grim ethos of life in the camp. Concern for others was a better recipe for human happiness than the cultivation of excellence in the arts and sport, or other competitive endeavours which brought honours but which isolated individuals even as they were praised.

Success was a trap, with its seductions, its vanities and its blunting of sensibility towards others less well placed. Although at junior high school I longed for the aesthetic appreciation, the stimulation of my intelligence and the challenge of the sporting programs pursued in the camp, I acknowledged that not everyone could enjoy these. To be cherished, on the other hand, was everyone's right and within everyone's reach, given a good community like the one that had taken me in. It provided a better recipe for community living. Of course, we were also obliged, as the New Testament suggested, to develop all our talents.

Boarding house and school programs were interleaved. Every morning after Mass we had a filling breakfast of porridge and white bread with jam. We took it in turns to serve at table, to help clear the dishes and to wash up and prepare the tables for the next meal. Then back up the stairs we went to complete our cleaning tasks in the washroom and dormitory. The boarding house was closed during school hours after we came down to the morning assembly in the playground. Thus, like the day students, we were not truly 'at home' during school hours. I'm sure most of us deeply missed our mothers, fathers and siblings.

Our midday meal consisted of hot food in a communal refectory. The smell of boiled cabbage and mashed potatoes, and sometimes of boiled corned beef, wafted through the building. My German nostrils were not as affronted by these smells as were those of my Australian peers. They longed for grilled chops or a golden roast of chicken with baked vegetables for lunch at the family table after Sunday Mass.

After all the day students had gone home, we changed out of our uniforms for relaxation. But the place was bleak, uncomfortable, unheated. Warmth and joy came from the cultivation of friendship and faith; from scholastic successes; from queuing up to hit a ball with a friend around the one concrete tennis court; or by assembling players for an impromptu game of basketball on the two courts that made up the remainder of the playing space in front of the large covered shed, our rain shelter.

I was a competent goalkeeper. I had been putting on a brave face, to all outward appearances coping quite well with the challenge of not having a working language. Inwardly, I was becoming increasingly disenchanted at not achieving the all-round excellence on which, in the competitive camp school, my parents and teachers had commented. The longer I failed to attain even average skill in English, the more my general confidence dwindled. I longed for the athletics that required no language.

But athletics were not permitted at a school where female modesty was a higher priority than individual physical skill. I became increasingly inwardly lonely while continuing to smile and exhibit good manners. Quite early in my schooling at the convent my spiritual retreat from the world began.

I was to discover later that in state schools subject areas were regarded as specialisations and had teachers who taught them in different classes. There every student experienced a number of teachers. In our school we had one teacher almost exclusively for every class, except for the fringe subjects without academic status. Our teachers were expected to be skilled in all areas, flexible and exceptionally hard-working. Their lives of service were heroic. Their lessons were of less value than the commitment they demonstrated to any kind of task.

Our evening meal usually consisted of weak soup and a cold collation, with perhaps a dessert of preserved fruit and custard, or a hot pudding with jam sauce. After the camp food I thought the boarding school meals a novelty and quite delightful, despite the constant grumblings of my companions. They told me gloomily that the soup stock was made by swishing a piece of meat through it. The flavour of strong pepper and Worcestershire sauce in clear broth was its distinguishing feature.

I even wrote to my parents about the delicious meals. Sister Beatrice, who censored our mail, was amused when I tried to translate my letter home for her, conveying my enthusiasm for tinned peaches and simple boiled custard. At first I wrote to my parents on toilet paper because I did not know the word for paper. Even if I had, I would have been too shy to ask for some.

The nuns supplied us with envelopes and stamps for the letters they obliged us to send home. When they discovered my problem, we had a hearty laugh about my letters on paper from the loo. They were discreet enough not to tell any of the girls, because the joke would have haunted me forever. Nuns and girls were never close in any case. Religious regulations forbade it.

The homework hour was conducted upstairs before the evening meal at six.

It lingers in my memory as the *Heimweh* (home-sickness) hour. I associated it with the declining sun, the last light on the slate roof across the yard, and the sad fact that yet another day was disappearing forever. Weeks were slipping by fast, and I still did not know how to perform all my assigned duties. For some days I had sat during homework with my hands crossed, mute, expectant. This was the time of day when the boarders would practise their pianos and violins below. I felt a deep sense of longing for home, wherever that might be. I wanted to be with my parents, but even more than that, there was a longing for consolation of a greater kind.

The scales from the courtyard below, or a difficult passage in a Clementi, Czerni or Busoni exercise, repeated over and over by frustrated learners, were heard by this lonely listener as the chatter of musical voices. They were like so many conversations, vying for a place. This practice irritated others. To me, such endeavours were a solace and a reminder of the ways in which music transcends the languages that divide us from one another.

The negative aspect of this reflection is the girl with her violin case in her hand, waiting for a teacher to appear. But that teacher never came. My parents could not afford lessons for music or tennis. It was a fact, not a grievance.

Our homework was supervised by a tall, lean and dignified nun with a kindly disposition, Sister Lucy. She was like the carved Gothic madonnas I had seen on German Fine Arts calendars. She was much liked by the girls, probably because she did not smother us with either kindness or threats. She treated each of us with respect. A liberating wind from heaven blew between us and her. I longed to return to infancy, to curl up in the arms of this mother and be comforted. But she took little notice of me because I was not in her class and she did not know how to communicate with a mute. I was to become her student two years later, but we were never close. She claimed no favourites. That was a part of her mystique. She was to become an inspiration in my life. For decades, she was the most-loved nun in the school among past students.

Why was Sister Lucy so popular? She had 'presence' without arrogance. She was our comfortable link between religion and 'the world', since she did not despise the world. No task was beneath her. She assisted us in whatever menial work we had been assigned. She was modest by nature without any hint of obsequiousness, and did not need to put pride aside.

I loved her cool friendship, lacking sentimentality. You could say she had innate dignity.

I acquired quite early in my time at the school a constant playmate, Frances Hendriksen. Her paternal forebears were Scandinavian seafarers. More than anyone, Frances guided me into the English language, although I was not interested in the games of 'fathers and mothers' she frequently proposed for our playtime. They were innocent games, re-enacting the kindness of the home life she missed so much. I did not share her model of a free rural family life and had no interest in emulating the world of adults. As a twelve-year-old, her affection for dolls left me cold. But I welcomed the companionship she so kindly offered.

Frances' greatest attraction for me was her exceptional talent for the piano. She was so skilled that she was expected to become another Eileen Joyce, the convent-trained girl from Kalgoorlie who went on to play on the international stage. Frances had learned the piano from the age of five. She was called upon to give recitals at school feasts and our association gave me entry to the music practice rooms. This brought me to the attention of the tall and blonde Janice Callander, who offered to give me some tips on the violin, and invited me to play simple duets. I accompanied Frances in my short repertoire, which included Toselli's *Serenata*, Mendelssohn's *Spring Song*, and a Gavotte and Entr'acte from Thomas' *Mignon*. I had not been taught well and had not even learned the *vibrato* that makes a violin sing. Frances and Janice tolerated me with encouraging patience.

I was happiest at this time, and also when singing in the evening Glee Club. Sister Beatrice conducted this because of her love of music and to keep us out of mischief.

The school library was a tiny cupboard. The sorts of literature the more precocious girls wanted to read were books on the Catholic Index of Prohibited Books. Curiosity prevailed, and I joined them. I do not know how they obtained such forbidden fruit as *The White Lady* and Alexander Dumas' *The Count of Monte Cristo*. The latter I did not read until years later, and then I wondered what all the fuss had been about.

Frances was a pious girl. Some of this rubbed off on me. We visited the chapel as a pair. Obviously missing her father, she made long appeals to the plaster statue of Saint Joseph in his brown cloak. He held a white lily in one hand and his adopted son, the child Jesus, in the other. She also appealed to its companion, the plaster statue of Mary Immaculate, with her painted blue-and-white mantle and veil.

It seemed odd to me that anyone should address a piece of stone and expect to get some sort of answer, either real or symbolic —even if, as she did, you placed a flower in its hand. 'Does the magic happen only if one says the correct words, or does one have to believe sincerely for prayers to be answered?' I remember puzzling as my heart remained unmoved by the statues in the chapel.

I accepted an invitation to accompany Frances to her family's farm near Apollo Bay at the foot of the Otway Ranges, during the second semester break. I was not sure how I would cope with yet another set of strangers. I learned to smile and nod my head in feigned understanding. We communicated poorly, but there was some understanding between us. We caught the tram near the school to the great railway station in town, then took a train to Geelong before changing to the Great Ocean Road bus.

Life was so secure then that two twelve-year-old girls could travel this long distance alone without concern. The winding Great Southern Road left me thoroughly carsick. But Frances' family was charming. Her father was a dairy farmer and fisherman of Scandinavian descent; her mother had family associations in the art world; her older sister Norma, a fine violinist, was also home from her convent school—and there was a younger brother.

15. *Ad Maiorem Dei Gloriam*

We divided our time in the township between the seaside and the farm. Soon after our arrival, we were obliged to attend the parish ball.

We walked as a light-hearted group along a dirt road to the local hall. The night was moonless, but the stars up in infinite space were crystalline sparklers on layers of black velvet. This was seeing the world as only country folk could. The track went past bush, dark and menacing to me. The Hendriksens walked with assurance, carrying cakes and drinks, while I stumbled along, trying to find my feet in the dark. Even the camp in the country had always been lit up by searchlights.

The 'hop' was fun. The dancing included the usual set pieces: the Parma Waltz, the Pride of Erin, the Tangoette, the Modern Waltz, the Barn Dance and the Foxtrot. There was appropriate music from a local band. I was always defeated by improvisational possibilities, but I tried my best.

Frances and I were asked to give a demonstration of a Minuet to a tune by Mozart. We danced delicately, and I always took the boy's part, because by then I belonged to the taller half of my age group. We danced in the way we had been taught to perform at our school ball, girls dancing with girls.

My friend and I spent most of our time at her family's farm on a hill which overlooked the crescent bay with its breakwater and little fleet of fishing vessels which moved out into the heavy seas. Frances' family had created a garden of primulas and violas each side of a creek flowing down rocks to a gully full of tree ferns. We spent long periods there and, in the evenings, coaxed the family cows back to the milking shed along steep zig-zagging tracks.

Mostly we sat on a low tree and pretended we were Heidi in the Swiss Alps. Frances really wanted me to play the grandfather but I could not wrap my mind around the part. She then realised it was unfair that I should always be the man to her child. The German-Swiss book *Heidi* crossed the boundaries of language and gave us common ground. Frances was still much more a child than I, and found satisfaction in such simple games of make-believe. I felt closer in experience to her elder sister Norma who, however, soon tired of my undeveloped technique on the violin.

One day I was left alone in the farm kitchen. My mother had not equipped me with clothing appropriate for the cold Victorian coastal spring, since we had been living inland the previous year. I was still wearing my bright red dress with the white polka dots and the small winged sleeves. Frances and her family had withdrawn. Were they all sleeping? Had Frances got sick of having me around? I was uncomfortable at the thought that they had begun to find me boring. Was that why I was stranded on my own?

The smell of lunch still lingered in the kitchen, a whiff of the long fillets of barracouta fish cooked in batter. There were no books to look at or drawing materials for me to use. The door of the slow combustion stove was open, a layer of glowing coals exposed. I warmed the front of my body, then turned around to warm my cold back. Had I begun to dream contentedly? I was such an absent-minded girl, never really concentrating on dull domestic tasks.

Suddenly I had the eerie sensation of the brightness of flame behind me. Was the whole oven on my back? Was I on fire? In terror I ran into the middle of the room. My movement fanned the flames. I began to scream, beating at the fire with my hands. No one came to my assistance. I kept on calling out. No response. What would my mother think if she found I had suddenly died? In a frenzy, I managed to beat out the flames.

Mrs Hendriksen had by then entered the kitchen to see what the commotion was about. She was appalled by the black shreds that were now the back of my dress. 'I heard you calling out, and thought it must be a mouse that had frightened you. Nothing to worry about! But what happened?' seemed to be what she said. I clearly understood her mistaken notion of the mouse and that she was most concerned at what my parents might think of the family's carelessness. She took pains to explain everything clearly to me. Then she told me, by demonstrating with actions, that I should have rolled myself in the carpet on the floor to put out the fire. It was a lesson I have never forgotten.

Fortunately, I was not hurt. Only my hands were slightly singed. My mother's reaction when she found out was typical of her: 'What is a mere dress, after all? Thank God you are safe!' But I fretted for my favourite dress.

Back at school, my association with the Hendriksen family brought a treat. One day a fine car came to collect my friend and me. The arrangements had been made and I was waiting with Frances in one of my better dresses in the visitors' parlour. The nuns watched us proudly as a chauffeur drove us away. At the Princess Theatre, just down the road, special seats had been reserved for us by Madame Rambert, a friend of Frances' mother. Her London-based ballet company was touring Australia. It was my first visit to a public theatre.

I cannot now remember the whole program, but what stood out was a delightful sequence of sketches: a Rossini-based suite with a Tyrolean setting and improvisations of milkmaids on their stools, beside imaginary cows. Then there was a sophisticated piece about metamorphosis, *Lady into Fox*, very dark. Most notable as a musical discovery was the enactment of Hector Berlioz's *Symphonie fantasque*, with vignettes illustrating the poet's dream, the ballroom, the pastorale, the frightening walk to the gallows, and the witches' sabbath.

The Ballet Rambert experience gave me a momentary insight into what it must be like to be privileged. Frances and I were the subject of much comment when we returned to school, and she reported proudly that a whole box of chocolates had been delivered to our seats in the balcony, as if we were indeed little ladies. 'You don't say!' 'Really?' 'What were they like?' 'You lucky ducks!' There was no envy in the other girls' curiosity.

As for my own family, at first my parents came on Sundays to take me out for the day. Then, after I was able to read the instructions, I caught public transport to Williamstown, where my chubby two-year-old brother Herbert waited at the gate. I was his second mother, the distance of nine years being significant early in life. On some boarders' weekends we made the long trek to Mornington to Peter's boarding school. Peter was far worse off than I, being younger and so far away. He always seemed to get a worse hand than me from whoever dealt life's fortunes, but he put up with his disadvantages more cheerfully. He languished in a place so far away, and then had to watch us depart into the distance as a family.

Peter and I spent the long summer vacations with our parents in Williamstown, mostly out on our own, so as not to disturb the Dragon Flower landlady with our games and squabbles. We often took little Hobby (his name for himself) with us. We attended the noisy local matinee picture shows, where manners lost out to high spirits as children rolled Jaffas down the aisles.

'It would never have been allowed by German parents!' I could hear my mother's voice declare. We explored the old harbour works, the beaches and the rather desolate Shelly Beach of the peninsula, our parents accompanying us with sacks to gather black-bearded mussels from tidal rock-pools.

This sometimes smelly foreshore was beside a rifle range and a race course, although no one ever seemed to use them. It was a quiet place, with few others on the beach. The land seemed to jut out into a bay of nowhere. That was Port Phillip Bay. Once in a while a stately ship made its way across the horizon to one of Melbourne's wharves.

Bathers flocked to Williamstown Beach, further south along a curve of the bay. In summer that strip of beach became a tourist resort for the season. The suburb was also a depot for cargo ships, and sea captains and pilots lived there. The dominant population was lower middle class, and few people owned cars. The *basso profundo* of ships' horns was to them as typical of this place as the rattling and whistling and shunting of trains. This peninsula suburb had a weathered, old-world look after the War, and gave the impression of being the end of the line in more ways than one, a kind of fast-emptying cul-de-sac before people moved to more lively districts.

Occasionally on Sundays a band gathered to perform in the rotunda of a park not far from the cemetery. Once Mr Zubek, who had been interned with us from Iran, appeared on the beach with his costly violin, took off all his clothes, and performed to the astonished bathers a brilliant passage, engrossed in his virtuosity. Police were called to escort him away. He once rented the Melbourne Town Hall to give a concert. Only a few people came. He wanted to give me violin lessons but my parents wisely found an excuse.

One of our less welcome activities was to lug sacks of empty wine bottles in a wheelbarrow to the bottle-o near the Catholic church. Mr Zapf, to whom my parents were indebted for a place to live, had a steady thirst. We were permitted to keep the bottle money: the carrot at the end of the stick. Peter and I never had pocket money, except for hand-outs to cover the cost of attending a film, with an accompanying ice-cream or sweets. There was also a small amount that our boarding schools kept in a kitty for obligatory activities. There was never even a small sum to teach us to be responsible for money. And while our father was home, mother was dependent on his weekly hand-outs.

We were becoming more and more embarrassed that our parents did not attend Church like the parents of our friends at school. In my class it was: 'Hands up whose parents do not attend Mass!'—and my hand always went up. I wished I could spare my parents the dishonour. They were too good, I thought, to suffer disdain in the minds of others for refusing to conform. Our mother made one valiant effort, but after the red-faced parish priest at Williamstown thundered from the pulpit against mixed marriages she seldom set foot again in Sunday Mass.

My mother reacted with equal disgust to the apparent lack of true religious fervour of money-grabbing priests and the restlessness of undisciplined Australian children. For her, this made attendance at Mass an ordeal. We were becoming acculturated much faster than she. We had to pay for our parents' non-conformism by being above reproach ourselves. But Peter and I were spared lectures. In my case, the nuns were proud of our developing strength of religious purpose.

On every boarders' weekend when our father could afford it, he took us for excursions into the hills beyond Melbourne for a brisk 10-kilometre walk, or to the beach at Carrum beyond Mordialloc, where the Port Phillip Bay water became clear. During summer mother treated our sunburn with homemade yoghurt which she grew from a bacillus she had acquired from the Victorian Department of Agriculture. The department was friendly to interested people and also provided literature on how to preserve fruit and vegetables. Since yoghurt was not generally available in Melbourne shops for another decade, I admired my mother's initiative in this new and frightening adult world.

Like other foreigners, my parents grew capsicums and zucchinis, and baked their own wholegrain bread long before these were available in Melbourne. Fortunately, our peers never saw us with these exotic foods. I could well imagine their pursed lips: 'Ugh. Ugh. What's that awful stuff you're eating?' Even much later, in 1954, a visitor to our house asked about a finely shredded capsicum salad: 'What is this grass we are eating?'

Life was safe in Melbourne but it was a rule-bound, conforming society. Foreign ways were exotic and only interesting to those with a sense of adventure. They were threatening to those who preferred the personal security of a predictably homogeneous existence. For years I became an 'Australian' conformist in all but religious observances. I hid my ability to speak German and my German customs. But I fought for my right to be over-religious (as they saw it) against my parents.

Although near town, my school was on the edge of a suburb that had become a slum. It was a refuge for the poor, the homeless and criminals, we heard the adults explain to each other. There was something exotic about that for me, something mysterious and not to be trifled with.

To return to boarding school after the Christmas holidays became a pleasure. There was always an affectionate reunion. Friendships do not just happen. They are constructed by daily exchanges and, like good wine, they are enriched by the texture of soil and season. Our friendships were woven out of jokes and mishaps, pranks, longings for ourselves and for each other. My primitive new language was beginning to be sufficient to participate in the incessant talk that went on among the girls, although I always remained the least talkative. In time I was perceived as a listener who had less to contribute.

It was the same with Peter. We became better in written than spoken English. Peter and I were not wimps deep down, and my acquiescent behaviour sometimes annoyed me, because people could be with me in real empathy but not show any interest in hearing me talk.

Deserts of lonely conformity stretched outside school, while at home the growing gulf between my foreign parents and me began to cause some anguish. Over time, religion became the comfort which filled that vacuum for me. The problem with religion, however, was that my heart was forever longing for something it could not give me. At the same time, the hearts of my peers were yearning for film stars. We were all probably longing for love, reassurance, self-confidence.

We all began Latin together in Year 8. The textbook, *Latin for Today*, was immediately disfigured by some of my classmates into Eating for Today. My parents forbade writing on books. Here at school I could copy the others. I was delighted that for once the whole class participated in a new subject in which I could keep up. I learned the words with my German dictionary, Latin and English at once. Latin was such an orderly language, with predictable sounds, unlike English which went all over the place and which presented me with ever-new pronunciations. Think of the various sounds of words associated with the letters *ough*! And when did I ever master that cat-like spitting of 'the'? Probably never, completely.

One day, shortly before her departure from the boarding house, Sister Beatrice took me and Peter, who was visiting, on an outing to St Peter and Paul's Orphanage in South Melbourne. She was to be transferred there.

This was her personal contribution to our vocations. Every cleric then had an obligation to seek out vocations for 'the religious life'. There was a dichotomy, obvious to us, between the religion of ordinary people living in the world and the self-sacrificing minority who offered their whole lives in service. We picked up the message that it was an obligation to search one's soul for a message. It would say: 'I ask you to devote yourself to My Work, My Word, My Way.'

To be with nuns and to belong to them became yet another emotional pressure. This was an instructive visit. If I felt sorry for myself for being stuck away from my parents, entering the bleak yard of St Peter and Paul's Orphanage to hear about the lot of orphans was a reminder that deprivation is a relative thing. There are always those significantly worse off!

A kind of yeast was working in me. My body was slowly preparing for adolescence, God's ploy to distance one from one's parents. Into my space, something else was moving. I was beginning to fall in love with my religion and all it stood for—the good things, of course. The bad things about it were studiously ignored.

I had leapt into the pool of faith. Did I want to join Sister Beatrice one day and work for orphans? She actually asked the question. The thought was daunting but unrealistic for a twelve-year-old. But a seed had been sown.

My adolescent body was meanwhile betraying me. I was beginning to come out in brown spots! Nobody else suffered such an affliction. I was turning into a spotted and speckled human hound. More spots constantly appeared until one day a young boy turned to his mother in the street and said loudly: 'Look at that girl. Look at her spots!' I was shocked. With a body of moles as numerous as the constellations of stars in the sky, you had no chance of falling in love with your own looks. It gave me a ready excuse to loathe my material self and turn to the spirit within. A fine skin is a privilege, an outer sign of inward refinement, I had thought, quite wrongly. And yet the school motto, *Mirror Without Stain*, reinforced this daily.

I knew that the cover of a book does not convey the quality of the writer. 'Whitened sepulchres' only seduce some observers, said the nuns, quoting the Bible. God was doing His best to guard me from worldly vanities, to prevent me from being taken up by my own looks. The Will of God was one of the central supports of our theological education, and we were to accept graciously what we were given. Not that we ever dearly understood what the Will of God actually was.

I never thought my predicament was unfair. I simply could not understand it. You win some, you lose some is secular wisdom about equality. That I could understand. The rain of God falls on all equally, whether you deserve it or not. It was a lesson in one of the holy books, another that transcends language barriers. My field lay open to God's rain.

Nowadays as an old woman I think I was privileged to have been spared so much that happened in the twentieth century, from 'man's inhumanity to man'. Even as a girl I felt no deep self-pity while struggling to find a footing in a foreign world. My energies were absorbed in that exercise, despite the long days of loneliness. Self-pity comes much later. People feel it for themselves, or their forebears, or their communities long after the initial struggle is over. But where was my sense of being different supposed to lead me? I would have done anything to fit in. But how to interpret the signs?

My peers at school totally ignored the problem of my spots. It was never ever mentioned to my face. They practised the art of personal tolerance to a high degree, despite our induction into one large ideological stream. This forbade admiration for Communism, for instance, especially after the Chinese Revolution of the late 1940s heated up the debate. Within the Catholic community, it was implied that there was nothing special about becoming a nun, despite the status it enjoyed among the clergy. Religion was like the seasons, a part of the rhythm of life. All you had to do was listen very carefully to find out whether you were called to sacrifice your life for the good of the community, and a deeper association with your maker.

15. Ad Maiorem Dei Gloriam

Non-believers had a ready answer for girls whose hearts were uplifted by stories of the fruits of religion and who desired to embrace the life of a nun. Nowadays, scepticism is more widespread and the convents are almost empty. But then they were full to the brim. I was to hear the criticism of sceptics even in the midst of my fervour because, unlike most of my peers, at home I did not move in a 'Catholic environment'.

'Nuns are running away from the world. It is easier for them to have someone else provide for them, to make decisions on their behalf. It is a form of cowardice. They are afraid of love and marriage,' my parents repeated, to put me off. I thought I knew better. But how to deal with such conflicts? Obstinacy was my instinctive approach. Sometimes I could not hold my tongue.

The example of my combative parents and of others preoccupied with what seemed like a banal struggle to keep food on the table and to clothe and educate their children had turned me off marriage and family life. Nothing had prepared me for an urban existence where one leaves in the morning to go to a desk and returns in the evening to a newspaper and to confront domestic tensions.

Unlike my brothers, I was far too self-absorbed to understand the charm of extended childhood. I felt deeply indebted to my guardians. The power of their self-sacrifice inspired me. Bue above all, I was falling in love with what can only be called a sense of God, as a combination of what being human and being spirit stands for, something beyond one's ordinary grasp. Only in dreams could I sometimes experience cognitive impossibilities; for example, how to live in two-dimensional space, or to understand the concept of $1,000,000?

I could feel something strong tugging away at my feelings, but I had no perception of who or what it was I was seeking with all my heart. I had no sexual stirrings, despite what sceptics might think. It was obviously associated with adolescence, with that outreach of soul most of us feel so strongly then. I was thirteen when it surfaced, at first very gently. It is, I think, an idealism which members of youth leagues feel all over the world. They may be aspiring servants of Communism, or of one of the world's religions, or of the *Hitler Jugend*. While love is the driving force, most of these groups that harness youthful self-sacrifice also have a structure of authority that promises assurance, a place where young people can distinguish or lose themselves, as well as meet kindred spirits.

16

Mirror Without Identity

During the first part of 1948, almost to the day of the anniversary of my first Holy Communion, my parents came to an arrangement with Mr Zapf. He intended to buy a house in Blackburn from a migrant from Alsace-Lorraine who was an elder of the Ringwood district Lutheran Church. We were to share that house. In return my mother was to run the household for all of us, including Mr Zapf, his wife and their two children, after he had brought them out from Austria.

I'm not sure what the precise arrangements were. In retrospect they seem rather foolish, especially as the house had only four rooms that could be used as bedrooms. There was further potential for five, by converting the garage. The pressing financial needs of my parents made them vulnerable to this deal. It tended to make them and us beholden to Mr Zapf, who had money in a Swiss bank account.

My mother especially was placed in the position of a kind of servant to him. It was not a problem at first because he seemed to be a man of impeccable manners and charm, who expressed deep admiration for her. And my father was neither a possessive nor jealous man.

Rudolf and Elfriede accompanied their friend Willy to view the house and garden on the green eastern outskirts of suburban Melbourne. There properties were subdivided from large orchards which stretched in the direction of Doncaster.

The house, which stood on two blocks, was within easy reach of the city-bound train. Its garden had a number of well-established fruit trees, grapevines and two varieties of passionfruit, as well as a large vegetable garden well-fertilised by the chook run. Here Elfriede could indulge the skills of her rural origins, practising a degree of self-sufficiency. 'You are after all a country girl, Friedel!', my city-born father used to remind, praise, tease and reprimand her, according to his mood. I heard this over and again. When his emphasis rested on '*only* a girl from the country', her retorts were as blistering as ever.

In early 1948 it was painful for me to accept the decision of my parents that I must leave boarding school. I was just beginning to feel that I belonged to a community of friends. Indeed, I was soon to discover that day students did not even associate in the playground with the boarders. The two parts of the school were kept apart. I do not recall any regulations that caused this divide.

The transition to becoming a day student in late May meant that I had no real friends for the rest of the year. All clusters of friendships had been formed during Form I, since the school did not take new students until the end of Form II. My isolation on the fringes of established groups is an experience familiar to migrants everywhere.

Peter fared even worse. He was taken away from Mornington and sent to the Convent of Notre Dame de Sion.

We became accomplished train travellers, although Peter often opted for a bicycle, carrying his younger brother between suburbs.

Father lined the fibro garage and turned it into a sleep-out for Peter and me, to prepare for the arrival of Mr Zapf's family and also my mother's sister. Happy with this retreat, I gathered my thoughts there to emerge to do battle with my elders about our widening ideological differences.

It is a universal need in adolescence to find one's true identity. I was not simply a replica of my parents. As my womanhood rushed in, with its all-too-frequent excessive menstrual cycles, I began to look into mirrors in an attempt to see myself as a stranger would. *Who am I really?* I looked in vain. My identity was locked into the observer. I was only able to see myself looking at myself. I could not get rid of me. Each person, I realised, was physically different from every other person I had known, and yet I could not really perceive myself as others might, except when walking along a street and suddenly catching sight of myself in the window of a shop. It was as if this was someone else's moving shape.

16. Mirror Without Identity

I asked the mirror to tell me who I was because I was so unsure about so many things. I badly needed a recipe for my future development. I was merely drifting on a current determined by my school. My parents did not fit into what that demanded from life.

The mirror reassured me that I was a person with a slightly foreign appearance minding my own business—nothing more. For a moment I would see an 'objective' image; as soon as I tried to judge it, hold it, analyse it, my ego got imprisoned in the exercise and my ability to see myself as others did vanished. I was just an ordinary person with a lot of spots on her face and body, I concluded. And yet, I had my own consciousness, separate from anyone else's. Each person had this. *Why?* Why would God waste time giving us such a unique sense of self if it was not for some purpose? Could Nature alone furnish us with the miracle of self-awareness? I was beginning to ask serious theological questions addressing the great divide between atheism and Christian belief. My intellect was beginning to grapple with questions of faith.

It is difficult now to recapture the simplicity with which my young but isolated mind addressed such ideas. I began to think that the human axis between good and evil, which the Catholic Church monitored and mediated with the sacraments, was not a ridiculous fabrication. Slowly the rational elements in theology began to dawn on me, and develop.

I was aware of grotesque injustices and horrific human actions that ran counter to the notion of an all-loving God caring for each of us. 'How can God allow such things to happen?' was a problem. In the anecdotal theology derived from the Old Testament, the first truly human pair, known as Adam and Eve, representative of all men and women, were granted unbounded happiness together in eternal life, before their Fall. This was conditioned by their 'innocence'. In Middle Eastern style, the setting was a walled garden filled with natural earthly delights, but to Adam and Eve the walls only became obvious after they lost access to the garden through their foolishness. God had given them the responsibility of freedom of choice.

The moral was simple: not to taste the fruit of the Tree of Knowledge, which was synonymous with che fruit of experience. 'Trust me,' God implied, and also that 'Once you begin to doubt me, disobey me, challenge me, deceive me, hate me, try to outwit me—the all-innocent, the all-good One—you will lose what you have now, and you will pay dearly for it.' God did not go on to explain the mystery of the nature of evil.

As children we had only glimpses of that drama of sin and atonement. We swallowed the story of Adam and Eve literally, as did most of our teachers. Like other myths, that Biblical story is highly condensed but clearly carries meanings larger than itself. Literal interpretation destroys its complexity. As adults we can see that it not only reflects human realities but also has culture-bound shortcomings.

My first religious knowledge was superficial and cliche-ridden. Slowly, very slowly, different interpretations began to dawn on me, although I was instructed never to doubt, that understanding comes from faith, not the other way around. Trust me. I hear those words so clearly.

The background to our learning about the sacraments of the Church was the concept of humanity's 'original sin'. Each person shared at birth, through a kind of litmus paper effect in our soul, humanity's propensity to perform evil acts. These dishonoured God by defiling ourselves and damaging others. Baptism wiped away original sin and bestowed an entry to a community of believers, the Church .

Confession reinforced that cleansing. One had to be forgiven grave sins by God, through a priest, in order to receive the sacrament of the Holy Eucharist. This provided the strength to resist evil. The Eucharist reverses what was forbidden in paradise: 'Eat the fruit and you shall die' in Eden becomes 'Eat and drink the body and blood of Christ, and you will have eternal life.'

Concern for our common humanity was often over-ridden. To blame 'the Jews' for the death of Jesus is simply racist. It confuses and distorts communal theology, because what in history may have been the actions of some Romans and some Jews is taken to signify 'all people', much as Adam and Eve represent 'all people'. Out of my half-understood literal interpretations of the Garden of Eden story as a child, has grown my personal Tree of Knowledge. Its crop of adult reflections was produced without the aid of specialist horticulture. The richly textured human story of Eden and the Fall can be examined by anyone who can be bothered to deconstruct it.

16. Mirror Without Identity

My beginnings in religious indoctrination were painful, as they must be for any novice training in doctrine and religious practice, be it Muslim, Buddhist or Christian. There was some degree of choice: whether to opt for fundamentalist fanaticism or a tougher engagement of the mind.

Often I took the easier way out. However, I was also far too rational to blame myself during confession for not accepting my father's immoderate punishments. Perhaps his lack of control, which had become a habit in the camp, and must be viewed as belonging to those times, set up an unfortunate tendency in me to forgive and defend myself far too readily. Perhaps I should have tried to develop a truly contrite heart.

Committing real sins to forgive would of course have been more meaningful. However, I did get the message that my soul must necessarily be full of previously unrecognised black stains that had to be washed away by the priest's power to forgive.

The secular world continued to produce its own, seemingly unrelated, dynamic.

At school we were, however, encouraged to see everything from a moral and theological position. At that time there was also a vigorous campaign in the wider community against buying Japanese-made goods. No one seemed to worry about German manufactures. As I cringed from my family's unfortunate associations as former German-Austrian 'enemy aliens', I projected the image of a wimp. But I learned, too, that acquiescence and meekness are not necessarily indicative of weakness. I felt bound, not so much to conform to the new society as to pursue a place in life that matched the physical singularity we each carry.

I was aware that the forces of adolescence operate to keep us in touch with our peers, and that this is a tide our parents try to hold back. Our culture wishes us to remain in touch, I thought, so that we can agree about some basic communication with other people.

You get a sharp awareness of culture when you enter a new one and make comparisons, looking back at the old and experiencing the tensions it sets up with the new. Otherwise a lot of customs acquired from childhood, as well as preferences and biases, are taken for granted, like the image in the mirror. Adolescent culture produces a new layer, a sub-stratum, and its own vision for the future.

Our education at school was often reduced to a kind of mass-producing sausage machine. It ignored basic facts about our physical development and our transition to adulthood. Most girls were by then able to have babies but the topic was never raised. Our teachers imparted moral, religious and academic information, usually in that order of importance and often without insight, analysis or discussion.

Heroes caught our attention. Our parents had models of what they would like us to become, and our religious mentors had others. So many streams of intention were—and remain for youth today—in conflict with one another.

We were, however, taught to cope psychologically with alienation. Everything we did was to be offered up to God. Our model for long-suffering endurance raised to heights of significance was Saint Thérèse of Lisieux, 'God's Little Flower', as she described herself. She echoed the sentiments of Milton in his sonnet on his blindness, when he evoked angels at the throne of God: 'They also serve who only stand and wait.'

With similar sentiments in mind, each new page in our exercise books continued to be ruled up, with the letters AM+DG, every day. We thus 'offered up' everything we did, every humiliation, every pleasure, every disappointment.

These were our gifts to God. He knew every thought in our minds. He would deal with the grace that flowed from such an attitude—provided we were free of grievous sin—as he thought best. Somebody else could profit from it. Behind such offerings hung the mystery of 'the Cross' and the figure of Jesus who had allowed himself to be crucified, we were told, to free us from the bondage of sin.

While Sister Josepha continued to raise her voice in my friendless classroom, and I 'offered up' all my actions in a half-comprehending manner, home life briefly became more attractive. Beside our house in Blackburn ran Maple Street, with the one-sided remains of a gnarled old avenue of trees. They had their heads chopped off in winter only to re-emerge at the end of that bleak season covered in broad floppy leaves.

On this dusty road, I learned to ride a bicycle that father had placed in our care. It was a wobbly exercise, like learning to walk all over again, so difficult was it at first. Then, suddenly, like an infant taking off for the first time with a wobbly gait, I shot off crookedly. Unlike the problems of learning a new language well, it happened amazingly simply. It was joyful and exhilarating, like the pleasure of learning to run on stilts, but with so much more freedom.

Peter and I shared the experience in turn. On our bicycle excursions, we took Herbert mushrooming and blackberrying. We passed the ice-man delivering his large lump to each house and noted the places where the milk and bread delivery horses left their droppings. To please our parents we would return furtively with shovel and brush and bucket, and make a hasty collection, before passers-by spotted us helping ourselves.

We also shared a talkative sulphur-crested white cockatoo, which had come with the house. He was chained up by one leg in the workshop. His captivity was a reminder of what it feels like to be imprisoned. I was told that, bred in captivity, he would not survive in the wild. His curiosity, however, had not been stunted by his prison. One day I found my small watch dismembered, cog by cog. I had absent-mindedly left it near his perch on the workshop bench outside my bedroom. I was distraught. Money was scarce at home, and a watch was essential for a life determined by strict timetables.

My brother Peter was far less of a prig than I, more outgoing, more ready to embrace life. But his compassion made him a magnet for stray animals. He was only permitted to keep one: a mongrel fox terrier with a jaundiced temperament, who nevertheless developed a certain kinship with me. Peter befriended other fringe dwellers, whose parents were divorced or eccentric, like the boy whose parents had worked in a circus and now made an itinerant living, renovating houses, then moving on.

Both my brothers worked harder than I at assimilation. Their cultivated Australian language made them less conspicuously foreign than I remained.

My father was then working as a draughtsman at Woodall Duckham, and Mr Zapf for the Geelong Harbour Trust. Mr Zapf came home on weekends to a house made fragrant by mother's impeccable domestic attentions: sheets 'white as snow', aromatic sachets in clothing drawers, home-baked breads made from various grains, herbs in the cooking pots, bottled plum cordial, vats of cabbage in brine, cucumbers and onions in pickling jars, yoghurt setting, yeast rising, Silesian *Bienenstich* honey cake for Sunday breakfast.

Little was ever thrown away. My mother's mending transformed rags into new garments. Rugs and painted cloths adorned the walls; a *kelim* turned a box into a seat. Books were cherished as if they were her lovers. She imparted that love to us. There was a rich cosmopolitan flavour in the environment mother created wherever we lived. People always commented on the pleasing aromas as one entered her house. The range of her skills and her attention to celebrating feast days traditionally was well beyond what I observed in the homes of my friends. Life there, by contrast, seemed empty and dull.

It seems strange, therefore, that the fine environment created by our mother could not dispel in me the view that Mr Zapf's house was a stifling red-brick box. Its plaster walls were hung with disposable objects. Here was yet another prison. Owned by Mr Zapf, the house was full of my parents' belongings, and yet seemed a shell in which we camped.

As time went by, I joined the thousands of teenagers who become disillusioned with materialistic goals. While my mother's home was comfortable and inviting, it lacked for me a spiritual base, a set of ideals that addressed the fact that one day we must all die and account for our time on earth. How had we spent it? I was one of the many fish netted by the Irish Catholic cult of the dead.

At school, my Latin was developing well. Learning it was just like getting on a bicycle. The language had an order and poise that made other crosses easier to bear. My facility with religious ritual was also improving. I had caught up sufficiently now, if without any real understanding, to front up to the confirmation rails with the other twelve-year-olds. Wearing our obligatory white dresses and uncomfortable black patent leather shoes and carrying long white candles, we sat with a hundred boys and girls from other colleges in St Patrick's Cathedral. We listened to the voice of the ancient Archbishop Mannix drone on, like a man speaking in a cellar. He seemed to go on forever. What he mumbled I could not understand, and I wondered if anyone would later explain it to me.

We had been taught at school that we were now old enough to accept personal responsibility for the vows made by others on our behalf at baptism. We were to willingly embrace the Church and its community, both living and dead, and give assent to its basic credo for living.

16. Mirror Without Identity

Once I was pondering my half-understood preparation when there was a rustle at the end of our pew. Sister Josepha was whispering to us, each row in turn, that we must repeat the words of the Archbishop and 'take the pledge'. We were being asked to vow not to touch alcohol until we turned twenty-one.

Word by word the old man dictated our vow. The girl beside me whispered: 'Quickly, cross your fingers.' I knew what that meant, having seen Deanna Durban do it on film. I crossed them quickly, just in case! Instinctively, I knew that one should not be pushed into making false promises.

At home, my parents drank wine. Sometimes we were given it too, diluted with water. I would not be bound by this promise. It was not that I had any desire to drink, and I sensed that it was cheating to say words you did not mean. As it was, because I could not properly hear or comprehend the old man's speech, I simply mumbled a set of sounds so that Sister Josepha did not notice my secret dissent.

Afterwards I was never entirely sure whether I had taken the pledge or not. Everyone else I met had taken it. Why would I be different? I was too frightened to stand out. Probably I would have been counselled if it had been known at school. Breaking the pledge was deemed a mortal sin and unconfessed mortal sins could land you in Hell after you died. It was too horrible a prospect, even though I never understood how anyone could be eligible for eternal suffering. I preferred to wipe this thought from my mind.

At confirmation, each of us had been given the name of a saint we had personally chosen as protector. I chose one about whom I knew nothing, merely because she was Barbara in both English and German. Her story as virgin-martyr, I was to discover, appears in *The Golden Legend*. Her father locked her in a tower and unsuccessfully attempted to kill her when she became a Christian. He was struck down by lightning. Barbara is the patron of miners and gunners, and of those suffering gun-shot wounds.

In contrast to my mother's enthusiasm at home for the beauty of Pentecost and all feasts associated with the Holy Spirit, how tawdry my confirmation had been! It was probably the fault of my ignorance, for the virtues invoked spring from a tradition in which wisdom has weathered the competition of the glittering prizes of this world, its machinations and its vanities. A few years on, we might have better understood how to explain the seven gifts of the dove god, the Paraclete which, apart from the supreme virtues of Faith, Hope and Charity, now descended into our hearts at confirmation. Like majestic angelic godmothers and godfathers they were to come to us one by one. We rattled them off only half-aware of their significance.

For some time I was not aware of any strengthening of character associated with my confirmation vows to live by God's laws. I was also never sure about the existence of the Devil. A religion that stated that an all-powerful God was all love made the existence of damned creatures a problem. Yet even then I knew that evil was a potent force at work in the world. Perhaps I felt that to delve too deep would be to contact a dangerous and fearful reality.

While at our school we learned little about secular politics, we had a continuing worldly commentary through the stories of members of our faith who faced political or religious persecution. These were also a warning about the dangers of the world, and the power of Satan, the arch-demon. We were taught, too, how ultimately weak evil was before the grace of God, thus insulating our souls from damnation.

Protestants occupied an ambiguous place in the struggle between good and evil. Their animosity towards Catholics proved that they lacked ultimate wisdom. The lesson was not lost on me that Catholics were equally lacking in what I had by now come to regard as the greatest of all precepts: 'to love thy neighbour as thyself', which meant 'do unto others as you would have them do unto you'.

Protestants were presented as generally much better off materially than Catholics, and as people who prevented Catholics from getting jobs. So we were told. Catholics retaliated by forming their own networks, and their own secret societies, even though the Church officially forbade this. It had outlawed the Masons.

A sceptic like my father argued that the Church's laws had their own protective purpose: it outlawed what it could not control. I knew no Protestant children with whom to exchange either taunts or information. We lived in a cocoon, in a citadel in which we knew 'the world, the flesh and the Devil' were fighting on all fronts. We were full of excuses when sceptics gave irritating examples of where our Church had gone wrong, or spoke of sinful popes or the wickedness of the Spanish Inquisition. While compassion was our goal, I was well on the way to becoming a fervent bigot.

16. Mirror Without Identity

By now I was in Year 9. It is the school year during which girls are most frisky. At the beginning of that year our class of twenty had reached the grotesque figure of sixty-eight, through an influx of 'scholarship kids' on junior government and diocesan scholarships. These newcomers were from working-class families, and most were Anglo-Celtic. They came from homes too poor to afford private education without a scholarship.

They had been rote-fed numerical tables and spelling lists, drilled in the solving of problems and interpreting adages and aphorisms. They were keen on grammatical rules and knowledgeable in identifying capital cities, rivers, lakes and mountain ranges around the world. They leapt like trout and otters from the bland instructional waters of our classroom. Like dolphins they leapt to do their tricks and take the morsel of praise. They left us undrilled plodders in their wake.

Sister Lucy had to cope with the lot, and cope she did with unbelievable fortitude and commitment. To go to the lavatory in a hurry one had to crawl under desks in front, so tight was space. The geography of the classroom was indicative of students' origins. You could draw a plan showing the division of space according to previous schools attended. Desks were allocated as you entered the room, two by two. Naughty performers were of course later shifted, away from distractions.

Having left boarding school the year before, I now had little contact either with boarders or day students. I sat next to a girl I will re-name Paula Brown, who was thought physically precocious, but not intellectually so. She dreamed only of boys. Her parents permitted her to attend mixed dances without supervision! I acquired a kind of split personality, belonging both to 'straight' girls and with the company of one girl who was 'bold as brass', who had chosen me, her desk companion, as her friend. I spent many a tedious lunch hour listening to her drooling over this or that film star, or enduring the banal pop tunes she and others hummed incessantly.

Knowing where my real interests lay, I tried to extricate myself from trouble but succeeded only after a number of disagreeable conflicts. I finally found the strength to break away from such associations, but only after an unpleasant party at Paula's home.

My parents were excited that I was becoming 'social' at last. Mother sewed me a fine dress in a style fit for the 1920s. It was in a slinky long style in navy silk with huge white polka dots and a scalloped white cotton collar framing my face. Everyone else turned up in mid-length flouncy skirts, responding to that ghastly song they were all singing, *Walking my baby back home*. Its pimply hero seemed to revel in the fact that he had dandruff on his comb.

The heroes of that particular party were all older teenage boys 'on heat'. Some had left school, some were 'at Tech' or were working as apprentices to tradesmen. There were no parents present. Each girl was paired off with a boy, and passionate petting made the dark air hiss and glow with heat. I did not like it. I did not like the boy I was with. I was fourteen, he at least eighteen.

I endured being trapped until at last I found an excuse to leave. To catch my train home, I had to walk alone through the dark deserted building sites of outer suburban Reservoir. Unfamiliar with the area, I just missed the 9 o'clock train connection and had to wait for an hour on the empty platform. What if someone had stalked me?

When the train arrived, I felt nervous about the 'dog-box' railway compartments. I could be trapped in such a space with someone undesirable, away from any supervising conductor.

At the station in town my family was waiting to take me on the next part of the journey home. My father was agitated with concern and the long wait, and shouted at me. My mother saw that I was distressed, but thought it wisest not to comment. Later I told her how stupid that gathering had been.

Although our Mercy nuns, by virtue of their vocation to serve as angels to the underprivileged or sinful, made compassion for others their most shining example, we could not confide in them. They seemed too remote. We never 'told on' each other in class. This was the worst thing you could do in an Australian school.

Often, however, I felt deeply out of place. As the fevers of adolescence laid me low, I felt like dying. I did not want to go to all the trouble of discovering and applying myself to a meaningful life. I felt this most deeply at jolly social gatherings or, paradoxically, in the natural silences which amplified my loneliness.

When our parents took us for walks around Blackburn Lake in spring, orchids appeared briefly and birds flew out of the sedges by the water. But instead of glorying in life's renewal, acute pain gripped my spirit.

16. Mirror Without Identity

These were but passing beauties. Something was missing, was profoundly missing. If only I could die! Longing and nostalgia gripped my heart—for what, I did not know.

A verse from the Bible resonated with my silent cry of pain: *We sat down by the streams of Babylon and wept there, remembering Sion.*

Through religious teachings, Jerusalem had become a homeland of my soul. It stood for all the homelands I had lost and all the homelands I was seeking. In tandem went the verse: *If I ever forsake you, my God, may my tongue cleave to the roof of my mouth.* These words provided a potent and reassuring psychological brew. I drank them deep.

Later in Year 9 I acquired two friends who shared my need to rise out of teenage malaise. As a threesome we spent much time at the houses of the other two, closer to town, debating how we could accomplish our dream of imitating the life of our teacher, Sister Lucy. Maureen Thomas, the only child of ageing parents, lived in a free-standing brick box on Clifton Hill. Blinds covered the windows to protect the furnishings from the sun. Margaret England was the only child of working parents who ran a vegetable and fruit stall at Victoria Market. She lived at Princess Hill in a tiny one-storey Victorian terrace house that, like a Siamese twin, shared a wall with its neighbours. It too was dark.

During the long Communist-organised (so we were told) Victorian train strikes late in 1949, I was generously offered lodging with the England family. Her parents, however, knew less about our preoccupation with the spiritual life and becoming nuns than about Margaret's tennis.

Our yearnings, which lit up our hearts, but which elders viewed as morbid, were endlessly discussed during long sessions at Melbourne's General Cemetery, conveniently near Margaret's home. No one thought that we were in danger there.

After some delay, Mrs Anneliese Zapf agreed to come to Australia with her two children, Erika and Peter. They arrived with her parents, Mr and Mrs Neumann, and her lover. The Neumanns thought that their daughter might do well from a divorce settlement.

Mr Zapf had known nothing of this.

On her arrival in Melbourne, Mrs Zapf immediately declared her unwillingness to live with her husband, who of course had paid for their passage. She was, however, prepared to have my mother look after her children on alternate weeks 'for the sake of their father'. This arrangement, fortunately for Peter, Herbert and me, who now had to compete for our mother's attention, lasted only a few months.

It was accompanied by an ugly divorce case, which I was obliged to attend. Some time later, Mrs Zapf died a terrible death from the tetanus she had contracted after a fall in a horse paddock. Her devastated children were cared for by their grandparents until their father was able to look after them himself.

Meanwhile, Rudolf had sponsored my mother's twenty-nine-year-old sister, Else, and paid her passage to Australia. Else had been reluctant to leave her relatives and friends in East Germany to make a new life in a foreign land with an older sister she hardly knew. She had declined a marriage proposal during the War to look after her ailing mother with whom she had fled from their home in the fire-bombed streets of Breslau. They had escaped before the advancing Red Army, pushing a cart. My grandmother had died soon after.

Else joined our Melbourne household shortly before my father departed for Iran, where Mr Zapf had arranged jobs for them both. She took English lessons at night at a state school in Mont Albert until the elderly teacher, a married man, fell madly in love with her pristine beauty and began to stalk her. To avoid him, Else quit her lessons. Her subsequent work in a factory paid so little that she had to earn extra money from caring for children and cleaning houses.

My brother Herbert gives a charming account of how he and Else taught each other English from the backs of cereal packets. She was like a nanny to him, and he grew to love her dearly. Although I esteemed her highly and we became the best of friends for over forty years, in 1949 my affection for her was temporarily moderated by my frustration at having to compete with her for my mother's attention. I came home from school in search of a willing listener to my day's happenings, but I often found the even lonelier Else had beaten me to my mother's ear.

Else was such a truly good person that she tended to see the best in anyone she met. My tougher mother at times found her gentle simplicity frustrating.

16. Mirror Without Identity

Else was one of those rare people not embittered by the War. Her sufferings had, if anything, made her more tolerant, even of those better-placed than she. She nevertheless suffered a version of shell-shock from the bombings that had turned her once-noble city into a rubbish tip. Whenever civilian aeroplanes flew over Melbourne, she began to shiver and shake, re-living the bombing raids that had demolished her city.

Life in debt to Mr Zapf had its problems. The presence of four adults in the house pushed the children into a separate group. We lost some of the close contact we had enjoyed with our mother. It propelled me even closer to the family of the Church. When no one else was in the kitchen I was permitted to listen to radio programs. One day, Mr Zapf, entering, became impatient with my deep focus on a reading in modern English of the Prologue to Chaucer's *Canterbury Tales*. The words 'pilgrim', 'priest', 'nun' brought out his intolerance of the Catholic Church. He had once been expelled from an Austrian military academy when discovered kissing a young nun-servant in the laundry.

On this occasion, he walked over and, without my permission, turned off 'his' radio. It was 'his house', after all. I was furious at his rudeness and autocratic style. My mother feared I might retaliate. Although I turned my back on him emotionally, I nevertheless continued to dutifully kiss him good-night on the cheek, as I was expected to do.

My mother was proud of my moral victory. Of course I would not have been able to overcome my hurt feelings had it not been for the lessons on self-denial we were given at school. Mr Zapf continued to give me gifts on feast days. But although the *Complete Plays of William Shakespeare* and a large compendium of de Maupassant's marvellous short stories were much appreciated, my genuine gratitude went to their authors rather than to the donor. The French collection of stories in English translation still circulates among members of my family, into the third generation.

I loathed having this landlord in my life. My experience was to be a cautionary reminder whenever I later extolled the virtues of extended families, on ideological grounds.

My dislike of Mr Zapf was probably because of his more general interference in my life. Another attempt to turn me away from religion was his appeal to my mother to give me sexual instruction. 'Those moles of hers,' he said, 'will attract suitors to her like flies to the honey-pot.' 'Flies? Those ugly creatures that spawn maggots,' I thought, with beating heart.

I expressed my dismay to my mother. She told me to ignore the remark. She refused to approach the subject of sex, perhaps because she noted my disdain at Mr Zapf's interference, which I thought highly irregular and slightly creepy. It was also because 'she is not ready yet'. 'Nonsense,' grunted Mr Zapf. 'No girl is ever not ready to make love.' I suspected voyeurism. My mother came to my rescue: 'She'll learn in her own good time.' I embraced her in spirit for her enlightened wisdom, and for keeping me out of his emotional reach.

I was growing into a copy of my mother when young, but a less attractive, spotty version, handsome perhaps, but not beautiful or elegant as she had been. The likeness must have made me more attractive to Mr Zapf. My religion encouraged ritual splendour but dowdiness in personal presentation. As individuals we were extremely important in the eyes of our God-lover, and so were all the others, as numerous as the grains of sand by the sea.

Catholicism was full of riddles, of perplexities, of mysteries. We had been taught at school to beware of glamour for its own sake, to beware of 'the world's vanities'. We were told that 'the Devil has work for idle hands'. I was more innocent in some ways but in others more serious, more grown-up than many of the girls in my class. I did not fall in love with stupid film stars. But I was in most ways still a mere child.

Others with healthy sexual appetites thought mother was wrong not to pull me sharply into line. A friend of my parents from the camp, Mrs Lydia Zachen, gave me an American novel by Betty Smith, *The Tree in the Yard*. 'A description of teenage love might do the trick,' I overheard her telling my mother.

I read this noble book about poverty-stricken youths in Brooklyn without much pleasure, finding it tawdry. My mother was right: at home I was an obstinate child, and I was unable to empathise with the miserable lives of the protagonists. I found instead many an absorbing romance in copies of mother's *Womens Weekly*. Both she and I followed a serialised story by Elizabeth Bowen, awaiting each issue of the magazine with some eagerness. We were both beginning to read English with a degree of competence.

But the world still claimed most of my attention. I became increasingly aware of the biological rhythms of my body, of easier and worse days. I was not without some longing for glamour. From my mother's magazines I sketched many a smart costume and fashionable hat, but avoided fulfilling her own ambition, and overcoming her lost opportunity of becoming a successful fashion designer. This was left to her cousin Vera, who had migrated to the United States.

My father's contribution to curbing my religious zeal was to show me a large German book translated from French, *Der Ewige Jude* (*The Wandering Jew* is its English title). I was to find out for myself how wicked the Jesuits in the Catholic Church could be. After reading this huge volume from cover to cover, I handed it back and voiced my dismay. 'It's full of propaganda! There are so few good people in it,' I pronounced.

My father was surprised and thought me lacking in sophistication, which may well have been true. I have not read the book since. '*Solch ein dummes Mädchen!*' (Such a stupid girl!), he muttered. Although I stubbornly refused to listen, I nevertheless did sometimes wonder if that refrain did not carry some kernel of truth.

He then told me in graphic detail of the Spanish Inquisition and how a Spanish plumber had told him of the quarrels he had overheard among nuns. I did not want to know. My mind was made up. I would not waver in my belief in the soundness of the Catholic Church.

Such experiences only deepened my conviction that I could not follow in the footsteps of my parents. But there was also the indoctrination of school. It was a none-too-subtle recruiting ground for the Sisters of Mercy, whose reception house was at Rosanna, not far away. Girls had already left school to join the order. The religious rhetoric of that time included elevation of the religious life over and above marriage, the latter being given very secondary billing in the competition for religious perfection.

My understanding of the Church's history confirmed my idea that it presented us with a magnificent record across every area of human endeavour: courage, devotion, compassion, service, justice, artistry and knowledge. The Church was teaching us about 'what really mattered' in this perplexing life. I closely investigated its various branches, from fixed and silent contemplative orders to itinerant missionaries.

In September 1949, my father and Mr Zapf left for Iran for an extended period. Mr Zapf had organised jobs more suitable to the talents of both than would have been possible in Australia. They left my mother to run the household with Else.

Both of them had to rely on us children to complain about defects in electrical goods or the ineptitude of salesmen, and to translate instructions between German and English. The women learned English through us, very slowly, and with some embarrassing moments when they tried out the slang expressions of the boys. We children did our mother's bidding grudgingly, far too weak to disturb the peace. With Peter's and my extreme shyness, we always had to be forced into action. We could never act easily. My father's over-exacting will, his many heavy-handed punishments that made our brains shake in their sockets, his domestic tyrannies as we children viewed them, had kept us insecure. We had to steel ourselves to become our mother's liaison officers and messengers into the world.

Under the administration of the two women, the atmosphere at home was warm-hearted. My mother's governance of the family was on the whole reasonable and liberating. Occasionally she sulked in silence for long periods when we failed to behave as she preferred. If we had not been told how we had offended, our guilt was even more painful to bear. She, on the other hand, must have been frustrated that her fine linguisitic skills in German had no use in Melbourne and that we children now surpassed her in the language that mattered.

17
The Wreck of the Deutschland

After my father had left to work in Iran, I was surprised by how much I missed him. What a gap there was in my life! He had established a strong bond of affection with me when I was very young and that had survived our ups and downs. Why did he have to go away? I admired his straightforward approach and his professional standards. In my eyes he was an accomplished person with a head full of knowledge. He took his responsibilities for us seriously.

My father's absence deepened my longing to do something meaningful with my own life. Compared with the only model of family life that I knew really well, and that had not convinced me that affections between men and women were necessarily lasting, or even joyful, the model of the Holy Family, Joseph–Mary–Jesus was unreal and insipid. I began to feel the need for something deeper in my own life.

My increasing involvement with the ideological positions of Tridentine Catholicism at my school, with its deep monastic influences and its otherworldly Jansenism—the flavour of Irish Catholicism inspired by French Puritanism—gave me the burning desire to bring my knowledge to those who were ignorant of its priceless treasures. And so I wrote my father a letter, saying that I wanted to devote my life to following the Master's 'bare, sandalled feet through desert sands'. Hundreds, even thousands, I wrote, had felt the same prompting with joy. The Middle East, where I had spent my earliest childhood, had begun to call me back, this time from the pages of the holy books. The urge to become internationally Catholic started to take up some of the space previously reserved for Germany-Austria as a home for my spirit.

My father was shocked by my intentions and immediately confronted me with '*Solch ein Blödsinn!*' (Such nonsense!). He had by now saved some money and so strong was his antagonism to my scheme that he was prepared to sacrifice the family's interests by offering me an air ticket to get me away from Australia. His sisters agreed to have me live with them in Vienna. I would have the opportunity to attend the Vienna Kunstgewerbe Hochschule, a technical high school devoted to the teaching of arts and crafts, and after that a good career.

Nowadays I regret the loss of such an opportunity, but then everything else that was good in my later life would be different too. While I was very tempted by the chance to study theatrical set design, or even glass-blowing or gold-smithing, I rightly suspected that this was a ploy to woo me away from my religious vocation. 'No,' I told my mother, 'I want to be educated first, before I go anywhere.'

My aunt's husband, Oswald Dittrich, whose father had been the first to take Western classical music to Japan, began sending me Asian books about Buddhist monks, in German translation, to engage my mind. To no avail. I remained a stubborn child when it suited me.

My mother gave vent to her frustration of missing out on living in Iran by grumbles about the artlessness of Australian daily life, the slovenly excuses people made that 'near enough is good enough', 'she'll be right mate', 'don't bust your boiler tidying up the mess'. People here, she complained, had little taste for ceremony, and nor did they make the effort of teaching their children good manners or how to respect their elders as was done *zu Hauss* (at home). Life for her was drab. There was no beauty or enough ritual in day-to-day living.

After seeing the artistic interests of the community in the camp, we children felt that culture shock as well. During Easter in Melbourne in 1949, no one painted Easter eggs by hand; before Christmas, no one made Advent wreaths to hang from the ceiling, with candles to be lit every week; no one painted Advent calendars with windows to be opened daily to reveal a symbol of remembrance: a shoe filled with sweets, a deer leaping over a pine sapling, a heart with a spray of flowers, a loaf of bread, a dove, a child in the snow, an angel, a star. Later '*Nicht wieder Schokolade!*' (Not chocolate again!) was mother's dismissal of chocolate Easter eggs which, she said, offered nothing but commercial sweetness to the stomach.

17. The Wreck of the Deutschland

It was an interesting remark, coming from an accomplished maker of Austrian chocolate cakes. 'No one in Australia, except in the churches, does anything about the feast of *Aller Seelen* (All Souls),' she grumbled. 'No one here observes a person's name day,' my Austrian father would certainly have added, had he been with us.

'Here the seasons vary so little,' my mother continued to grumble. Christmas in Germany was usually celebrated with knee-deep snow outside, while inside the houses were made fragrant with branches of pine, with freshly baked gingerbreads and apples brought out of storage and tied to the tree. In Australia, my mother complained, the candles melted from the heat on Christmas Day and 'you feel like crawling into a refrigerator'.

'At home,' she went on, 'the evergreen pines symbolise eternal life and the candles the return of the sun after winter. Here Christmas has no symbolic partnership with nature. Why don't they make up their own meaningful customs instead of importing them?'

We Girschiks followed our home traditions. Our father was particularly keen. He was a man of rules. As the year moved to its end, our mother was upset that her man was going to be away for Christmas.

She also complained about Australian food, which she found dull. Those who waited on others in restaurants, she noted, often expressed their resentment at having to do this, spoiling the rare occasion on which she was invited to dine out.

My mother demonstrated good sense in her sole parenting. One day when she found my brother reading Man magazine in the wood-shed, she told him calmly: 'If you want to see naked women, come into the house. We have lots of books that show them even more beautifully. Besides, you don't need to hide what your friends have given you. They are good boys.' Her tolerance was remarkable yet she could never quite bring herself to give us formal sexual instruction.

In Australia, we children were more open to experience than our nostalgic mother. We enjoyed the greater freedom that is part and parcel of a lenient way of life. As a child in an Australian home you could express yourself, voicing disagreement more openly. You also had many more choices.

Both my brothers cultivated a broader Australian accent than I. Their street slang was also proficient. Our highly disciplined upbringing, where at the table with our father we were 'to be seen but not heard', was not without its virtues. We developed a talent for patience. From our background, we acquired focus and application to our tasks. Our emotional repression and our excessive diffidence, however, we could well have done without. We cherished the delicious sense of freedom once the fetters were removed,

Time had lapsed since my father had sent his invitation for me to study overseas. With my Australian courage I approached this forbidding person by writing courteously. I did not inform him that I was afraid of losing both my education and my religious ideals. I could not bear to repeat the confusion of the first months at my Australian school.

My father warned me that the opportunity would never return. I remained obstinate.

At school my two friends and I confided our ambition to become nuns to Sister Lucy. She took an exceptionally practical approach. She told us to think carefully about this prompting in our hearts. 'You are too young now,' she said in an encouraging voice. ' Leave it for the moment,' she cautioned, 'and if this feeling does not go away, then perhaps you ought to think more seriously about it later.'

Sister Lucy (whose family name we found out was Murray) was so tolerant that the girls in her class tried hard to find out how old she was and where she had come from. This is what we learned from various sources, including a girl whose sister had 'entered'. Sister Lucy was Aileen, the daughter of a publican who ran a hotel in Brunswick and whose wife had died while the girl was quite young. 'That's why her father sent her to board with the nuns at Nicholson Street,' one girl opined. Rumours continued: Sister Lucy's father had been a sea-captain, it was whispered. As Head Prefect she had been expected to enter the order, as every other Head Prefect was said to have done. First, however, she went to university and completed a science degree. Having enjoyed the university's social life, she then entered the Mercy training house at Rosanna in the full knowledge of what she was giving up.

We somehow discovered that she was about thirty-four when she came to teach that huge class alone, except for the single relief teacher. Sister Imelda sometimes took us for part of an afternoon. All our teachers were nuns except the stout woman to whom I owed my swimming certificate, our physical education teacher, Miss Carey, and another robust woman who wore flowing gowns, Miss Murphy. She taught us elocution and took us through recitations of such poems as Hilaire Belloc's verses: *Do you remember an Inn, Miranda?* Another favourite was by Thomas Moore, the Irish musician: *Rich and Rare were the Gems She Wore.*

With a name like Murphy it was not surprising that our recitations were drawn from Catholic and Irish versifiers. I could never understand what was appealing about having verse spoken in chorus, especially if the poems were boring. I suppose it was easier than having us sing correctly. It also taught us to speak 'like ladies'.

The excessive Irish Catholic content was not a problem for me. Irish teachers belonging to an order founded in Ireland, with others who had come from there, expressed their nostalgia for a place they would never see again. This was understandable. We caught their longing, their romanticism, their sense of a true Catholic homeland, the great land of saints and scholars.

Vivid memories of the camp and revelations about the atrocities of the Nazi regime in Germany and elsewhere were weakening my attachment to Germany. Like a painting on transparent paper placed over another scene, Ireland began to slide across my sense of a true homeland. Such is the power of words and song to help construct an identity. The Irish nuns talked of Saint Patrick, the Irish slave of the Romans in England who had converted the Irish to Christianity; of Saint Brigid, that marvel of womanhood whose mother had been a Druid and had taught her the secret arts of nature; of the adventuring monks, Saint Brendan and Saint Columcil. Behind such talk was nostalgia for their homeland. Their heroes now also became ours.

In our motet choir we sang liturgical music in four parts, and the haunting melodies of their homeland. Their love became ours as well, as in the Gaelic *Shule Agra*, mourning Johnny, 'my darling love', who has gone for a soldier.

I misunderstood, thinking it was *the land* that had been taken away, not *the lad*. That was obviously what I preferred to hear. The loss of one's land brought tears to my eyes. I, too, had been dispossessed. Not able to understand death, to me it seemed far worse for people to lose their homeland than for one person to lose a son in battle. Death is hard for the young to grasp. That's why we could long for it without serious misgivings.

Silent, O Moyle was the other beautiful dirge that we often sang. It is a song about the coming of Christianity during Ireland's tribal past. Cathleen ni Houlihan, for whom another song was named, was honoured for her embodiment as both Ireland and the Virgin Mary. Sentimental hymns of love and praise were, however, much more common.

The influence of Dr Percy Jones, the priest who conducted the St Patrick's Cathedral choir, who had compiled the diocesan hymnal, and who prepared sheet music for special occasions, gave this Irish influence an artistic impulse. For me, the quality of the Irish messages made it easy for us to open our hearts to the Irish heritage of Australian Catholicism. We adolescents were inevitably couched by the cruel story of the Irish colonisation by England after the Reformation. We sympathised with the Irish dispersed around the world as a consequence of the potato famine behind which the evil genius of the English lurked.

The cult of the dead which attends Catholic cultures in rural parts of the world found a ready response in someone who had no particular faith in the future and who had cultivated an inner life at the expense of social skills.

Yet as I progressed through school, I heard much about heroic English Catholicism, of priests fleeing from their would-be executioners into a 'priest's hole' in the house of protectors. We learned of great English martyrs, mystics and theologians who preached wisdom and tolerance and a love of history. I had a feeling that English Catholicism was more tolerant and rational than the Irish version. But I did not have the intellectual equipment to argue my way beyond what was daily to hand.

Sister Lucy was one of the few nuns not born in Ireland. Neither were some of the younger nuns Irish-born. Yet they all shared their Irish Catholic heritage. Sister Lucy's grey-blue eyes were like the sea, but took on a green metallic sheen when she was angry. This seldom happened. Her good nature overcame such temptations.

Our huge class respected her because she respected us. We were only uncontrollable when she was relieved by the mild-mannered geography teacher, Sister Imelda. We made her miserable.

One day Sister Lucy called 'the three friends' and from the small cupboard that was our library took out *Three Daughters of the United Kingdom*. She told us we should read it, because it had a moral: that nuns don't grow on trees, and that it is hard work being a nun.

This book presented a typical scenario of the times with considerable sensitivity. It suggested that one of us would remain single in the world, another would marry and have a happy, large family, but only one was likely to become a nun. Statistics were beginning to show a slight decline in vocations.

We each read the book and were equally impressed by the choice of roles. But like many adolescents, our minds were set on being heroic. Each of us thought the same. Each of us wanted to be *the nun*.

Sister Lucy never singled us out for our piety, but she pressed into my hands separately a copy of Francis Thompson's long narrative poem, *The Hound of Heaven*, a potent reminder of how God will hunt down a person, will claim his own, which means each one of us. One could also interpret the poem in the light of religious vocations. Religious vocations, after all, were a gift from God, as our teachers never tired of telling us. 'He calls you. You do not choose Him.'

With her inimitable sense of fairness, and her reluctance to proselytise, Sister Lucy suggested to me one day that I might go to university, as she had done. 'I believe it would suit you very well.' She spoke gently, without labouring the point.

From her, this was a daunting compliment. I was struggling at school to understand the English language better and get on top of my subjects. I never ever caught up in mathematics, having missed the essential building blocks of learning, and with no remedial teaching available.

We understood that few girls from that school went to university at the time. Sister Lucy's simple remark was to have far-reaching consequences for my life. I honour her respectful encouragement.

Two years later I read Gerard Manley Hopkins' long narrative poem, *The Wreck of the Deutschland*, about five nuns, refugees from Germany's anti-Catholic laws, who went down with the ship during a storm close to the English coast. The Germans later accused the English of waiting thirty hours before sending a rescue boat. Some 157 passengers were drowned, and the tragedy nearly led to war between the two countries.

Lucy's personal sacrifice, living such an enclosed life when she had such a fun-loving, sunny nature, I now viewed as the symbolic equivalent of the death of the *Deutschand* nuns, an immolation of herself for reasons greater than personal happiness. She was 'the lily' on the ship. She had done it in the cause of love and duty. I did not know it at the time, but through our rather remote relationship, she subtly inspired me to accept my lot, displaced in Australia with no geographic home to call my own.

Indeed, here were signs that the seeds of new acceptance were beginning to take root. *The Wreck of the Deutschland* was fast taking hold in my mind. Horrible details of the Nazi Holocaust were becoming public knowledge, to cries of disbelief: 'The shame of it all!' And the attendant shame of Nazi ideology, underpinning it! How deceived we had been as children by the songs about our *Heimat*. They had merely hidden dark political goals.

Of course, you never cease to love what is loveable in any great relationship in your life. My affections for grandparents and parents were still strong and loyal in my heart. I continued to love the music of my ancestors, and was inspired by the fine photographic studies of Austrian buildings, such as the Vienna Opera House and the monasteries along the Danube. They became models for the architectural drawings we were asked to do in Sister Bernardine's marvellous art classes. They made a fine complement to a watercolour I painted of a view across the rooftops of the slums of Fitzroy.

The fiercely competitive internment camp ideology had left me with an unfortunate competitive instinct for performing at least as well as others in school subjects. I enjoyed the notion of high standards and human excellence, but disliked the ill-will and snootiness it bred. At the end of that year, in a class of sixty-eight, I came twenty-third. That's how competitive it was: I can even remember it.

Everyone's name was placed against a number on the blackboard so that we could take it all in, over and over again. I was absorbing the idea that I was not particularly intelligent, an impression increasingly endorsed by my father, who understood me less and less. He was disappointed in

17. *The Wreck of the Deutschland*

what he saw as indifferent results. I did not even do the sum that would have shown that I 'came in' just below the top third of the class, a good achievement given the handicaps of my background.

Sister Lucy, however, had lit a candle in my head which protected me through many painful hours. All around me was the message that God had willed us to do certain things. It was our duty to listen and pick up on that. No one really understood what a debilitating thing it is to be so dependent on dogma. We were not properly guided in a practical way to make something of our lives, except in moral and religious terms. Part of my religious scruples consisted in the fact that like so many teenagers I was ready to do whatever my idealism demanded. Camp politics and the other-worldly version of Catholicism presented at school had turned me off politics. They were at once dangerous and trivial, I believed.

There was a fair amount of anti-Communist rhetoric at school. But it did not leave any deep impression on me. In a fumbling sort of way I longed for liberal values, while swallowing precepts that encouraged moral, rather than political, censorship. At home, after my father's return to Iran, my mother and I fought out the battles between Luther and the Catholic Church. My ammunition was pat answers. My mother was worldly-wise. She was unceasingly devoted to us, working for us until late at night, repairing our clothes, cooking us fine food, mopping our floors, tidying our drawers.

Sometimes when I came home from school I might find some loving kindness laid out on my bed in the shape of a white cotton jumper, a new pair of sandals, or a drawing pad. Her love was constant. My adolescence rewarded her in less generous ways.

She also had a clever, sharp tongue. Her habit of sulking, not talking at all for days if she was offended, without giving a reason, heaping guilt on others, persisted. It was her weapon. I recall some nights, after a spirited argument about faith, we would both be sobbing our hearts out, with our arms around one another.

The religious mania that was filling the vacuum of my displaced culture kept us apart. Ideologically, remembering the camp, I can over-simplify the situation by describing my fanaticism—or romanticism—as 'new wine in old bottles'. I was so consumed with the other-worldly outreach of soul that I attended Mass in town daily before going to school.

My mother thought me crazy because in those days one was not permitted to eat or drink anything before receiving the Eucharist at Mass. She continued to cut my lunch in her delicate way, so that I could catch up on food at lunch-time. When my father had done this, in contrast to the thin, white, refined-flour sandwiches of my peers, my father's crude slabs of wholegrain bread and fillings of uncooked smoked cod, smelly cheese or plum jam had little appeal. At that time my lunch regularly found its way into the rubbish bin. 'Think of the starving millions', a familiar exhortation, fell on deaf ears. It occurred to my blunted sensibility that my smoked cod sandwiches were not likely to appeal to anyone else either.

Except for water, I often fasted until I reached home late in the afternoon. Then my mother's delicious cakes and several cups of tea restored me to normality.

Since no one else in my class behaved with quite such a degree of quiet fanaticism, I began to think that something was indeed moving my spirit. I really wanted to try for a life that was different, not simply banal. But how to get there? To think I was different was dangerous. Vanity and pride may have been motivators. And yet, I still often felt so wretchedly alone, confused and troubled. My struggle with language and its application to school work no doubt gave way to the religious and moral imperatives that provided me with an attractive choice of escape.

My mother was both proud and alarmed when I told her one day that toleration is a form of weakness. In those days I still belonged to those thinkers who needed black and white categories. That's why I was also committed to knowing 'the truth', as if it was something one could fit into a mental box.

The candle that Sister Lucy had lit in my head was a crucial influence. Whenever I stayed with Margaret in Princess Hill during the long strike at the end of 1949, I travelled by tram. I gazed with great interest at people pouring over work in lighted laboratories in the medical faculty buildings at Melbourne University. Why did their absorbed activity touch my heart? The word 'university' and the notion of wishing to understand became a new influence. This was a long way from the ideologically restrictive German political program into which I had briefly been plunged in the camp.

17. The Wreck of the Deutschland

I have a lasting image from that time of my life. It was a Persian miniature in a book belonging to Mr Zapf, which I used as a model for the cover of a leather photograph album I was embossing for him, in gratitude for giving us somewhere to live. I worked on it in Sister Bernadine's craft class. A prince is on a journey on horseback. He stops to speak to a wise falcon: 'Where can true happiness be found?' he asks. The falcon answers in riddles: 'True happiness cannot be found in this world!'

I was isolated within myself, far from my brothers, my parents and most of the people with whom I had contact. Only my family guessed what I was going through. Like so many wretched migrants, anxious to be accepted, and therefore anxious to please, I was outwardly an extremely cheerful person. I was certainly no threat to my peers. Everyone seemed to like me. I did not challenge their opinions. In this sense I was too polite—a coward.

The following year took me into the much smaller Intermediate class of about thirty-six. This was a relief. Suddenly the girls had changed. They had come back to school after the Christmas break as adults: comely, respectful of school, interested in their books. On the threshold of adulthood, they now seemed much more calm within themselves.

I tried to study British history in Intermediate but found it too difficult. I lacked the skill to take down fast dictation in English, which was the way the subject was taught by the oldest of the nuns, Sister Borromeo. 'When James the Sixth of Scotland became James the First of England …' she droned, mumbling with age, making only a few headings on the board.

That opening sentence is etched into my mind like a 'keep out' sign. It was the gate to other people's territory. I could proceed no further with the wordy exactitudes of history. Algebra was equally problematic. My mind had become too twisted by trial and error to proceed from foundations to lucid logic. Geometry, however, with which nearly everyone had problems, came to me with great ease. This joy was short-lived. There was no one to teach it at the higher levels.

Latin was another subject that suddenly stopped at the school. An administrative ruling, which dictated that the nuns would move to another religious house every few years, deprived us of a teacher, as well as a community of scholars.

My imaginative English teacher in Form 4, Sister Phillipine, made a breakthrough with me in English expression by presenting us with little essay topics on a wide range of descriptive and interpretive subjects. She also began sentences, which she then asked us to complete. Reading us a sample of Dickens's prose, she gave us a comparative exercise. For instance: 'One night as the rain was beating against our windows I heard a knock on the front door,' she read. 'Complete the paragraph.' We spent part of that year engaged in such delightful prose exercises.

I was also taking art lessons and my work was often on display in class. Sometimes one of my intricately decorated frames surrounding a saint, holy scene or general notice appeared behind glass on the school's general notice board. My conspicuously talented art and craft teacher, Sister Bernardine, contributed to an illuminated address sent to Pope Pius XII by all Melbourne's Catholics. I was proud of such a teacher, a woman who was able to appreciate the magnificent nudes of Michelangelo without false modesty. It was known that in some schools nuns and brothers tore out pictures of nudes in school texts.

The nuns never talked about themselves. I found out later that Sister Bernadine was the child of a noted Irish Catholic country doctor with the family name of Carr, and that she had probably been sent to board at the Nicholson Street convent from an early age. Her sane influence on me was greater than I perceived at the time.

I was fortunate to have an artistic outlet, for during the whole of the Intermediate year I was without friends. Margaret and Maureen were now in the commercial stream of the school, preparing for secretarial studies. The two streams did not mix, and nor was there mixing between classes. I began to belong to the whole school community.

Much of our daily lives seemed to us endless endurance tests of grey-coloured banality. To learn under those conditions was like pushing a barrow full of bricks uphill, with only occasional respite. Somehow I continued to pass whatever test was expected of me.

My religious preoccupation continued. At home I tried to read serious books of theology which I had borrowed from school, and to compose music in two parts with the aid of my recorder. While sick with a heavy cold, I made an attempt to build a model of Salisbury Cathedral from glued cardboard and paper, using illustrations in an encyclopaedia probably owned by Mr Zapf.

17. The Wreck of the Deutschland

Hopeless attempts at making music and constructing complex scale models demonstrate the continuing influence in my life of my father's family background and career. He had spoken to me often enough of them. In his absence his presence still haunted our home and my imagination.

I dragged my willing brothers and unwilling mother by train to St Patrick's Cathedral to Sunday High Mass, and to evenings of liturgical music during Easter week. My mother, who missed her husband keenly, was astonished by the resemblance in stature to my father of chubby Dr Percy Jones, the priest choirmaster. I thought my father was much more a lookalike of the Australian politician Dr Herbert Evatt, or the Russian composer Schostakovich. Because of the splendid way Dr Jones led the choir in procession into the Cathedral and the music produced with such vigour by his boys, my mother enjoyed coming with me.

The musical programs of the ABC also provided us with a fine education. My mother and I came to Berlioz that way, through the *Shepherds' Farewell* in the *Childhood of Christ*. This stood out from the usual Christmas music. A performance 'on air' from a record of the splendid Berlioz *Requiem*, with double orchestra and chorus answering each other from balconies across the nave of Strasbourg Cathedral, showed a maker's hand so original that years later we identified it immediately, after hearing only a few bars.

The ABC broadcast performances of orchestras and visiting celebrities, like Ginette Neveu, before she and her magnificent Stradivarius violin were burnt to death in a plane crash as she was leaving Australia. Baritone William Warfield, and later his wife Leontyne Price, sang with aplomb on behalf of all American blacks still entangled in discrimination. We discovered Erna Berger, the petite German soprano, who sang Mozart with such angelic purity, sincerity and warmth that Wolfgang Amadeus should have leapt from his grave to embrace her.

Every weekend for years, a whole opera appeared on radio. When our household first acquired a radio in 1948, it was as if electricity had suddenly been connected to the house and the switch turned on. After life in the camp and the boarding school, the marvel of music on radio was unimaginable.

My mother was making noodle dough when I heard my first-ever opera, *The Magic Flute*, sung in German. It was such a marvel that for years I recalled the names of the others that followed it, one by one. With my father away from home it was no doubt easier for a child like me to have control of the home radio. It was also lucky that my mother and I had shared tastes in music and literature.

Years later I met women who had been more precocious in their music and reading than I when they were children. Unbeknown to me then, there had been many of us, marooned in philistinism, quietly storing up nourishment over the years through books, the radio and our own imaginations.

My spiritual life continued to both nourish and confuse me. While I found Catholic theology rich and purposeful, but riddled with mysteries, I could never entirely believe deep down that Catholicism had the monopoly of 'truth' or that there were physical places beyond death called 'Heaven' and 'Hell'. I could understand that Hell could be found on earth. The degradation and genocide of the Jews, victims of the Nazi regime, was such a Hell, I understood. So were things such as the imprisonment and torture of Cardinal Mindzenti. My mind still could not grasp the notion of eternity.

Once while in a dream I crossed boundaries which in conscious life I could not comprehend. But they did not confirm me in a belief in the impossible. Nevertheless, in every Mass we were obliged to declare our credo, a statement of our Catholic belief in which the forgiveness of sins was the humanising ingredient. We were then also asked to believe that during the Consecration the wafers turned into the real flesh of Jesus Christ and the wine into his real blood we had to consume for our own redemption. We were assured that this was not 'magic' but reality.

I still did not believe, but felt I had to. I was satisfied that if this was not 'true' the symbolism was extremely important.

A strange phrase in the Credo made a particular impression at that time. 'And on the third day [after His resurrection] He descended into Hell.' I now took this to mean that Jesus stepped into Hell to share the pain suffered by others, before departing to continue as an invisible presence both in Heaven and on earth. Love must be prepared to walk through Hell if it was sincere and true, this told me.

The novels of Graham Greene, which I read much later, dwell on a similar interpretation: that evil is a mystery; that God's ways are strange; and that God does not necessarily favour self-righteously virtuous people.

While the basic structure of the Mass was unchanging, the readings and lessons of the Gospel contained within it had historical, pedagogical and ritual significance to us. The Mass was still entirely in Latin, but we had learned enough of that language to make a general—if tantalisingly incomplete—interpretation of its drift.

Priests, some nuns and classical scholars reaped the benefit of the moral lessons, the epic stories and the poetry conveyed each day from the Bible as well as repeated at Mass. My daily familiarity gave me a sense of ritual intertwined with literature from the Bible and sacred Jewish texts, which we did not study at school. The Old Testament was regarded as simply the pre-history of Christianity, but I loved what I heard, if not relating well to the violence of the battles. Jesus was the revolutionary who, as reported in the Gospels of the New Testament had set many traditional values on their heads, favouring the poor, untutored, alienated, despised, incapacitated, modest and those who genuinely placed the welfare of others before their own.

Jesus rejected tribalism that insisted on retaliation. His ethics set out to break cycles of violence. The seeds of Christian humanism are there. But extracts from the Old Testament—the 'old dispensation'—were also woven into every Mass. Thus was a sense of history respected by the Church.

I got hold of a translation of the Bible and discovered memorable beauty enshrined in its Psalms. Jewish experiences focusing on the deep love of their God had universal appeal and resonated with my own experience. My soul, too, longed for its God, like the doe that thirsts for water.

We learned only the meaning of the main structure of the Latin Mass, together with translations of passages used on Sundays. The priest spoke at and to the altar, with his back turned to the congregation. There was much boredom associated with not knowing precisely what we were hearing. Our emotional highs came from the introduction of music, the aromatic smoke from the censor attached to its golden chain during the procession at High Mass, or during the fairly short ceremony known as Benediction. Then the golden artefact in the shape of the sun on a stem, the ciborium, was held high for worship. It housed the living presence of Jesus.

As in ancient times, the role of the priest was that of mediator between the divine and the human. It is easy to slip into modern cliches rejecting churches and religion as superstition unless one tries to recapture what it was that then gave meaning and support to so many believers.

At the time I could not argue for my religion with my critics using words appropriate to the wealth and complexity of my experience. I now see that religion was my walking stick in times of emotional instability. But it also fuelled my withdrawal from ordinary reality. I could not understand how so many Catholics could live their faith like unthinking clocks. In that sense I was a typical convert, a 'pillar of the Church'.

Throughout the liturgical year were commemorations of the days of the deaths of saints. If a saint was also a martyr, then red was worn as a remembrance of the blood spilled for the faith. At the time Australia had no saints of her own. Everyone named after a saint shared a day of honour with them, a custom more fully developed overseas as one's 'name day'. In this way one also had a strong identity forged as a 'citizen of the world' and of an international Church. 'Everyman' was also us. That was the odyssey of life.

Such internationalism did not free us from a sense of being beleaguered at home. The very entrenchment of Catholic practice, its esoteric mystical ritual, its hierarchical religious chain of command from Rome to every Bishop and his flock, and the belief daily drummed into us that the Catholic Church was 'the one true Church' made us suspicious of everyone else, especially Protestants.

We were not permitted to attend Protestant services, marriages or baptisms, except with special permission, which was usually denied. My Aunt Else married an ex-internee from the single men's camp, Alfred Erlanger, a Berliner by nurture who had worked in Iran. His father had been a Jewish businessman who had married a Christian woman.

Both sets of parents were against such an inter-faith union and both disowned them after they married. Else and Alfred married in the German Lutheran Church at East Melbourne. I had to seek permission from the school chaplain at St Patrick's Cathedral to attend the ceremony. I was told that I could go provided I kept at a 'proper distance', towards the back of the church. This was extremely liberal. I had not expected to be given permission. It was not that we could not mingle. The idea was not to give the impression of approving of heretical beliefs.

Nevertheless, my Lutheran relatives and I never had any religious disagreements as I grew up. Alfred's son was to marry into a Jewish family, while his daughter reclaimed her Jewish roots. Their mother, my aunt by blood, was always truly ecumenical. Alfred taught his children enlightened tolerance. He thereby undid the destructive intolerance of his four German grandparents.

I joined the Young Catholic Students movement, the YCS, just as most of the girls in the school did. It was the school student youth arm of the Church, dedicated to promoting the faith in every part of our lives, including travel on public transport, should the opportunity for conversation arise. We were permitted to carry our beliefs into a world perceived to be hostile to Catholicism.

The internationalism of the Catholic Church enabled us to cross boundaries in religious art and music to secular knowledge. Although our theology channelled us into a bigoted sectarianism, I nevertheless adored Protestant music such as Bach's oratorios, especially his *Sleepers Awake*, which, in my opinion, contains one of the most beautiful love songs ever composed, between the soul and God, the bride and her bridegroom. Like every piece of music I love, I played it over and over again. I also loved Handel's *Messiah*. For me it was unrivalled in its ability to raise the heart to an affectionate recognition of what we used to call 'divine inspiration'.

Art always transcends sectarian boundaries. My Catholic bigotry was being subtly subverted on several fronts, while my need for a German-Austrian 'nationality' had weakened. I was becoming Australian by stealth.

18

Intelligence Testing

Fifteen years old, but still very innocent, I approached my second last year at the school. During the holidays my mother, concerned over the cost of textbooks, strongly advised me to apply for holiday work at a recently established pottery near our home. Although I feared having to ask for work, I did as she had told me, offering my services as an artist to decorate ceramics. I expected to be scorned but they only said 'no', kindly. I then got holiday work near home at Melbourne's first frozen pea factory, Pict Peas, manually shelling the peas. With young and dexterous hands, and on junior pay, I was an asset. The company, which had been established by a retired army major, had imported the idea from the United States. I felt proud paying for my own books when the school year began.

Our class had shrunk yet again in Year 11. So many talented girls had left to earn wages to assist their families. In 1951, only twenty of the original sixty-eight passed the Leaving exam, and there were only three in Matriculation in that year. Sister Perpetua, the Irish-born Head, taught both classes in nearly every subject, in the same room. While one class worked with her, others were busy on a set task.

Naturally we were often drawn into what was happening, so much more interestingly, in the other class. The room was in a wing once allocated for the 'babies', our name for the primary school boarders. With its lower ceilings, this room now used by the seniors of the school had a feeling of intimacy. From a window at the back of the class one had a fine view over the city-scape of north-west Fitzroy and Clifton Hill.

At my desk near the back of the class, I found myself most lethargic after lunch. Then I could indulge my daydreams of my childhood in Iran. I pictured it lovingly in my mind. Images appeared and reappeared unchanged from one session to the next. That's how I came to remember much of that part of my life.

Sister Perpetua was an accomplished, if somewhat frightening, teacher. When she was not becoming angry, with disturbing frequency, with a new girl from Geelong, or with one with Yugoslav parents (which I thought unfair), her voice continued on in its modulated soft brogue. There was little comic relief or the communal spirit we had encountered in our previous two years.

In the Leaving year I listened with fascination to translations from the French while later, in Matriculation, I heard the Leaving class read from Thomas Hardy's exciting novel, *The Mayor of Casterbridge*. I followed its plot as it unfolded and heard it discussed daily, instead of concentrating on my indifferent French, for which I was frequently reprimanded. There was no library I could explore.

During my years at the convent, most parents presumed that their daughters, when they came of age, would marry a good Catholic boy, perhaps one encountered at a parish dance. The philosophy that permeated my school and many others at that time presented the vocation of marriage as of secondary merit to that of a 'bride of Christ'. Our nuns were dearly hoping that some of us would 'enter'. We were even taken to a profession ceremony at the Rosanna convent at which postulant nuns took their final vows of poverty, chastity and obedience, as they lay prostrate on the ground before their Mother Superior. They then received for life the 'habit', the religious uniform of the Mercy order. This was all exotic to us.

I had begun to have second thoughts about entering the order and pursuing its way of life. Referring to her Lutheran upbringing, my mother said: 'Once you put your hand to the plough, it becomes a commitment of service. There's no turning back.'

Father Catarinich, a marriage counsellor, was invited to visit and give the two senior classes sexual instruction. His coy embarrassment at talking so intimately to young girls about the marital embrace and the involuntary extension of a part of the male body (he could not bring himself to say penis), made him flushed and Sister Perpetua turn a bright beetroot. However well-intentioned the exercise might have been, we longed to hear the voice of a female doctor, not that of a priest or nun. I remember discussing the matter with Ursula Bayne, my new friend in Leaving, a girl of exceptional maturity and critical sanity, who agreed with me that Father Catarinich's visit was useless, and more embarrassing for him than us.

For me Ursula was a good antidote to my religious fervour. She was still grieving the death of her father a year or so before. Her doleful contralto, with which she hoped to sing opera one day, carried on from where her father's funeral had ended. Her ambition to become an opera star took her out of school at the end of the year and into the Defence Department, which she suffered patiently in order to help her mother make ends meet and to put some cash aside for singing lessons. But before she left we made marvellous educational discoveries together in class, especially in English literature with a text on the eighteenth century, *A Varied Company*, and an introduction to modern poetry curiously titled *Feet on the Ground*.

I missed Ursula's perceptive responses and her sharp retorts when, the following year, I struggled through Biology and found that, while allowed to dissect the female of the species, we were not shown male rabbits. We were ladies, after all.

My mother was not far behind the school in Victorian decorum, despite her worldly background. When I told her that a priest had given us sexual instruction, she breathed a great sigh of relief. 'Thank God for that. Now I don't have to do it!' she said. She could not bring herself to question me about what I had or had not learned. She would have discovered that Father Catarinich's instructions had been good for virtually nothing. They did, however, have something positive to say about sex and procreation, and were not just a litany of *don'ts*. Although he explained that monthly menstruation cleaned out the womb of a woman for the growth of a sacred human egg, he said nothing about female sexual responses or the joy of sex for its own sake. His kind of sex had a purely procreative function.

Both at home and at school, then, we girls were being short-changed—but did not even know it. This negligence, this silence, this *Schweigen* was symptomatic of the times. As late as the early 1980s some parents were still aghast that their daughters were 'studying' sex education at state schools, in lessons from visiting doctors. Imagine the silences of the 1950s! There was as much *Schweigen* from our mothers and the nuns on the topic of sex as there was about Nazi ideology and Nazi war crimes after the War among Germans and the Austrians they had once assimilated.

We girls never discussed sex among ourselves. There was immense social shame at the thought of conceiving a child out of marriage. Most of us were not aware of the negative effects on our maturation from the kinds of messages we were given.

Although the wages of sin and eternal hellfire were not major preoccupations of the school, whenever we came into contact with priests we also encountered a mechanical, legal set of instructions lacking moral probity. If you had committed a mortal sin by not attending Mass on Sunday or a Holy Day of Obligation or if, for instance, you had eaten meat on Friday or had sex before marriage, you were destined for eternal hellfire unless you confessed your sin and were forgiven in the confessional, or unless you made a fervent personal act of contrition alone.

'Imagine if you are run over by a car and you don't have time to repent your mortal sin—you are damned forever,' was a stock example, a form of mental terrorism. Ursula and I remained unmoved.

Who allowed such 'hellfire' priests to thunder at us during a 'mission' or during a 'retreat'? These required us to spend one day, or several, in the company of religious 'experts'. Our retreats took us to the convent of the Franciscan Missionaries of the Sacred Heart at Essendon. Priests did the talking. We were expected to spend most of these days in silence and reflection. But chatter behind cupped hands was incessant.

After twenty months in Iran, Mr Zapf and my father came home to us in Blackburn. On that first afternoon, one incident left a deep impression. I was standing in the backyard garden when I saw both my parents rush past me into the small outside toilet, where there was barely standing room for two. They were in such a hurry that they were blind to my presence. I instinctively withdrew from the scene, wondering what the urgency was. Despite my ignorance I perceived that this was to do with adult passion, which obviously could not wait until nightfall. Presumably the presence of others inside the house posed a problem. Like two bisons on heat, I thought, they rushed to perform what later I understood to be one of the oldest acts in the world.

I shrank from this display of raw passion from elders who had been sending confusing messages to us about restraint and the nature of sex. On the one hand it was deemed particularly dangerous for unmarried girls, but on the other it was obviously the life and blood of marriage, a noble condition.

18. Intelligence Testing

My father's language at home was peppered with what my chaste mentors at school would have found 'filthy' jokes. And yet he was firm about the need for young girls to be 'modest'.

In the respectful retreat of my sleep-out that day I thought about the association of sex and toilets and did not like it. I was sitting in a chair. Many German youngsters of my generation were not permitted to lie on our beds during the day. 'Beds are for sleeping, for being ill and for dying,' my mother used to remind us. Desire, pleasure and procreation appeared not to exist. My father would add: 'They are not for lazing around on!'

Rudolf was demanding. We did not enter our parents' bedroom. That was their private retreat. I did not speculate about what might be going on in there. My father always rose early, turned up the volume of the radio and made sure everyone else in the house was up too.

My older brother and I became neither voyeurs nor sexually prurient. My younger brother was the least inhibited. He had a serious heart condition which was supposed to confine his life to twenty-five years. Until he was about eleven he was more gently treated by his parents, if not by his older brother, whom father continued to beat (when he was home) until the age of eighteen. Then Peter showed who was strongest. This violence was sometimes redirected downwards between the boys.

Soon after their return, both men took mother for a holiday to Queensland. Else looked after the three of us. While away, our elders investigated the possibility of buying a guest-house together in Gympie. I was to be taken from school to work as waitress and housemaid. Gloomily I envisaged myself having to terminate my education.

On their return, I heard that the scheme had fallen through. The business was cheap because the place had been allowed to run down. 'Saved by the bell,' I told myself, and gave silent thanks.

The four adults established their own life from which we children felt excluded, like Lazarus from the rich man's table. Teenage loneliness peaked again at home as adult laughter in lighted rooms floated into our dark garden and my sleep-out.

On one such night, after another mating of the bisons scene, my loneliness and depression descended. My mother was once again completely absorbed by the men in the house, and my aunt was being courted by a newcomer.

I stealthily collected the big carving knife from the kitchen and decided to send myself to oblivion. I could not have been wholly serious because I chose the garden for this ghastly act. It was a melodramatic plot worthy of the opera *Madama Butterfly*. 'Perhaps afterwards they will miss me, at least,' I thought, with pathetic self-importance. Trying to fathom how to 'do myself in' swiftly, without fumbling, how to gather the strength to do it properly, and which point of my body to aim at without wavering in my courage, presented problems.

Suddenly I looked up at the sky and saw something surprising. Up there, high above, was a dark, deep corridor directed into outer space. It was crowded with little lights, some bright, others obscured by swirling mists. The lights were suspended in darkness and yet I knew they were attached to that dark wheel of sky that was set on its own course beyond the earth. You might see the wheel turn if you waited long enough.

The stars shone cold and indifferent, bent on their own destinies, indifferent to my presence and my plight. I was struck by my own insignificance and the absurdity of my pessimism. Did I really want to leave my parents miserable on my behalf? And what would I get out of my own disappearance?

Chance had again protected me from disaster.

I stepped out of self-pity, forced to concede that life on earth was precious, not made for premature endings. I knew that mine was not a unique dilemma. Thousands faced it. What I needed was better knowledge and perspective. I was so ignorant. So confused. So lost. Lacking in true courage. What I needed was a big sense of humour, even larger than my mother's and aunt's. 'Beware of self-pity,' I told myself, 'it is your trap!'

And so I put back the knife, careful not to be caught. Although on a number of subsequent occasions I was seriously tempted to run away, I was never again tempted 'to end it all'.

Soon Mr Zapf and my father decided to go their separate ways. By late winter father had purchased a three-acre property on the outskirts of Melbourne. The day that we moved into that damp and misty valley on the back of the furniture truck that made its bumpy way up the long drive to the house, an avenue of acacias was in bloom. The house in Croydon, which had advertised itself as *Glenfarn* and as a 'villa', was a roughly constructed timber rambler, extended room by room, without

18. Intelligence Testing

any eye to style, as need had arisen. Its internal walls were pasted over with newspapers a couple of decades old, under some sort of linen cover. Our interest in these subsequently caused my father irritating delays when he began to re-line the interior of the living room with cheap timber and stop up the holes in the floor.

The latrine was in a tiny garden hut along a path from the kitchen. Mother removed the colonising spiders from the shelter for our sake and for the sake of the man who came to remove the bucket. Much later, my father organised a septic tank.

I was given my own room and three acres on which to roam. I revelled in the freedom which, for my mother, must have become a new responsibility. There was a cow to milk and butter to churn, chooks, ducks, vegetables and fruiting trees to tend. Two paddocks were subdivided so animals could graze in them, in rotation. Our rural splendour was confined within four wire fences.

Despite all the repressive messages in my life, and despite the stand-offs between my father and me, my youthful urges were not altogether extinguished. My body began to sprout little leaves of spring desire after its frozen winter.

One day when our parents had taken us to the Royal Agricultural Show in Melbourne, I was watching young Herbert ride a pony on a merry-go-round when I saw a slender boy with fair hair of about sixteen or seventeen. He was assisting with the collection of tickets. He was entirely self-contained, not interested in anyone else. There was not a hint of showing off.

He did not see me as he spun around. He seemed like those wild tulips that grew in Iran's stony country, although he was probably a suburban lout. All I knew was that I had instantly fallen in love with the physical presence of a young man.

It was a generalised feeling, and had nothing to do with lust. I had only ever been exposed to an occasional fleeting view of the naked bodies of my two younger brothers. I wanted more. I wanted to kiss this young man and feel his arms around me. So powerful was my surge of love that I could not get his image out of my mind.

For three nights I tossed and turned in my bed, unhappy that we would never meet. Although I knew that he would probably be unacceptable as a companion in real life, he remained my ideal for a long time. I met the same type later in Thomas Mann's *Death in Venice*. Through the eyes of the old man I longed to be loved by that beautiful young boy, and to recapture those parts of youth that I too had obviously lost.

My sense of freedom in our new home was soon matched by a number of congenial friendships in the area. I had never had neighbourhood friends. In fact I had only ever had four real friends outside my family.

During the holidays I worked in a factory near Auburn Railway Station to pay for my school books. It was more like a large workshop, and each woman worker assembled a different tiny section of a radio used in aeroplanes. While I regarded this work as important, its daily repetitions were tedious enough to make me feel privileged to be still at school.

During the weekends, in the evenings, we teenagers from several Catholic schools explored the countryside or strolled across the nearby golf-links. Romance was beginning to float around us in the moonlight. We occasionally embraced and allowed ourselves to be moved. During the weekend we played golf or visited each other's houses. We were never at ours for long. My parents were too rule-bound. We spent hours talking elsewhere.

One of the boys home from the Christian Brothers boarding school in Geelong wrote poetry. He was a footballer, covered in pimples. He walked about at night on his own in the moonlight, relishing the silence, the beauty of the bush. 'How deprived we girls are!' I said without a touch of envy. 'We cannot walk around alone at night in contemplative splendour. I have to be home by nine o'clock.'

I wished I had been born a boy. Boys have all the privileges, I thought. I wanted to change roles but not my gender, despite the physical inconveniences we girls suffered.

My father was becoming vexed with my indolence on weekends. In view of my work in the factory and because I had passed my subjects for the Leaving Certificate, I reflected on the irony of his words: 'Life is not meant for sitting around and doing nothing.' But he said I was wasting my time staying at school. Nor would he give his permission for me to enter a convent. He spoke of celibacy as a defiance of the natural order, a crippling of the rights of the body. I should seriously think of leaving school and finding a job, he said. He could not support me forever.

When I resisted the idea, he took me to vocational guidance at an intelligence testing agency.

The test took four hours in an upstairs office in inner Melbourne. How had my father known where to take me? I stumbled out of the test exhausted. The Melbourne summer was peaking that day at 110 degrees Fahrenheit. The bitumen pavements were melting under our shoes. This was not a good omen.

The results of the test were not immediately available. When my father received notification, he was jubilant: 'I told you so!' The report was a dispiriting summary of my failure to meet average scholastic requirements. But it was obvious to me, immediately, that my own stated preferences had been given some consideration—for instance, that I enjoyed English Literature and Art, but not History or Science. I regarded them as rigid, rule-bound, not open to interpretation. No consideration had been given by the testers or the assessors to my cultural formation, to my educational vicissitudes, to my mother tongue. No concession was available for my use of English as a second language. During my visit they had found me personable and included this impression of me in their recommendation. 'She will never manage Matriculation, least of all University. She will suffer a nervous breakdown if she persists. She has some literary flair—an 80 per cent rating—and therefore will make a fine secretarial stenographer. She could also be a compassionate nurse and an attractive air hostess.'

I had not the slightest interest in healing people's wounds unless obliged to do so as part of religious service. I was certainly not attracted to serving people tea in the air, and had in fact never been inside an aeroplane. I was not at all attracted to flying in any form. I realised that one could learn to do such tests. So I stood my ground. 'If I have any say in it,' I told my father, 'I will stay at school and make it through my studies.'

My father did not appreciate having his will thwarted. Towards the end of the holidays he and my mother came to see the nuns. He waved the report of the intelligence testers at them. Sister Perpetua called Sister Lucy to help her deal with this troublesome parent. Both women filled my father's head with carefully worded praise. And then they told him they certainly saw the potential at school and in their religious order for my style of concentrated work. 'She's slow to learn, a bit of a plodder. But what goes into her head stays there. That's not something you can say of many of my students,' Sister Perpetua explained. 'She will overcome her challenges.'

My father grudgingly gave in to the nuns' faith in me, and I was permitted to return to school. Hurray! Had I put it into words, my joy would have found appropriate expression in the poetry of Psalm 34:

> The angel of the Lord is encamped
> around those who revere him, to rescue them.
> Taste and see that the Lord is good.
> He is happy who seeks refuge in him.
> Revere the Lord, you his saints.
> They lack nothing who revere him.
> Strong lions suffer want and go hungry
> But those who seek the Lord lack no blessing.

Those angelic nuns at my tent, pitted against my father's strong lions—that's how I viewed my escape.

Matriculation year began in the other half of the classroom. There were six of us left. It was a promising six: Pamela Brady, Kathleen Kehoe, Pamela Poynton, Judith Wison, Mary White and I. Each of my lovely comrades came from a family who had been several generations in Australia. We got on well as a group and were to spend the rest of the year in co-operative work, without competition. We were all to sit external examinations, but we approached them together, in good humour.

The ethical lessons of the nuns were beginning to become transparent to me. In contrast to the competitive and artistic education of the camp, and to an ethos there favouring exclusive cliques, the Mercy nuns offered me rather a bland education, but one rich in compassion and humane values. Even its puritanical streak did not dilute the basic message found in the New Testament: that love was the greatest of all qualities and concern for one's neighbour the cornerstone of civilised living.

The school at that time had no speech night, nor prize-giving ceremony, no board of honour. Three of us, as if by random selection, were made prefects, a mere formality, because it was the custom. Although they put me on top of the three, all of the seniors were now role models for the younger girls. We were asked to help keep order in the playground, encouraging others to keep up the good name of the school in comportment and cleanliness and behaviour on public transport. We were not expected to be arrogant bullies or superior beings. Nothing much distinguished the three prefects from the other seniors, except that we three were given particular tasks, especially in liaison between girls and staff. We were popular as a team with younger students.

Mostly we concentrated on our studies, despite the disruptive setting, one room for two classes. We also became involved in the social life of the school. This included fundraising activities for the Young Catholic Students movement. YCS discussions were prompted by the Apologetics we had been studying systematically since Year 11. These were a set of common questions about Catholic dogma to which answers had been attached. We committed the lot to memory. They explained our beliefs, when we were asked to do so, with pat answers. We were like mechanical talking dolls.

We were also forced to be resolute. Lessons in Church history provided examples of the Church's resilience and durabilty despite enemies who set out to hoodwink its members. We were given models of illustrious thinkers and scientists in the history of the institution . Their steadfast example would prompt us when our individual reason came into conflict with our faith. In the end the institution always triumphed over human failings, including its sinful members. I took this view on board, but did not allow it to concern me too much.

Although I found studies quite difficult, I also found much joy in reading *Our Mutual Friend* by Charles Dickens and Thomas Hardy's *The Return of the Native*, Shakespeare's *Hamlet* and *As You Like It*. The Victorian-age poets, Tennyson, Browning and Arnold, brought me much pleasure. I shared these treasures with mother, who consumed them greedily. A marvellous book of speeches and essays, *Prose of Purpose*, still chimes in my mind. It offered an introduction to great speech writers and essayists through excerpts which we used for exercises in precis writing.

Eleanor Dark's attempt to re-create Australian history in *The Timeless Land* failed to convince me. It stayed as bland as its title, but was nevertheless a subtle introduction to Australian studies after my experiences with English and continental Romanticism. It was like stepping from Governor Phillip's ship onto the shore of an arid continent, Aborigines with spears on the periphery.

My delicate scientific drawings showing every scale of a fish were waved aside impatiently by my teacher: 'This is science, not an art class.' They were, however, kept for years by my much more appreciative family.

Unfortunately, my father lacked the ability to explain technical things to me. I tried to understand him in vain. We were like chalk and cheese. Had he been wiser he may well have helped me construct scale models of buildings. His influence had made me observant of architecture.

My desire to join the Mercy nuns received a decisive set-back during preparations for the school fete, when I caught two nuns quarrelling like angry seagulls over spaces for their stalls. Such incidents, along with Sister Perpetua's obsessive targeting of the two girls, made me review my plans. How could I live with people who 'picked on' others daily, as Sister Perpetua did? And how face a repetition of the verbal sword fights I witnessed at home? So far I had been protected. No one had ever singled me out for abuse at school. But would this protection last? In an Australian setting, I was too weak to defend myself. To date my energies had been employed in making myself tolerated and liked. Since the departure of Sister Beatrice and the death of the music teacher, Sister Winifred, who else shared my taste in classical music? Was I to be deprived of one of my greatest sources of inspiration? To what purpose? Catholicism was no longer meant to be masochistic.

I secretly thought: perhaps I can still make it to University.

What is interesting in the story of my Matriculation year is its comment on the skills of so-called professional intelligence assessors. At the end of the year, I obtained sufficiently good results in five of my six subjects to entitle me to a Commonwealth Scholarship to Melbourne University. Another indicator that I was not a mere battler was when I won, unaided, two of the three top places in two Victoria-wide school essay competitions.

Then, of course, I had finally to face the question of the convent. The Christmas holidays were an agonising time. Was I influenced by my parents at last? Did I lack the conviction that I could be happy placing my future into the hands of women with whom I had only marginal cultural empathy?

I shrank from making an immediate decision and wrote a letter to Sister Perpetua telling her that I would not be joining the order just yet. Since I had given her to understand that I would probably be doing so,

18. Intelligence Testing

and reluctant to mislead her, I found the writing and posting of that letter one of the most difficult things I had ever done. After all, I owed the nuns a considerable debt of gratitude. They had stood by me when I really needed them.

I did not receive a reply. There was only *Schweigen*.

The University had suddenly come within my reach, but I had no means to get there. Sister Perpetua had failed to tell me about my entitlement to apply for a Commonwealth Scholarship. My parents were relieved that I had not sought admission to Rosanna, which would have required my father to provide me with a nun's dowry and even a 'wedding' dress.

But my father still held out against giving me any financial assistance to pay for further studies.

'You girls waste our money. You say you want to study for a profession and then you only end up getting married,' he said. Perhaps he was right. At the time, however, I did not intend to become someone's wife. I was now set on a University education to better equip me to make an informed choice about my future.

19

A Banquet of Life

Later in life I realised that Melbourne in the 1950s housed a tightly structured society. Access to people was relatively simple. You could seek out anyone you wished to meet. This network of contacts was to play its part in my own life.

After I discovered that I had matriculated, enabling me to study Arts at the only University in Melbourne, I visited Newman College, the Catholic residential male college where the chaplain for Catholic students was based. I had made an appointment to see him and waited in a side corridor of the Spanish Gothic warren surrounding the dining room.

I caught sight of a tall, silver-haired man in a black university gown with large sleeves. He had magisterial bearing, but his face was placid and his expression benign. He held out his hand, emanating warmth. Before I had even opened my mouth, he said, with a firm handshake: 'Welcome to University.' It felt good. But I was taken aback when I heard my inward voice announce boldly: 'The chains have fallen from me!'

The Jesuit priest before me, Father Jeremiah ('Jerry') Golden, became a soothing presence in my life and something of a friend. I was not the only one to feel comforted by his tranquil spirit. Other students and even staff attested to his reassuring influence.

It seems odd now that such a sense of liberation swept through my mind and body, since I knew that my problems were far from over. I was aware, however, that I had crossed from one zone to another, and that perhaps life would never be as difficult again. And in some respects that was how it was.

Born in Ireland, but educated from the age of twelve in Sydney, Father Golden still spoke with a soft Irish brogue. He gave me practical advice. He told me to see the Commonwealth Scholarship branch in town, to review my case. He also told me to visit Miss Alice Hoy of the University's Secondary Teachers' Training Unit to negotiate a teachers' training bursary. He told me about the Catholic association of university students, the Newman Society, and suggested I put down my name for its annual camp at Point Lonsdale. 'That's where older students meet "freshers" and induct them into University life, and clubs and activities for Catholics,' he directed.

Since the nuns at the Academy, for their own reasons, had not alerted me to the requirements for a Commonwealth Scholarship, I had no hope of picking one up now that they had all been announced. 'It's a pity,' the clerk told me, 'but we depend entirely on entry forms being lodged on time!' My lack of knowledge about how the secular world functioned was demonstrated by my ignorance of the way the government does its business through its agencies. I had no idea that allocations of funds had to be streamlined and accounted for within strict budgets on an annual basis. I was to find out later that a living allowance was means-tested against the income of one's parents, who were still held responsible for providing for a student's keep.

Since my father was secretive about his earnings and assets, I had no idea whether I qualified or not. He was certainly anxious for me to become financially independent. I had not even known how he compensated the nuns for my time as a boarder and paid school fees after I became a day student. Consequently, I had felt over-beholden to the nuns when I need not have been over-grateful.

I was equally innocent as I approached Miss Hoy. She expressed cordial interest in my applying for a teaching bursary. The Department of Education was short of teachers, but only in some subject areas. Were I to take up a bursary, which paid for my study costs and which provided a modest living allowance, I would have to sign a contract that on completing my studies, I would teach in a state school for three years, probably in a rural school. Should I fail to complete my degree, or not meet my obligation to serve the state of Victoria on my graduation, I would be obliged to repay all that money.

Given my feelings of insecurity, that was a problem. But I kept this to myself 'And what is it you wish to study and teach?' Miss Hoy asked me kindly. 'My interests in learning and communicating are in this order of significance,' I stated with self-conscious German high seriousness: 'Philosophy, Fine Arts, English and German Literature.' 'Oh,' she replied in astonishment, 'we don't teach Philosophy and Fine Arts in our schools. We have enough English Literature teachers. There's little demand for German. However, if you're prepared to teach French and History, then we can offer you a bursary on the basis of your results. They would need to show that you have application. I do see that French and History are your weakest Matriculation results.'

'In that case, Miss Hoy, I will have to turn down your kind offer,' I said, primly. 'But thank you for your generous assistance.' I offered a half-knee curtsy to the elderly lady. 'A pity,' she muttered.

I walked away with mixed feelings. I now had time to study with enjoyment and fulfilment. History at school had been dictated and learned 'off by heart' with the assistance of one textbook. There was no interpretative dimension. And our one Australian History text had been written by a geographer.

French had been a struggle for me. I could not overcome the surge of negative feelings which continued to link me to a time when I had to deal with English without a systematic bridge from German. Emotions dominated mental activity. On the threshold of puberty I had been forced to jettison my own much-loved first language and get into a muddle with a strange tongue. I had learned without systematic guidance. Traces of dyslexia affected me afterwards. What I wanted to say sometimes came out of my mouth as its very opposite, and 'sorry' was too often on my lips.

A great impediment to my accepting a bursary was the legal obligation to repay what the state laid out for me in training. What if I could not find a job? What if I wanted to teach for the nuns? If I did want to do this, it would take six or seven years to make that a possibility. I could not even think about such obstacles.

I was always hasty when I needed to be decisive. I had said 'no' to Miss Hoy and did not regret my decision to avoid French and History. I was not ready to study a subject as difficult as History at that time. I realised that it required massive amounts of reading, guided by an understanding of structured and thematic chronology.

As for English, I had lost my accent and it was now fluent, but a long way from being either correct or elegant. At Matriculation level, I had won those inter-school essay competitions. But my imperfect English was still slowing me down. It has been said that it takes at least six years to learn a foreign language really well. I had an almost pathological fear of speaking in public to an audience.

But I was not lacking in courage. I hid my extreme self-doubt by becoming defensively opinionated. Many of us lack confidence. This should not be used as a manipulative tool to gain sympathy and approval. But I was still confused about the different order of counting in English and German, differences in sentence structure, and the use of idiomatic language and prepositions. I frequently lost the mental clarity to communicate well. Besides, I lacked the linguistic skill to serve my personal need to see deeper meanings in everything, something attributable to both my German and Catholic upbringing.

While I waited to begin my new life, I worked on a conveyor belt at the Vacola tomato bottling factory near the Glenferrie Railway Station, counting rubber rings. This work made me realise how lucky I was to be going to University. I felt I ought to have some rapport with the girls who worked there and did get on reasonably well with them. But we had hardly any interests in common and I simply endured the tedious work, probably much as they did. I felt very sorry that they seemed to have fewer options in life than I.

Fortunately my mother supported my strong desire to continue my education. Some time in January 1953 her well-connected Irish-born neighbour, Mrs Yourelle, learned of my interest in University. She took a lively interest in my development, and had herself adopted two orphans. She was friendly with a woman whose husband worked at the University's School of Agriculture as a personnel officer. During a morning tea session between Mrs Yourelle and Mrs Johnson, his wife, my mother's friend learned that the School needed a student to work as a technical assistant to Miss Yvonne Aitken, a Lecturer in Botany. She was conducting research into leguminous nitrogen-fixing plants, like subterranean clovers, peas and lucerne. The aim was finding ways of increasing soil fertility, testing their capacity to prevent soil erosion, and providing fodder for animals in drought-stricken country. Her fieldwork supported her studies for a doctorate.

19. A Banquet of Life

Mrs Yourelle arranged for me to meet Mr Johnson and he in turn made an appointment for an interview with the Professor.

To my shame, my father also insisted on turning up for the interview, as if I was too dumb to cope on my own. Fortunately, the two men took an instant liking to one another. What Professor Wadham thought of what I had to say, I never learned. After answering a few questions and reminding him with foolish honesty that his name had been on two of the questions set for our Matriculation Biology paper which I had failed to pass, I was immediately employed full-time, with three hours spare time a week for my own study.

I did not know at the time that Miss Aitken had lived just behind my parents' Croydon property, and that she was still friends with a pair of women—a same-sex couple—who had owned *Glenfern* before the person from whom father had purchased it. 'Small world,' I said to my father.

Thus began that marvellous but exhausting year of travelling long distances between my home in Croydon and work in town at the University, thirty-seven kilometres away. I had to juggle thirty-seven hours of paid work with twelve hours of lectures and tutorials in Fine Arts and German Honours. I did the latter illegally as a part-time student, and also took some evening classes at the National Gallery Art School.

I was involved as well in the politics of the Newman Society's 'intellectual apostolate'. It became a year with too many commitments. But I nevertheless thought of it as a banquet of life.

My mother refused to take board from me. Instead, every pay day, I bought her something practical or beautiful. I also offered my brothers pocket money when I could afford it. I had experienced how embarrassingly dependent one could be without money.

With so much going on in my life of new-found freedom, I made some big mistakes. Other students made them as well, especially those from same-sex, lower-ranked religious schools. Traces of trauma from my earlier youth, so well repressed in the secure environment of school, now surfaced as I made my own choices. 'What will I do with my life?' became an urgent preoccupation. I spent far too much time probing that question instead of throwing myself into proper professional training.

The religious idealism generated by the Newman Society unfortunately diverted a number of us from the path of focused study. The girl who had studied so well at school now wasted a lot of time after a full day's work. Instead of going to the library, I enthusiastically joined the activities of the idealistic Catholic student community.

The Newman Society's summer camp at Point Lonsdale introduced newcomers to their program. The free social life which happened around simple huts under a lighthouse on the beach had its serious component: the Society's 'intellectual apostolate'. The conference program listed speeches and discussions on theological topics, including the role in the Church of an intellectual laity.

The Newman Society's intention was also to strengthen the ties between Catholic men and women, and unite them against the liberal secular ethos of the University.

At the core of the Society's thinking was that Catholic students ought to have a leavening influence on University life, and challenge the content of their study. Using exemplary scholarship, they ought to influence secular knowledge and civic morality through their expansive Catholic vision.

Secular intellectual life was ideally directed at the search for 'truth' and the greater reliability of knowledge of the natural order. The Newman Society sought to reconcile the secular ideals of the University and a liberal Catholic vision based on the writings of people such as Jacques Maritain, Yves Congar, Charles Péguy and Teilhard de Chardin. As I understood it, a complex ideology emerged in which the Incarnation of Christ had its relevance to the natural order. Implicit in it is a theology in which all creation has its place in the mind of God and evolves its sacred character to reach the purpose for which it was ordained.

The environmental implications of such a philosophy only emerged three decades later, although the poet James McAuley was already addressing the issues. He said that even rocks had a place in the redemption of matter.

Admirably, the Society aimed to challenge the University's purely utilitarian and vocational goals. An element of proselytising was inevitable in its moral program. We were proud to be linked to the avant-garde theological liberalism that emanated from France. It was an attempt to break with the Jansenist taint of conservative traditions with which Australian Irish Catholicism was then saturated. Such a project demanded from us intense application and intellectual clarity. We needed to know what we were defending. Such heady sense of importance is not unusual among people who feel insecure. But our young hearts were also fired by the desire to 'do good' and by the adventure of participating in the sacramental life of a Church still evolving within history towards its final destiny.

The Newman Society of 1953 consisted of a small cluster of leaders. At the helm were two academics, Max Charlesworh and Vincent Buckley. Max was a gracious, lucid philosopher who was an authority on Thomist theology, while Vincent wrote poetry and taught English Literature. While Buckley styled himself a public intellectual, it was Charlesworth who, later in life, became much more what his colleague had set out to claim for himself.

Max remained essentially the activist scholar while Vincent surrounded himself with a court of tough young men whose putative working-class origins and macho self-consciousness were cultivated with lashings of booze and disdain for so-called 'bourgeois' living.

Unlike other Catholic Action bodies, such as the Campion Society or the Young Catholic Workers, the Newman group was less involved in social issues of a political kind than in the mystique of their 'intellectual apostolate'.

I am pleased to say that Buckley and Charlesworth and the other leaders rejected the politically divisive, anti-Communist program of Bob Santamaria. Father Golden had the support of Archbishop Mannix in rejecting Santamaria's attempts to involve the University's apostolate in his own brand of political intrigue.

Many newcomers like us were confused and befuddled by the theology of Vincent Buckley's camp. Max Charlesworth, a true scholar, stood somewhat apart but made it his business to communicate in rationally accessible ideas. The quasi-mystical component of the theological investigations undertaken and extolled by the leaders of the Buckley camp demanded opinionated assent. Instinctively some of us thought we understood what they knew so positively. But I could see as well that the composition of this almost exclusively male leadership, with only a sprinkling of women, had severe drawbacks. Acceptable women were required to condone the almost prescriptive alcoholic over-indulgence of the leaders, and worship at their throne. It was all based as much on the cult of personality as it was on intellectual engagement.

Even then I saw this as a serious flaw in the way the Newman Society functioned. Max had won a postgraduate scholarship to study at Louvain. On his return from Belgium, he became increasingly alienated from the Buckley cult of personality. By then Buckley and his acolytes had become dominant, and presided over all 'apostolic' activities.

While I admired the integrity of Max Charlesworth and his commitment to his wife and family, I was quite enchanted by Buckley's poetic gifts and his mission as a 'visionary'. He and I shared an empathetic but distant association. When in early 1954 I asked him if the 'will of God' meant that God was the great puppeteer who pulled the strings according to His plan for us, he had no answer. Instead he advised me to flee my tensions and confusion by entering an enclosed convent in France, there to write poetry. I shrank from the elitism and dismissive gestures of Buckley and his followers towards 'bourgeois' students whose minds they assumed to be filled with trivialities. In fact, many of these despised outsiders were actually training themselves by focused study to become responsible professionals serving the community.

The Newman Society was designed to promote moral conduct among its members while engendering a very relaxed style of interaction. Some of its self-styled leaders did not provide a fitting example in either the way they conducted their personal lives or in the time they gave to reading and study. They were, however, ever-ready to express authoritative opinions. The male chauvinist leadership spent their social time in an apostolic ghetto of their own choosing, emerging only for formal occasions. They loved it like that.

By 1955, much of what we had been discussing appeared summarised in a mystifying ideological text. Unsurprisingly, Max Charlesworth was absent from the list of its authors. The essays were based on speeches delivered at a Universities' Catholic Federation of Australia conference. They were written by the self-appointed leaders of the 'intellectual apostolate', with official sanction by Co-Adjutor Archbishop Simonds. Needless to say, the collection was edited by Vincent Buckley. Entitled *Incarnation in the University*, it makes little sense when read today by someone not trained in theology. How did we understand it even then?

Outsiders ridiculed these mystifications we treated with such awe. I thought I understood instinctively what it was about and did not then see its contradictions. Few of us were equipped to have any real impact on the life of the University. Our opinions were still raw. Few of us studied philosophy at all or beyond the first year. But what was marvellous about *Incarnation* as applied to everyday and academic life was that it endowed secular life with a sacred character. This included secular knowledge. It eliminated the divide that had always existed in our thinking between spirit and matter, soul and body. Ordinary activities could be luminous, it told us. It extended academic studies beyond purely professional goals. We were excited to be seekers in a process of development, on the edge of new things.

There is no doubt that real value was extracted by many of us from the enlarged view of the world the apostolate was offering us. Not all Catholic students belonged to the Newman set. The Society was designed for idealists. We exchanged books by contemporary foreign authors in translation, and the works of our gifted Australians. We attended theatre, shared and made music together, and spent many hours in discussion over endless cups of coffee. We loved the sense of community it generated. The word 'dialogue', so commonly used today, was at the time relatively new.

Ecumenism, found in the writings of Dom Bede Griffith, was one discovery which matched our further need to associate with people of different faiths. Dom Bede attempted to link his English Benedictine Catholicism with the austerity of Hindu monks in south India, where he had settled. He tried to relate what he had learned in his Catholic upbringing to the Hindu path for reaching God.

This was particularly important to me. Many of us at the University associated with students from Southeast Asia supported by the Colombo Plan. I found myself surrounded by groups of encouraging friends. There was a heady atmosphere in my extra-curricular engagements. From insular Australia, the University's and the Newman Society's activities strengthened our bond with a wider world.

I had acquired a special friend on my first day at the engrossing German Literature lectures. She was Liesl Husak, another so-called foreigner. I enjoyed so constant a friendship with her that one observer, having difficulty with foreign names, unwittingly gave us a composite one, Lysol Girkhish. The name stuck with a number of our friends.

Liesl had a great sense of humour and taught me Mozart's crude nonsense canons. We used to sing them in two parts while walking at night through the University's parks. We still sang together as we walked barefoot along the wind-swept beaches during my second summer camp at Point Lonsdale. As we scanned the waters of the Great Southern Ocean we laughed at the audacity of one of our favourite Biblical psalms: 'Bless the Lord, all ye whales.'

War had displaced Liesl. She was on her own. She had suffered her parents' death by starvation. Anglicanism attracted her, although her origins were Austrian and Sudeten-Deutsch (Czech-German). She thought that my early experiences in the camp had equipped me better for community life, since it had offered the possibilities for many friendships. She herself preferred the depth of loyalty of single friendships to numbers of friends.

When I turned eighteen, I received an official invitation to become an Australian citizen. The alternative was to retain my Austrian and Turkish birthrights. I did not hesitate to take this serious step. I felt I had no real homeland in which I had lived as a child, no place to which I could say I belonged, no bonded loyalty which I might betray. I was by historical accident a displaced person. Australia was now offering me a haven.

It seemed to me a land of opportunity in which ordinary citizens could compete with the wealthy and privileged. I was by now acquiring an increasing sense of psychological freedom.

I made the necessary arrangements to become an Australian citizen without involving my family. When I turned up at Ringwood Town Hall in October, I was the only person there. In an empty room the Mayor of Ringwood was dressed in full regalia, with robes and chain. His clerk acted as scribe and witness. With my hand on the Bible I was asked to foreswear all other foreign allegiances and devote myself in exclusive loyalty to Australia, its 'head of State, the Queen of England and all her heirs'.

With the signing of my name I dismissed my inherited connections with both Austria and Turkey. I had done nothing to earn Australian citizenship except to live here for a number of years. In Germany even a third-generation Turk could not obtain citizenship because of a law which attempted to control the privileges associated with the blood lines of Germans. I thought that was an unjust law based on a fantasy.

19. A Banquet of Life

There was no ceremony to celebrate my citizenship. I went back to the University and read some poems by Judith Wright to celebrate my official kinship with an austere and brave land. In *Bora Ring*, she found a way of linking Australian situations with the larger canvas of culture and tradition:

> The song is gone; the dance
> is secret with the dancers in the earth,
> the ritual useless, and the tribal story
> lost in an alien tale.

In *South of My Days*, she described the character of an Australian landscape in all its harsh beauty:

> South of my days' circle, part of my blood's country,
> rises that tableland, high delicate outline
> of bony slopes wincing under the winter,
> low trees blue-veined and olive, outcropping granite—
> clean, lean, hungry country.

The south of her days, so eloquently described in her poem, was to become the north of mine.

My brother Peter, and then my parents, became Australian citizens a few years after I did. When my parents were 'naturalised' at Lilydale Shire Hall, there were at least twenty candidates. Father's fine Viennese sense of farce got the better of him when the officiating councillor pronounced the 'Queen's heirs' phrase as her 'hairs'. To show off his knowledge of English, my father laughingly shouted out 'her *hairs*' so loudly that the clerk in attendance stooped to whisper in the ear of his superior to correct him.

At home, so energised was Rudolf by the occasion that he uncorked every bottle in his cupboard, obliging us all to 'drink up!' even when the essence for Black Tulip 'cocktails' was the only drink left in his liquor cupboard.

Well before then, in late 1953, I was being respectfully courted by a young man from the inner core of the Newman Society. His fine physical attributes were the product of the Irish-Australian working class.

My parents had taught me to admire social battlers. My escort was a hero. He had risked his own life in the 'rip' at Point Lonsdale to save a drowning fellow student. He drove me home late in the evening on the back of his motorbike. As our friendship deepened he called with his mother one Sunday to take me to the Dandenongs. He came right into our Croydon home to collect me.

I was concerned at the direction towards domesticity of this situation, but I was too timid to say anything. So it was fortunate that the young man spoiled his chances forever in my eyes by making scathing remarks about my 'bourgeois' parents. He reached that swift conclusion from one brief visit, based on the way my mother had furnished our simple, rambling wooden home in German style.

I was not myself conspicuously bourgeois in those days. On the contrary. At the first opportunity, while my friend was away chopping wood to earn money, I wrote to him that I intended to become a nun. It was at the time both a true and a self-protective declaration. Catholic students respected such an intention. To them it was not the world-denying final act it appears today.

My own paid work for Miss Aitken involved me in mostly the boring routine detail that is essential in experiments. But it also opened up new horizons, bringing me closer to my adopted homeland. Miss Aitken was a good role model for independent women. She and another woman lectured in Botany and Agronomy to classes of all-male students. A tall and gentle Anglican who lived at Janet Clarke Hall at the University, she took her faith seriously. She belonged to the Moral Rearmament Movement. Her hobby was watercolour painting, at which she was still awkward.

The family of my young colleague in the laboratory, Susan, lived in Ballarat. She was a Science student engaged to be married to a young chemist who practised in Charlton. She suffered her separation from him. We two laboratory assistants got on well and were equally bored with the work of recording numbers of peas and lengths of cross-bred clovers. We welcomed our field trips to the country to plant up experimental crops of legumes, as far away as Walpeup beyond Ouyen in the Mallee, Dookie Agricultural College, at Scoresby near Ferntree Gully, and Newstead near Castlemaine.

Once we arrived at Ouyen at 4 am and had to wait until 7 for a train connection to Walpeup railway siding. On arrival we found only a wheat silo beside the track. Then we were met and taken to the agricultural research plots. We slept in a shearing shed on sleeping bags on the floor, and during the day watched the mournful crows flap above the red earth in which we planted our crops.

Wherever we travelled I took a drawing pad and pencils to record my observations through pictures. The paints travelled with me in tins. I dipped my brushes into creek water to record how bushfires had left some weathered community of ghostly gums that had failed to come into leaf again.

The constantly nagging pain in my heart was easing. I found solace everywhere in the countryside. The hybrid clovers I looked after in the University's glasshouses carried the names of their places of origin: Walpeup, Traralgon, Scoresby and Tallarook. These names still evoke the fragrance of freshly cut clover. At home in Croydon, for the first time, I began to help my parents with the gardening they practised with such skill. And my father also took us on long day trips around Victoria.

At University my over-full calendar began to affect the studies I really enjoyed. Examinations loomed. I needed to 'swat' in preparation for German and Fine Arts. Full-time work was a major impediment to this. Arriving home late at night at Croydon, I was obliged to walk the three kilometres from the railway station along the unlit bush paths that shadowed the roads. I feared I would be kidnapped.

My father refused to collect me from the station. He merely insisted that I was to come home by the last bus. This left the railway station at 7 pm. When I once discussed the matter with him, he said: 'You have a choice. You have made your choice to come later.' In my crowded timetable my 'choice' was 'no choice'. I had to walk in fear.

Enthusiasm for my 'banquet of life' was bringing on a gluttony of involvement. It also meant I half-completed many tasks. I had to do something. First I gave up singing with the University's Choral Society. Then the art lessons with Charles Bush at the National Gallery School had to go.

Then I was offered the opportunity of a twenty-hour job by the acting director of the Conservatorium of Music which was next to my place of work. I jumped at the opportunity.

My boss was the flamboyant Catholic priest, Dr Percy Jones. I had not known him personally, but had often watched his confident rotund figure in white robes as he conducted the outstanding St Patrick's Cathedral choir. He also trained it. In his home, I was to become his switchboard girl for twenty hours a week, have free lodging in an attic, and a little pocket money as well. Father Jones thought it 'a good deal'.

I thought that this arrangement would give me time to study in the library. I could perhaps use his books as well, and be rewarded occasionally by listening to the sound of music from a collection of records built up by an expert musician—if only through the key-hole.

When I arrived to take up my position at St George's Presbytery in North Carlton, I was told that the housekeeper whom I had been hired to assist was ill, and had gone on leave. I later heard she had left with a nervous breakdown. Surely I could do some of her work, Father Jones suggested.

I could make the beds, do some sweeping, cook the evening meal for him and two curates, and also attend to the phone.

My cooking skills were confined to one recipe, for a German apple cake. Surely I could learn to do a simple meal of grilled chops in a jiffy, he persisted. I was to be his servant. After two weeks I realised that I had jumped from a difficult situation to an impossible one. Both my father and Professor Wadham had been angry when I left the School of Agriculture job. I began to think they may have been right. So little free time did I now have, that when I did get some hours off I tended to fritter them away in the reassuring company of friends who called to take me to town.

Father Golden was concerned about my situation, and he was right. I failed Fine Arts and achieved indifferent results in Honours German, largely because of my woefully inadequate attendance.

He was able to secure me a position as a waitress-in-residence at Newman College when the following University year began. I was privileged, since at that time female students were generally forbidden to work at this all-male college. I was also able to obtain work during the long vacations as a nurse-waitress at Heidelberg Repatriation Hospital. This job I obtained through the University's Appointments Board.

19. A Banquet of Life

I put my written resignation on Dr Jones' desk I wrote that my contract had been to work for twenty hours answering the telephone, but I had found myself instead involved in all manner of housework for seventy hours a week, for the same small pay. I was not seeking more money, but my freedom.

Next day I found my letter scrunched up in the waste-paper basket I had to empty every day. I wrote the same note more emphatically and posted it formally, through the mail. Dr Jones was furious as he read out the letter in his study: 'What do you think you are doing?' he demanded. I repeated the words of my latest letter. He could do nothing but protect his pride by stating that I had been a disappointment to him. He had hired me because German girls were said to be orderly and industrious. I had, he said, embarrassed him when the Italian Ambassador was obliged to use his toilet.

I was surprised at the words which came out of my meek mouth. They stated that I was not aware that I had been employed to clean toilets. Dr Jones and I parted acrimoniously. But he did not bear me a lasting grudge and acknowledged me as a 'friend' when our paths crossed on a few future occasions.

My knowing where he slept was also a bonus when, a couple of years later, after a Newman Ball in the nearby Exhibition Building, a group of us gathered outside his bedroom at midnight to serenade him in harmony, through one of his own and other liturgical compositions. He did not appear, but we found out later that he had been deeply gratified.

Despite the increasing liberalisation of my ideas, subordination to the authority of bachelor clerics prevailed for a long time. Such attitudes can be summed up in a conservative poem that was being circulated at the time, which I loved. It was Gertrud von le Fort's *Hymn to the Church*. Two lines sum up my dilemma, the choice between adherence to painful authority and what the English divine, Ronald Knox, called 'enthusiasm': 'My will fell on your law as on a sword' and 'Your nights are like rich wine'.

But then I had also discovered *The Waters of Silence* by the American journalist who had become an ascetic monk, Thomas Merton. Merton and others kept the ideal of contemplation alive in modern Catholic society. A number of us were thinking of entering a religious order to better engage with this. I also met an inspirational Thomist scholar, Tony Barton, just before he began his training for the Dominican priesthood. He introduced me to his friend, Jim Provan.

My lifelong friendship with Jim had its origins in his loan to me of his grandmother's white bakelite radio. Instinctively he knew that I needed music in my lonely work breaks at Heidelberg Hospital. Our love of music and the Catholic liturgy which had influenced his conversion to Catholicism, initially cemented our friendship. Tony Barton's and my good friend, Kevin Keating, told me that on the night of James Provan's reception into our Church, he had walked like a cat on top of the bookcases in Barton's modest South Yarra flat, singing liturgical praises.

Tony Barton, who used to iron his shirts on the floor—so limited were his worldly possessions—influenced a number of us with his uncompromising virtue. The Jesuit scholastic John Cowburn also attracted a cluster of cultured people. Margot Boyd, Doreen Breen and Philip Martin became my friends.

The relative merits of the contemplative life and lay initiatives were challenged by the 1954 Newman Society summer camp. Those of us flirting with the idea of entering religious life stuck together. One hot evening while we waded in the sea near Deirdre O'Connor's home, Peter Wertheim outlined the virtues of the Franciscan order, Deirdre the Poor Clares, Margot and I the Dominicans. We knew of Jim Provan's love of the Benedictines, and that Peter Crane was to join the Jesuits, while his sweetheart, Christine Boland, had committed herself to the Franciscan Missionaries of the Sacred Heart who worked at a leper colony in north Australia.

Middle-aged John Dormer, a kind of Al Grassby of the lay apostolate, had appeared at the previous summer camp. He stressed the work of the laity in the Church. Educated at Downside Benedictine Abbey and at the military academy, Sandhurst, he had then served in the Spanish Civil War on the side of Franco. He had returned to Melbourne after a visit to France, an ardent promoter of the Belgian Cardinal Cardijn's Jocist teaching which was already an inspiration for our lay apostolate.

In France, 'worker priests' were sent to factories in ordinary clothes to serve those who had no time to go to Church or who had left it altogether. Dormer had memorised what he had to say to us and kept repeating himself in long and repetitive monologues. As the heir to Toohey's Brewery, and with his background as a British military officer, he had a certain cachet in some eyes. His dress was untidy and his mind bemused by the message he felt he had to preach. Repetition, he must have thought, leads to absorption. He always lived in rented rooms in guest-houses and gave little indication he had inherited wealth. He ultimately forfeited much of it through his communitarian interests and his improvidence.

About that time there also appeared in our midst, with motorbike and guitar, a young peach-cheeked German priest. He had been studying for the Catholic priesthood when he was forcibly conscripted into Hitler's defence forces. He had risen through Navy ranks to become the commander of a submarine and, while decorated for bravery, was also placed on a Hitler death list for rescuing enemy shipwreck survivors. Being taken as a prisoner to England had saved his life.

After completing his studies he was finally ordained and came to Australia. For a while he was a charismatic presence at Newman Society functions. A delightfully relaxed and loving human being with a sense of fun, a propensity to blush and no trace of repressive prurience, he preached a social philosophy that nevertheless embraced traditional values.

Women and men, he told us, were designed as two halves of a whole. Women were intended to bring out the best in men by rendering joyful service. Sylvester had been born in Breslau, and came home with me to enjoy my mother's Silesian hospitality. He continued to associate with my agnostic parents long after I had left home.

The Easter of 1954 was a particularly heady one. It was soon after the first midnight vigil at St Patrick's Cathedral that Margot Boyd and I decided to enter the Dominican order of nuns at Carisbrooke on the Isle of Wight. It was an enclosed contemplative order.

Margot was a part-time Arts student with a passion for music and she worked at the University library. She knew where we might go to become contemplative nuns. She turned up the correct pages in the British Catholic Directory and pointed at Carisbrooke. We decided then and there that we would go together.

Margot's parents were 'good Catholics'. When I told my non-conforming mother of our plan, she became so hysterical that I immediately abandoned the idea, temporarily at least. I argued with myself that something was wrong if God's will demanded such sacrifice from one's parents. I knew that Jesus had said that those who followed Him had to abandon their parents and siblings. It was a lesson that appeared repeatedly in our Catholic education. In our Church this was interpreted as a direction to priests, nuns and brothers. Marriage was not advertised as part of that theological scenario.

I decided to wait and see. Love for people was the most important imperative, I had come to believe. My father's disgruntlement I viewed as a product of his internment and of his lingering attachment to European formalities in a much freer society. I began to strengthen my evolving Christian humanist viewpoint as central to my search for meaning. The test of love should be that one was prepared to walk through Hell for those to whom one was committed.

The intoxication of our thinking left an imprint even in our dreams. I recall dreaming one night about the famous poetic lines: *As idle as a painted ship/Upon a painted ocean*. In my dream I found myself in the two-dimensional space of a painting. I was in an open train on a hilltop in a thunderstorm which ended abruptly as if the next slide had been shown. Grey smooth air lay all about. I stretched out my hand and found the air frozen. My hand in the frozen air activated the sound of a bell. Then the two dimensions opened up further into a glorious panorama: a beach far beyond the hill. The sound of the bell chimed the sound of peace right down the beach.

I have often pondered how the human mind can grasp in a dream a contradiction otherwise impossible to conceptualise, such as 'to be' and 'not to be', or air and ice, at one and the same time. Perhaps, I thought, that is what 'talking in tongues' is all about: a private trick of the mind born of desire and not readily communicable to others.

By June 1954 Dormer wanted to bring all the factions of the Newman Society together. To this end he held a party at his home in July. What this achieved for me personally was of a different order altogether. His party sealed my fate. There I met a teacher from Xavier College, James Griffin.

Jim and his best friend Vincent Buckley spent the evening talking to me. Vin asked me to sing the Nazi *Horst Wessel* song, as satire. I could not remember it. Had I ever known it?

19. A Banquet of Life

Jim won my heart on subsequent meetings with his fine voice and trenchant mind. His body, too, was palpably energetic and pleasing. He had been an outspoken critic of the way the Newman Society conducted itself. Vincent Buckley had heard it all at first hand. At first Jim's criticisms disturbed no one.

Jim proved a steadfast lover during our courtship. He neither left me for the Australian booze-ups of his regular male acquaintances, nor showed any of the controlling characteristics of my Austrian father. Neither Jim nor I had been truly happy before we met—so we told each other—with him taking the high ground in this commiseration.

We were both confused about the direction of our lives. I felt more comfortable with Jim than with others because he combined in his life an informal Australian upbringing with a deep interest and understanding of the history and culture of Europe, and of Britain and Ireland. Neither of us fitted happily into the social circumstances in which we found ourselves. We found inspiration and comfort in our loving association. He was an accomplished and well-read teacher and a beguiling lyric singer.

I admired his refusal to accept received knowledge at face value, and his nonchalance regarding social and materialistic advantages. We agreed on this. An independent thinker, who quite courageously defied social conformity, he told me he had known no truly happy day until I walked into his life. 'When I first met you,' he said, 'you were like a figure that had stumbled out of *The Book of Kells*.' That's the way he described my awkward shyness.

I was touched by his compassionate response to all the contradictions with which I was quietly wrestling. I held out a loving hand to his temperamental anguish.

Jim brought a new focus to my life. He had the ability to bridge Australian and European ways. His religious scepticism was a challenge. I perceived him not as someone bent on desecration or iconoclasm but impelled by the right for each of us to discover what was correct or true.

He shared my love of music and I thought I was being courted by someone with a future as a singer. I could live with a singer. On reflection, I could not have followed a religious path that did not include classical music. It is as essential to my well-being as the air I breathe.

We sometimes stayed up all night, innocently walking the streets of Melbourne. Then we began to become more intimate. On one occasion he serenaded me all night with songs by Schubert, Schumann, Mahler, Handel and Purcell. He sang old Irish folk songs and seventeenth-century Italian songs. I already knew them, but the depth of feeling he brought to them was particularly persuasive.

He told me, however, that there was a degree of narcissism in being a singer. He asserted that to follow a profession in singing would make his intellectual life difficult to maintain.

I consented to become his wife not long after we began to 'go out'.

My lover had of course taken me into his arms and away from the camaraderie of other Catholic students. We had embarked on a private journey. We maintained, however, some strong community involvements.

An image comes back to me when I think of our courtship. It is afternoon. We lie in each other's embrace in the faded boarding house where he is living. The pious school I once attended is nearby. It is the Academy's sports' day. We can hear the girls barracking for their teams behind the high, grey convent walls. I can see the four colours that attract their screams. I reflect on how far I have moved in just over three years.

I hear again the German verses from *Tristan and Isolde* which he and I speak in unison. T.S. Eliot had quoted them in *The Waste Land*, which Jim knows and I have been studying. It links German and Irish legends, and our forebears:

> *Frisch weht der Wind*
> *Der Heimat zu.*
> *Mein Irisch Kind,*
> *Wo weilest du?*
>
> [Fresh blows the wind towards the coast.
> My Irish child, where do you linger?]

Indeed, I think, is he waiting for me, or I for him? Each is thinking of the other. We are both 'the child' which the poem is calling from a legend about lovers. He identifies with his Irish antecedents. The Nordic legend is familiar to German writers, and I know it.

19. A Banquet of Life

In the latter part of 1954, Jim and I became not only inseparable companions, but lovers. Then the feathers began to fly. The inner core of the Newman Society behaved as if they owned me. Father Golden, John Dormer and Vincent Buckley tried to separate us. The friendship between Vincent and Jim broke up over this issue. My self-appointed guardians conveyed that I belonged to the established community. I had no right to leave it with an intellectual sceptic. Father Golden began to spy on us and had me in tears in the rain one night for the best part of an hour.

When John Dormer could not win me over to abandon Jim and become a key worker in his apostolate, he followed us at the end of the year to Portsea. Jim and I were working in a hotel dining room to make money for a planned overseas trip. Ostensibly he came to paint with me, but then he made the preposterous suggestion that he and I could conduct a celestial platonic association while Jim possessed my baser body. He told Jim to leave the apostolate alone and stick to his schoolteaching. He then wrote a sprawling ninety-six-page letter to this effect.

I had never encouraged his attention in any way. If anything I was aloof, almost rudely so. All this now seems strange. But it is how ideologically oriented associations often run their affairs. Officers in the various Christian churches and in political parties can be equally careless of individual rights. None of this was unique to the Newman Society.

A number of people outside the University were also opposed to the prospect of a marriage between two people they judged as so different in temperament and attitudes. Never mind the friendship and camaraderie that underpinned our love affair, which included our writing small essays to each other on the principles of aesthetic judgement, and attempting to teach each other philosophy from a textbook in the sand caves along the beach. Jim and I were both comrades and lovers.

One woman warned me that if Jim went overseas, I would never see him again. Another of his 'friends' bet two bottles of champagne that a marriage between us would not last. My English tutor, Tom Dobson, wrote to my home address after I announced that I was quitting my course to save money to marry abroad: 'Please put off your marriage until you have completed your studies. You are one of my more promising Literature students,' he urged. I was of course flattered that the intelligence testers had been so wrong in their cliched predictions for me.

There were other people who failed to understand the person I was and my potential as wife, mother, companion, teacher and scholar. Many young women were similarly disadvantaged.

High on the list of those intractably opposed to my marriage was my father. Like Tom Dobson's, his viewpoint was also unexpected, but much more novel. In April 1955, not long before he left for Rome on the Otranto, and with the respectful formality then expected when daughters had not reached their 'majority', Jim had asked my father's permission to marry me. He had invited my parents to dine with us at The Italian Society, our favourite cheap restaurant. The conversation was cheerful enough but Father Rudolf and Lover Jim made men's talk on politics, Jim treading warily, while Mother Elfriede and I somewhat apprehensively exchanged pleasantries.

When the coffee arrived, Rudolf abruptly asked: 'Well, Mr Griffin. There is something you wanted to talk to me about.' 'It's quite simple,' replied the host. 'I want to marry your daughter.'

'Well, I have nothing against you. You seem a decent young man,' Rudolf conceded, 'but Helga—she is not fit to get married.' He then proceeded to present 'Mr Griffin' with a catalogue of all my failings. 'Well, if that's all,' Jim replied cheerfully, 'I will take her with all her faults.'

This led to a brief but thunderous silence, and the subject was dropped for the time being. But my father's uncouth conduct put my mother firmly on our side.

I must have ignored the catalogue of my shortcomings, so used to them had I become, for I do not now recall what my father said so publicly and so rudely. And I held back my tears. My father could not abide to see anyone close to him in tears.

Jim was avidly interested in Italian Renaissance history and Italy's great traditions of art and architecture. In early May, on the eve of his departure for Italy for an indefinite stay, he rang my parents to say goodbye. As casually as he could, he informed Rudolf that he had put a deposit on my passage on the Otranto the following year.

Rudolf reacted angrily: 'Why did you do that?' Jim told him that if he saw fit to give permission we would marry immediately I arrived; if not, then we would wait until June, when I turned twenty-one.

19. A Banquet of Life

In May 1955 Jim sailed away. He was joined by his friend Desmond O'Grady and my friend Margot Boyd. Both had asked Jim if they might accompany him on the journey he had already planned. Margot was beginning her travels to the enclosed Dominicans on the Isle of Wight. Jim Provan and the Newman Society's motet choir were there to farewell the three travellers.

I usually told my mother almost everything. Such openness is surprising, given my shyness and reticence. However, while she and others knew that I had planned to marry my love, no one knew anything of our deeper relationship, or of the specific content of our twice-weekly letters after Jim had left Australia.

'Your Nordic name is to me like a distant bell ringing across wastelands of snow,' he wrote. Before his departure from Australia he and I had playfully speculated that we would honeymoon in the Scottish Highlands and call our first daughter Solveig.

His feelings for me were too precious to share with others. But even so, it is unlikely that if I had informed my father of this romanticism his heart would have softened. It may, in face, have hardened it further. At a time when few women were in the paid work force, a father like mine sought in a future son-in-law a sound financial provider, not a writer of poetic sentiments.

I wondered whether my father had learned anything from his internment. After all, he had lost everything, then had imagined and made a new life in this land of promise.

In June 1955 I dropped my University studies and moved back home. I was prepared to brave my father's boorishness in order to save money. I managed to secure a clerical position at George Taylor's Secondary Coaching College, having secretly (and immorally) put my age up to twenty-one to earn a better wage. I need not have worried about the rights and wrongs of this. Taylor's used me not only as a clerk, but had me coaching private students and migrants in English as a second language, for which I had no qualifications. I worked assiduously, preparing my lessons separately for each student. Unaware of my plans to marry, Mr George Taylor, his son-in-law Mr Whitehead and Miss Sexton, who together ran the institution, offered to have me trained as a secondary teacher in return for joining their staff. I had to tell them the truth. They were good about it.

Meanwhile, I kept up my association with people at the University. Some of Jim's older childless friends indulged me with their concern. Although much older than I, and better-educated, they provided me with protective assurances.

One night, two cars with six of my own associates, three women and three men, brought me home after dinner at a restaurant. Liesl was with us, and her male companion, John, who played the violin. I served tea to the group and took out my inadequate violin, hoping that someone with experience could make something of it. Our performance was quite good and we sang along in harmony.

Suddenly the door of my parents' bedroom opened and my father came stomping out in his striped pyjamas. Even though his residence was a three-acre farm with no near neighbours, he shouted at my companions to get out of his house. What were they thinking of, visiting so late at night and disturbing the peace?

My friends slunk out. I apologised to them in the driveway. It was all my fault. I ought to have known that parents raised elsewhere still valued the stricter formalities of their own upbringing.

I often brought friends home during the day, and mother was always ready to feed them and exercise her tact and charm, delighting in intelligent company. One evening, months previously, the courteous but eccentric John Dormer, whose nose was dripping from colds that winter, had absent-mindedly wiped it on a tea-towel while helping my mother with the washing-up. I was horrified, and thought that she would reprimand him. But she silently signalled me to stay calm and, after our guests had gone, washed all the dishes again. She retained both her presence of mind and her admirable style when she was enjoying herself.

All this time I was getting ready to leave to go overseas. My father still refused to give me his permission to marry Jim. I was not sure he wanted me to marry at all, except perhaps a man of means from his cultural background. His insistence on thwarting my intention to marry Jim made things bad not only for me but also for my mother. She continued to support my proposed marriage. Had she and Rudolf not done exactly the same thing, left home and got married against the wishes of his parents? She could be more rational than he and told him so, over and over again.

19. A Banquet of Life

She then arranged secretly to have a wedding dress made for me by a Russian dress-maker who lived close to Melbourne. She borrowed money from her sister's husband, promising to pay him back in small sums from the house-keeping money she was given each week by Rudolf. She had no money of her own, and could not buy presents independently. She was beholden to him for everything.

The white lace dress took a long time to finish, and I was obliged to make far too many compromises about its style. My mother was all fired up by what she presumed to be my future social life in Rome, at diplomatic functions. Jim had secured a position in the city as a translator with the Australian Legation. I did not share her optimism. The two older women designed a three-quarter-length dress with a halter neck and matching fitted jacket. It was to serve as both wedding and cocktail dress. But these two European women were out of touch. One did not wear white lace dresses at the cocktail hour.

However, since my mother would not be at my wedding, I humoured her dreams for me. While her own dress-making was perfect, her once-impeccable dress sense was now hopelessly out of fashion in Australia. I loathed the stiff tulip-shaped cap tailored to hold a veil. I was relieved when Jim's gentle and generous mother knitted me a lace wool shawl for our first baby. I knew immediately when I would first use it. Naturally I did not show it to my demanding mother.

My mother urged my father to present me with a useful wedding gift. But he baulked at the idea. He remained unmoved even when he helped my brother Peter choose an opal on a gold chain in a jeweller's shop.

I was to sail away on a Saturday in February. My father was prepared to drive me and my luggage in his Hillman sedan to the ship, which left at five in the afternoon.

On the day, I was packed and ready to leave whenever it suited him. But it was still only mid-morning. Suddenly, impetuously, he told me to come into town with him. Just the two of us. He wanted to buy me something. 'Another of his mad schemes!' I thought. I liked to be discriminating in how I spent his or my money.

It was already 11 o'clock, and we would not arrive in town until 11.30. On a Saturday, the shops closed at noon. But he was set on taking me. I was concerned that no accident happened to the car on the day it also had to take me to the ship. But off we went and in one shop father urged me to pick forty pounds worth of linen. It was a fortune! And how was I to pack all this so late? He assured me that he would provide me with one of his own suitcases.

In a space of less than twenty minutes I came away with two sets of double bed sheets with matching pillow cases, the first coloured sheets I had ever seen. We added four towels, a blue checked table cloth with serviettes, and a set of four table mats and serviettes with a fish motif. When moved by sentiment my father could be extremely generous.

20

Marriage in Rome

We leaned in silence against the lower deck railings of the Otranto, a one-class passenger ship, my middle-aged father and I. Our gaze followed the people who had just left us and were re-grouping on the wharf below.

Looking back as an old woman with much family experience behind me, I now question why he and I managed to make life so difficult for each other. Remembering that day, I see again on the wharf below us my elegant mother, vexed and sad, in her smart home-sewn cotton dress, high heels and black picture hat. She was flanked by my two brothers. Three young women who had been at school with me also attended her. One of them, Pamela Poynton, placed her arm reassuringly on my mother's shoulder. Behind my family stood a cluster of student acquaintances from University.

By this time my father should have been leaving the boat as well. Why was he still on board? It was usual for him to expect others to obey instructions immediately, and the signal had been given to leave. I wondered whether the wanderlust of his youth had gripped him again.

The two-funnelled *Otranto*, once a steamship, had been converted to diesel. On my first long solo journey away from home, she was on her second-last outward bound voyage. Adventuring students usually booked themselves into the dingy cheapest cabins, well below the waterline.

The voyage would finish for most at Southampton, the access port for London. I was to get off earlier, in Naples. When I arrived in Italy, I would be three months short of twenty-one, the age when parental consent for marriage was no longer legally necessary.

The silence between my father and myself diverted my attention to movements in the crowd. Late-comers struggled up the gangplank with suitcases, rugs, cartons. Behind us people pushed and shoved, clumsily in each others' way. Bouquets of flowers passed by in the hands of strangers, and with them, conspicuously boxed, was what I heard later was a wedding cake. I did not know then that the cake was for me, sent by my future husband's cousin. It would never arrive in my hands. Like so many good intentions, it was lost on the way.

A man's voice urged once more over the loudspeakers: 'All visitors please leave. All visitors leave now. Final call. All visitors leave now!' I felt my father stir at last and then his heavy hand on my shoulder. In an uncharacteristic gesture, because he was not given to either verbal or physical expressions of personal endearment, he leaned towards me and said with barely concealed tenderness: 'Don't hold it against me that I stood in your way.'

Although often voluble, sometimes even boisterous in company, he was reticent about his deeper feelings. After years of mutual stubbornness, we now cut our moorings, as I impetuously hugged him. 'Of course I won't,' I promised.

I could feel his silent struggle not to resist me. Perhaps unable to further soften our obstinate relationship, or afraid of the feelings his one moist eye betrayed, he turned abruptly and disappeared into the crowd.

Because of my astonishment at my father's expression of concern on the *Otranto*, I do not now remember whether any other words followed his departure from my side. I recognised the courage it had taken him to broach the problem between us. Had I lost a crucial opportunity to strengthen a new friendship with him? I wondered about this as I saw his determined face and stocky figure emerge from the throng below as he joined the family group on the wharf.

By now streamers were flying towards the deck. Those that landed formed a colourful canopy which trembled ever so slightly in the breeze that stirred from the sea. Others, failing to unite giver and taker, joined a graveyard of soggy paper between ship and wharf, in water lapping against the pylons.

20. Marriage in Rome

A group of students from the Newman Society began to sing. There was a cloying smell of engine oil and of musty mussels encrusted on damp wood. With a lump in my throat, I recognised out of the din below the a cappella music my friends and I had shared for the best part of three years. My gallant, handsome friend Jim Provan, and the singers whom he conducted, offered them to me in several parts.

The old music was beginning to link my journey spiritually with other travels, different times, other places. The performers were offering me a blessing for a safe passage. Many of them would dearly have liked to travel abroad as well. But most were bound by responsibilities.

They were still singing when the ship hooted and its loudspeaker began to broadcast a farewell. Passengers joined with the crowd on the wharf in song: *Now is the hour/ When we must say goodbye* … As the singing swelled and streamers flew, the pilot vessels began to pull the Otranto backwards, away from the wharf. She turned laboriously in a huge half-circle until she was pointed to the Port Phillip heads.

I was leaving with a cabin stacked with wedding presents from my friends. A wedding poem in my pocket was dedicated to us by Philip Martin.

As the ship moved out, we travellers moved towards the deck still facing the wharf. Hands and handkerchiefs waved as the gap between ship and land began to widen. It was like the fluttering of hundreds of wings.

It gave me a grand feeling, my floating away like that on board a stately ship in the late afternoon haze of a hot summer's day. I stared at the people on the wharf as if to capture the scene forever. Soon they began to shrink and disappear below the horizon, as the ship gathered speed. I then looked west to the high waters off Williamstown, sheened with early evening light. Later, as we approached the heads, a strong breeze accompanied the sudden cold change so typical, yet unexpected, of a Melbourne high summer. The bonfires Father Golden had said would be lit on the beach at Point Lonsdale to farewell me were foiled by a sudden wind.

During my journey to Naples I received mail from Jim at each port and at each I posted letters to him. At Aden I followed a large bearded man in flowing robes through a sinister-looking part of town to post my last letter at the office to which he had directed me. I felt uneasy. Was I being sensible? How safe was this town for foreign visitors? Did the white slave trade still exist? Imagine if I never arrived in Naples!

Already at dawn the temperature had risen to almost forty degrees Celcius. This desert township beneath its looming rock seemed eerie and sinister. All the other passengers who had disembarked had gone to tour an oasis.

But I got back on board safely. There I could read the air-letters from home and from Jim. He ardently outlined his latest wedding plans. He promised to be on the wharf at Naples when the *Otranto* pulled into port. I was to be welcomed with flowers, an unusual gesture for an Australian man.

After a brisk passage through the grey and choppy Mediterranean Sea, still throwing off the squalls of winter, we arrived in Naples on 23 March. Groups of companions from the ship left on tours to Pompeii. But some were so excited about my wedding that they stayed with me to catch a glimpse of the groom. But Jim was not there. I had done without breakfast to be sure not to miss his arrival. Time went ticking by, and still no one! What could have gone wrong? Had there been an Australian bucks' party, and Jim too unwell to come? What should I do?

He could hardly have changed his mind! My nervousness was catching. The three people still with me told me to forget about the wedding and come with them to London. At 9.30—which seemed like hours later—Jim appeared on the wharf in a state of agitation. A quick embrace and then we had hurriedly to lug my two cases off the boat to catch the train to Rome. There were formalities still to be completed before our marriage the very next day.

Jim spoke rapidly to me as we moved. Someone was trying to push him out of his job with the Australian Legation on which we would both now depend for a living. He was agitated, restless, shy. We were both reticent after eleven months of separation. I depended on his new knowledge of the Italian language and the force of his personality. He would lead the way and make all the arrangements.

He was feeling the weight of his responsibilities. What is expressed in letters and in the visible, tangible reality of a relationship are not the same. We had to become re-acquainted. Practical action made it easier. Whatever doubts he may have had about becoming responsible for me, he nevertheless shouldered his new burdens quickly and with aplomb.

He told me that he had stayed up all night so as not to miss the fast train to Naples at 4 in the morning. On the early morning platform he then found four trains listed for Naples, each one apparently 'quick':

20. Marriage in Rome

accelerando, diretto, direttissimo and rapido. He chose what he thought was the fastest but, some way into the journey, when the ticket inspector made his rounds, discovered that this route took far too long to reach Naples. He would miss my arrival. He was told he would get there more quickly if he left the train at the next stop, returned to Rome and there boarded the true rapido. There was nothing else to do. My promised bunch of flowers could not compete with this new program. In a man of such febrile energy, a long journey does not bring a calm state of mind.

His disappointment in not getting the reunion 'right' was unsettling. I now became the calm one. As we both waited to board the train from Naples to Rome, he informed me that, if possible, we would marry in St Peter's Basilica. To marry in Italy, I would need several weeks' residence, whereas none was required for marriage in the Vatican.

I was dismayed by the prospect of such ostentation. He reassured me gently that we would not be married at the main altar but in one of the minor chapels.

I heard all this from him as the train raced through the smooth, well-cultivated Italian countryside. Crops grew everywhere. There were grapevines on trellises between gnarled, bent olive trees. Fortified hill-top villages seemed to be part of a theatre set. They had the exotic quality I learned to love in Italy.

We lunched beside a large window in the dining carriage while Jim outlined what we had still to accomplish together that day. There was as yet no wedding ring. He had only just managed to get the tailor to complete his suit. I needed to buy a pair of white court shoes with heels, to match my white lace dress. We both needed permission to marry from the parish priest of the Aventine district where Jim was renting a bed-sitter for us from a widowed Hungarian potter.

In Rome Jim took me to the Corso to buy a plain gold ring and a smart pair of white shoes. Father Bill Smith, a Melbourne Jesuit studying in Rome, who was arranging our marriage, accompanied us to the *parocco*, the parish priest. He wanted to know if there were any pressures on me to marry, either from other people or through an unwanted pregnancy.

I laughed inwardly as I thought of all the people who had tried to prevent this marriage from taking place. The old priest laughed out loud when I told him that I had travelled across the world to be with my future husband. He signalled his lack of doubts by moving his hands sideways, as if to confirm 'that does it!'

We then asked Father Smith to join us in a meal to get to know me. He came back with us to Jim's room, took out of my hands an electric iron, and proceeded to iron my wedding dress. Jim later told me how relieved he had been on meeting this Austro-Australian girl. I was not the sophisticated 'slinky Viennese' he had assumed Jim might have chosen.

The obstacles on our way to the altar were by no means cleared. Father Smith instructed me to wear my black coat over my wedding dress and also the white knitted shawl Jim's mother had made me, rather than the veil under the tulip-shaped cap the sentimental Russian dress-maker had persuaded my mother to allow her to make. Until the ecclesiastical authorities had spoken, we were not to presume we had permission to marry in St Peter's before it had been granted. We agreed to everything.

That night we slept chastely in the hotel. Since it was Lent, and we would not be able to have a nuptial Mass, we were up at 6 in the morning to attend Mass and Communion at the great basilica of Santa Maria Maggiore, I in my disguised wedding dress. A fortnight later, at Eastertide, Father Smith, most ceremoniously, was able to organise a private nuptial Mass for us in the catacomb of St Priscilla.

We picked up Father Smith at the Collegio di San Roberto Bellarmino, where we left my suitcase with my honeymoon clothes under the bed of one of his Australian Jesuit colleagues. This was a cause of much hilarity among his celibate colleagues for months to come. (What if Very Reverend Father Superior had discovered it?) Then the three of us walked to the ancient Pantheon nearby, where Jim hailed a horse-drawn *carozza*. He directed the coachman to drive us on a tour taking in the Colosseum, the Roman Forum, the Piazza Navona and other landmarks.

Father Smith still had to go to the Vatican Vicariato to get the bureaucracy's permission to marry us. Because it was Lent, consent was not assumed to be automatic. An Australian Jesuit did not cut much mustard in the Vatican. Jim and I waited apprehensively until our resourceful Father Smith emerged, triumphant.

20. Marriage in Rome

Inside St Peter's he approached the Warden, a plump, pompous Italian monsignore in flowing robes, and showed him the necessary documents. 'What?' he gesticulated. 'You want to get married here. When?' '*Adesso* (now),' said Smith meekly. '*Impossibile!*' thundered the *monsignore*. 'Well, when can they get married?' Bill Smith pleaded gently in Italian. Would we have to come back in two weeks? we wondered. 'Come back in half an hour!' was the abrupt reply, with a patronising smile. There was no need for a tip.

Our small wedding party of Jim and myself, Father Smith and six others, walked across the piazza to a corner coffee shop. We ordered hot chocolate and yeast buns. Our companions were sincerely happy for us. There was the best man, Des O'Grady, the expatriate Australian writer, and his Roman *fidanzata*, Giuseppina (Gegi) Culotta; the bridesmaid, a pedigree Roman friend of Jim's, Adelaide Pettine-Zampi, who worked with him at the Australian Legation; a comical Australian bohemian, John Fitchett; and two former Dominican seminarians, Brian Dargaville and Bernard Delfendahl, who, anti-clerical and full of progressive ideas, nonetheless lived at the Dominican Angelicum. Father Smith was rather suspicious of them.

Ever-resourceful, Bill was the only one to bring a camera, to give us a small record of the day.

Within half an hour we had returned to the architectural wonder of St Peter's. We passed the modest marble Stuart memorial to exiled Bonnie Prince Charlie of Scotland and his father, the Old Pretender. We headed cowards Bernini's ornate *baldachino* below Michelangelo's great baroque dome. I noted on the other side of the basilica the almost black statue of Saint Peter, Christ's 'rock', his foot nearly worn away by centuries of devout kisses.

We were led into the *Tesoreria*, a gilded chapel beyond the end of the side aisle. There Father Smith led us through the officially designated words that bound us to each other. Jim gave me the gold ring to wear as the visible sign of my pledge. Being an Australian male, he did not have to receive one from me.

Then Father Smith delivered a sermon about our duties to one another and to the Church, with no less eloquence than if he had been in front of a cathedral assembly. It was an imaginative and caring talk. Our promises were then sealed in writing and registered in the basilica's records. Jim was given a little book, *La Famiglia Christiana*, lest he forget to procreate, and I received a mother-of-pearl rosary. These were gifts from Pope Pius XII to all those who married in St Peter's.

As we walked down the steps of the basilica, Jim turned to me. 'Helga,' he asked, 'do you want to spend the next few days in Naples, Capri, Florence or Siena?' 'Somewhere charming, quiet and not well-known,' I replied, 'the home of my friend, St Catherine.' 'Siena it is,' he smiled, and led the party in the direction of the Piazza Navona where Olimpia's pleasant *trattoria* had been chosen for our wedding meal. And there we were all merry.

21

Integration

This book is about my life before I married. Some early readers of this story of my youth have asked me: 'And what happened next? How many children did you have? Did you retain your religious faith? Did you ever complete your University degree?'

The landscape of my long-ago memories is of course larger than the slice of life I have presented in detail here. In this book I have taken the effects of War and the displacement of my family as the crucial features of the life I was offered, out of which I had to find my own way. I have offered only my voice telling about the camp, that period of my life on which those with no personal experience have been so eager to comment. Most older inmates could not discuss it for many years. Some still cannot.

My brother Peter says he had a happy time in the camp. And I reply: 'But you were a boy!' Other younger boys also remember happy games. Girls were more vulnerable. We are sad about different things.

My story is only one of those telling what happened to displaced children, often much more terribly, and all over the world. My experience of trying to forge an identity was something all children have to do. They are obliged one day to join the world of the adults who control the rules. It is a complex business for most. The demands of their parents and culture have to be set against personal temperament and vision. There are always episodes of wanting to escape from it all.

Beyond what I have described in this book lie important issues and a totally different set of circumstances: my adult life. My marriage produced seven children in ten years. Both my brothers made careers in Australia, married and also had children. Three of my sons and three daughters survived their Australian births and were raised by Jim and me in a number of locations, including Melbourne, Port Moresby, Townsville and Canberra.

Looking at her contemporaries and comparing, one of my daughters has remarked that our marriage, now in its fiftieth year, has outlasted the proverbial bottle of Tabasco sauce. The dynamics of traditional family life used to place less emphasis on the social and intellectual needs of the mother. Indeed, the practical necessities and basic work demanded by a large family obliterated the egocentric search for meaning and purpose of my younger days.

By working as an adult for others, without expectations and through exchanging love, I did manage to achieve personal integration. In a situation such as mine, one does not have to search for a role, or for identity. As some mystics say, by losing yourself you find yourself. The self is validated by becoming less important but also, paradoxically, stronger. Parents and others who serve people for no obvious reward will understand what I am saying.

The modern emphasis on personal fulfilment, worth and recognition tends to obscure such a reality. I, too, have been affected by contemporary demands that I balance my role as donor of my love and service with my personal needs. Over time, this has meant completing my tertiary education in altogether different subjects, mainly History, Anthropology and Archaeology, plus a Diploma in Education. These have helped me earn money for my family.

My father was eventually able to practise in Australia the engineering for which he had been trained. He laid the second railway line between Kalgoorlie and Perth, and oversaw the construction of the Art Gallery of Western Australia. He reluctantly abandoned other engineering projects when illness interfered with his energetic personality. This was not until his late seventies. My mother outlived him by four years.

'What about your religious life?' people ask me. I remain a Catholic by orientation, because of my love of the Church's great intellectual, artistic and liturgical traditions, and because of its international character. At the core of Catholicism is its Christian foundation, and the belief that at birth all people are of equal worth in the eyes of their Creator. Despite serious blots on its history, and despite the hypocrisy of many of its clergy, who have abused their power and trust, for me its worth is maintained by those courageous Catholics who have committed their lives to work for justice and the alleviation of the lot of poor and suffering humanity.

But as I grow older, dogma, formalities and the need to be certain have been replaced by an emphasis on humane values, on spirituality and ecumenism. I feel personally responsible for my actions without having to be told by an exclusive club of single men, our institutionalised, unmarried clergy, how to behave. The Christian Church is mine and ours as much as it belongs to those who make the rules about who is worthy, and who may fully belong.

I attended Mass and daily Communion for years in my maturity, and also stayed away from the Church for long periods. This was in reaction to the rules which the celibate clergy have designed and the laity are obliged to observe. I am amazed by the widespread accommodation of Catholics who do not speak out about their quiet rebellions, but pretend to be conformists. Like a dolphin I have moved in and out of the depths, absorbing the intensity of two separate, but overlapping domains, the religious and the secular life.

I receive much comfort in my heart as I contemplate the Australian countryside, with its durable, stoic character. It underpins my sense of what is sacred. But what matters is also anchored in the compassion that people bring to each other. I have little empathy with the second-rate quasi-pop music of our modern parish churches, an attempt at being up-to-date. When I am at Mass I pray for people who are victims of political regimes or religious persecution, the kind of cause for which Jesus died on the Cross. Religion should not be a numbers game, suggesting that popularity equals greatest relevance.

I have attended the churches and sacred places of other religions. I disown the traditional Catholic claim that only we have 'the truth' or that we can know exclusively 'the mind of God'. Nor have I ever understood the mystery of evil: how a well-educated nation like Germany could give overwhelming support to a criminal government and its lunatic leader.

Aside from the frame one places around personal experience in the telling of it, history has an odd way of presenting its own patterns and connecting currents in the landscape of memory. Reviewing and assessing my life, I can see four obvious themes in my life.

First, was it so odd that my family was brought here as prisoners against our will? After all, this continent was developed by prisoners who were dumped here from another part of the world. They then performed the basic labour that supported colonial life. Was our enforced transportation so different?

Second, a senior academic psychiatrist at a Sydney-based university has come up with the theory that people (especially foreigners) who have been placed in long-term 'detention' develop an obsessive preoccupation, not so much with the past as with the future. That certainly fits my profile after my release.

Third, most days of the week, I drive my car to the city of Canberra where I now live, along an arterial road that connects a major road and a highway. This road is called William Slim Drive. How did it come about that Slim, my father and I came into such strange alignment with one another? As acting Major-General commanding the 10th Indian Division of the British Army, Slim imprisoned my father in that Kurdish village in Iran in 1941 to try and find out what he knew. Information on Iranian politics and German nationalism was required, with the reward of becoming a British spy, an honour Rudolf declined. In 1953 Sir William Slim became Governor-General of Australia, the country which by chance had also become ours.

Fourth, the Australian community at Tatura has now forged links with people who were once imprisoned out of sight. They have funded a museum in their township which lovingly collects local memorabilia as well as relics from the internment camps. It has always surprised me how little is generally known of even the existence of these camps in Australia during World War II. The museum helps to keep memories and history alive.

In 1991, with my mother and Aunt Else, I attended a fiftieth reunion of Camp 3 prisoners at Tatura. We rejoiced in the tolerant and generous welcome of the Tatura local community as we made contact with a large number of ex-prisoners we had not seen since 1946. I met again my esteemed teacher, Lieselotte Wagner, a Templer who married an engineer from Iran and lived in Germany. But by the end of our day at the campsite, I was suffering distress remembering the bad things I had once known there. My aunt had to take me away. My mother, who had been much more deeply affected by her imprisonment, took the whole day in her stride, with aplomb.

Now there are reunions most years organised by descendants of the Templer community. The Palestinian Templers have become loyal Australian citizens. The previous German Consul-General in Australia, Hans Michael Schwandt, also used to attend camp reunions. My brother Peter and his son Lachlan reported to me his strong, positive speeches referring to the assembled group as once sincerely German but now sincerely Australian. He seemed fascinated by this chapter of Australian-German history.

A few months ago I received a notice from a researcher at the Tatura Museum, Lurline Knee, telling me that four letters from the camp had been sent to her from Vancouver in Canada. A POW had written two of them to his beloved wife in Germany and, amazingly, two were from my own father to his family in Vienna. One was from 1943, and the other 1945. Now based in Vancouver, Hans Michael Schwandt had rescued them for the Tatura museum at a philatelic auction. Collectors of stamps and letter covers were eager to buy them. Lurline Knee asked me if I would translate them for the Tatura museum. And this I did. But how did they get there? The only conclusion I have reached to date is that my Uncle Oswald Dittrich, an ardent stamp collector, traded them with Allied soldiers who occupied Vienna at the end of the War.

Fascinated by the mystery, my son Gerald, his wife and son drove me to Tatura to deliver my translation to Lurline Knee in person, at an open day at the museum. Other records were shown to us there, and we were promised a conducted tour of Camp 1, possibly the last of its kind, since the now eroded site has been privately purchased.

We were joined by my two cousins from Melbourne, Christine and Peter, whose father, Alfred Erlanger, had in 1941 been interned from Iran at Loveday in South Australia. In 1945 he was moved to Tatura, and to Camp 1. His children had never visited the campsite before.

Ironically, Alfred had left Berlin in the 1930s to work in Iran to avoid Nazi persecution of Jewish families, although he was raised a Christian. Unknown to my father in Iran, Erlanger was the paymaster of the workers on the Trans-Iranian Railway which he was building. Then in 1951 in Australia, Alfred and Rudolf had become brothers-in-law.

After a tearful encounter in the museum with written documents and images, my cousins and my own family strolled over to the abandoned site of Camp 1. I again experienced Tatura with its bleached, tinder-dry grass, prickly pear and eucalyptus trees. The barest remaining contours of camp life lay among a few piles of stones. All corrugated iron and building timber had long since been dismantled and sold during times of need. The barest remnants of Camp 1, mere indicators of garden paths, lily ponds, the theatre, bowling alley and meeting place *Kafe Wellblech* reminded us of what Alfred and his kind had endured. But we also remembered that he and other prisoners had created lives out of barren desolation, hope out of oppression.

Both my 2003 visit to the land of our mothers and to the Tatura campsite with my cousins the following year stirred new currents in our memories. Alfred and Else's daughter, Christine Robertson, sought out for the first time a stack of genealogical documents about members of our mothers' family in Steinkirche. Peter Erlanger dug up a memoir he had encouraged his father to write a long time ago about his imprisonment in Australia. As a man labelled 'Jew' both in Loveday and Tatura, he had faced malice of which he could never speak.

As for the next generation, my twelve-year-old grandson, Patrick Griffin, during that privileged outing in late October 2004, picked up some rusty barbed wire. He took it to school to show his classmates. It was evidence of his visit to the Tatura museum and to the disappearing campsite. This was where members of his family had been locked up for five years, playing their part in Australian history and in their own. He was able to speak openly about what until now has been concealed by *Schweigen*, the long silence.

www.ingramcontent.com/pod-product-compliance
Lightning Source LLC
Chambersburg PA
CBHW042043240426
43667CB00048B/2962